HACKED TO DEATH

Kate Webster rushed toward her former employer with her arm upraised, her hand clutching an axe. It struck the side of Julia Thomas's head with a glancing blow. Struggling with the larger and heavier Webster, Thomas lost her balance and tumbled down the stairs. Webster followed and drove the axe blade into Thomas's skull.

She dragged the body into the kitchen, where water was already boiling in a large copper pot. Set out on a table were a meat cleaver, an assortment of long-bladed knives, a large ladle, and two empty jars. Nearby were a large, black leather bag and a wooden box full of cloth sacks lined with thick brown paper.

Webster removed Thomas's clothing, picked up the cleaver, and hacked off the woman's head. She placed it in the leather bag, before cutting up the rest of the body. Through the night and the next day, Webster kept the pot boiling as she disposed of her employer, skimming the floating fat into the jars and stuffing the boiled flesh into the sacks.

BOOK YOUR PLACE ON OUR WEBSITE AND MAKE THE READING CONNECTION!

We've created a customized website just for our very special readers, where you can get the inside scoop on everything that's going on with Zebra, Pinnacle and Kensington books.

When you come online, you'll have the exciting opportunity to:

- View covers of upcoming books
- Read sample chapters
- Learn about our future publishing schedule (listed by publication month *and author*)
- Find out when your favorite authors will be visiting a city near you
- Search for and order backlist books from our online catalog
- Check out author bios and background information
- Send e-mail to your favorite authors
- Meet the Kensington staff online
- Join us in weekly chats with authors, readers and other guests
- Get writing guidelines
- AND MUCH MORE!

**Visit our website at
http://www.pinnaclebooks.com**

WITH
AN AXE

H. Paul Jeffers

PINNACLE BOOKS
Kensington Publishing Corp.

www.pinnaclebooks.com

*In memory of George Weiser,
a great literary agent and friend.*

Grateful acknowledgment is extended for invaluable research assistance to Al Leibholz; Lynn Aber, Portsmouth Athenaeum; Maryellen Burke; Joan M. Carroll, AP Wide World Photos; Sue Lindsay, *Rocky Mountain News;* J. Dennis Robinson, editor, Seacoast, NH; Nicole Wells, The New York Historical Society; and Jake Elwell, who started me on this path and kept me going.

CONTENTS

Introduction

With an Axe

The two brothers were talking in a field. We can't say for sure what they discussed. We do know that the older one was unhappy because he felt that his work hadn't been sufficiently appreciated by an overseer. Evidently, the brothers' words became heated and in a fit of fury the younger was killed.

Later that day, God demanded of Cain, "Where is Abel thy brother?"

Cain tried to dodge the issue. "I know not," he said. "Am I my brother's keeper?"

God replied, "The voice of thy brother's blood crieth unto me from the ground."

The Book of Genesis does not record the nature of Cain's murder weapon. Because the youths were in a field and blood had been shed, it's probable that Abel was struck with a rock. Many centuries would go by before descendants of Cain and Abel's parents invented the knife and sword, and several millennia would pass before guns made their noisy debut on the stage of homicide.

Since history's first killing, there is no counting how many human lives have been snuffed out in a manner deemed by the ruling authority to be unlawful. Certainly, there has never been a lack of ingenuity regarding devices with which to accomplish the deadly deed.

As Agatha Christie's fictional sleuth Hercule Poirot observed, "With method and logic one can accomplish everything."

One encyclopedia of murders and their methods listed death by the knife, dagger, razor, chisel, iron file, hammer, poker, bottle, tire-iron, sandbag, sash weight, mallet, brick, stick, stone, fire tongs, revolver butt, chair, candlestick, rope, piano wire, silk stockings, poison, manual strangulation, assorted firearms, and the weapon that is the common denominator of the cases of murder in this book—the axe.

While the instances related in these pages span two centuries (1831–1998), death by the axe is probably as old as the object itself. Practically from the day it was invented, the wedge-shaped chunk of sharpened stone or metal fitted to one end of a wooden or metal handle earned a place in history as an efficient means of taking human life. It also afforded quite a good living for men who exhibited a talent for wielding one as official executioners.

No one knows the axe's inventor. It's reasonable to deduce that its purpose was as a tool. Examples of the axe go back thousands of years to the Stone Age. When mankind found out how to forge metal, the technique was speedily adapted to making more efficient axes. Turning a tool into a weapon for soldiers swiftly followed.

Where and when the first person to employ an axe to kill someone for a personal motive is not known. Perhaps the earliest written instance of a monarch executing someone by lopping off a man's head is found in the New Testament's account of Salome performing a dance for King Herod and demanding that he dispatch an axeman to bring her the head of John the Baptist. In the two millennia since, other rulers sent plenty of subjects, loyal and not, to the chopping block, but widespread notice of these royal homicides by axe and those by commoners who took one in hand to assuage their passions had to wait for the arrival of printing and its offspring, mass communication in the form of the newspaper.

Before newsboys appeared on city streets to shout "Read all about it," no one but those immediately involved in a murder—the police, witnesses, relatives of the victim, the accused, judge, and jury—had any way of knowing all the gory and gruesome details.

Consequently, it was not until the rise of a sensation-seeking press in the first half of the nineteenth century that stories of murders became the grist of conversations among the general public. That is why the accounts of axe murders contained in this book begin in 1831.

Not every death of a person at the hands of an axe-wielder has been recorded for posterity, simply because there were no newspapers to send reporters to gather and record the horrifying details. But since that time few news stories concerning the murders of ordinary people have fascinated the public as much as those in which somebody took an axe, bashed someone over the head with it, and thereby reached the morbid place in history, lore, and legend attained by the men and women whose stories unfold in the following pages.

Except for the fact that they killed using an axe, it's unlikely they or their victims would have been noted and remembered by anyone beyond the times and places where these bloodiest of crimes occurred.

The perpetrators in this gruesome compendium include a jealous wife in the wilderness of antebellum North Carolina; a young handsome clerk in 1836 New York City; the brother of the gunmaker Samuel Colt in 1841; a maid in Victorian Scotland (1862); a German-immigrant fisherman in New Hampshire (1873); three young black men and a woman who were lynched for the murders of two North Carolina families in 1883 and 1885; England's notorious Kate Webster (1879); a murder in a small town in Iowa in 1912; a butler's lunchtime slaughter at Taliesen, the Wisconsin country cottage of famed architect Frank Lloyd Wright, in 1914; the assassination of Soviet revolutionary Leon Trotsky in 1940; Karla Fay Tucker, who, while awaiting execution of a death sentence for a pickax murder in Texas in the 1980s, became a born-again Christian and the center of a national debate in the 1990s on whether she deserved to die; a church deacon who killed two prostitutes in Tampa, Florida, in 1996; Rita Gluzman, who fled the Soviet Union and hacked her husband to death in Rockland County, New York, in 1996, and then found herself prosecuted not only for murder but as the first person charged with violating a brand-new federal spouse-abuse law; a gruesome slaying of a clergyman and his wife in Indiana in 1996; and another in Colorado in 1998.

Of course, no book on axe murders can omit the most famous case of all—Lizzie Borden, whom succeeding generations mistakenly believe was convicted of taking an axe and giving her mother forty whacks, followed by two-score and one for good luck aimed at her father. Lizzie got off because the police did not properly advise her that she was entitled under the U.S. Constitution to refuse to answer questions without having an attorney on hand.

If space permitted, there could be even more cases detailed, such as the October 17, 1863, murders of Ellen Jones and John Blair in Pennsylvania's Delaware County by George Wilkinson for the purpose of robbery. Said to have been the great-great-granduncle of actor Jack Nicholson, he was acquitted despite eyewitness testimony of a six-year-old girl. Jones's axe-shattered skull is on exhibit in the Mutter Museum at the College of Physicians in Philadelphia.

A month after Lizzie Borden stood trial in Fall River, Massachusetts, one Herbert Edwin Glasson found himself in a condition that Lizzie's New England neighbors termed "hard-up," and the customers of Glasson's butcher shop half a world away in the town of Carcoar, in New South Wales, Australia, called "in queer street." Glasson's meat business had fallen into such financial straits that he hadn't paid his assistant in three months, and the manager of the Carcoar branch of the City Bank of Sydney, John Phillips, was after him almost daily to make good on an overdraft. The latest of these unpleasant confrontations occurred on September 24, 1893. Faced with ruin, Glasson figured the way out of his financial difficulties was to sneak into the home of the manager, steal his keys, and loot the bank. He wound up killing Phillips and another person and fleeing with the wrong set of keys. Traced to a barber shop, he was found cowering in a corner in blood-soaked clothes and ranting, "I did not do it. I am mad."

The trial judge advised the jurors not to let "subtleties of the law of mania affect you." They didn't. Glasson was found guilty and hanged.

It's difficult to imagine a more idyllic country in 1914 than the lush green hills around Ruahine, New Zealand. Little wonder, then, that Arthur Rottman, a twenty-one-year-old German sailor, interned for the duration of the First World War, was pleased to accept an offer of a job by Joe McCann, who with his wife, Lucy, and their infant boy lived on a dairy farm. Everything seemed to be going along fine until December 27 when Rottman showed up at a bottling plant without Joe. His explanation was that Joe had to go away to help a friend who was a sheep-raiser to assist in the fleecing.

The next day, when Rottman didn't show up at the bottling plant, the manager was worried enough to go out to McCann's farm. He found Joe McCann with his head split open in a cowshed, Lucy and the baby also dead in the bedroom, and two bloody axes. Arthur was nowhere in sight.

He was, at that moment, at Cape Terawhiti near Wellington and asking for a job at a construction site. Because it was Christmas, all workers but site-supervisor William Kelly were off for the holiday. Kelly permitted Rottman to stay the night. The next morning, after reading in a newspaper about the murders at Ruahine, and wanting to talk about them, Kelly found Rottman to be extremely nervous and suddenly eager to leave.

After Rottman departed, Kelly informed police of the visitor's suspicious manner. When they located him, Rottman blurted, "I am guilty. I know I'm done."

Rottman explained that he'd had an argument with McCann about his being late on the job because he'd been drinking the previous night. As to how and why he'd struck McCann with an axe, and then proceeded to murder Lucy and the baby, he offered no explanation beyond claiming that he could not remember anything after the argument with McCann. Medical experts debated homicidal mania, frenzy, and madness brought on by drink. The jury listened politely and found Rottman guilty. He was hanged at Terrace Gaol, Wellington, on March 8, 1915.

Still unsolved are a group of murders lumped together as the work of the "Axe-man of New Orleans." Committed between 1911 and 1919, they created a panic similar to that which surrounded the maraudings of London's Jack the Ripper in 1888.

The first victims were two Italian grocers and their wives. The cases went unsolved. But in May 1918 another Italian resident of New Orleans, Joseph Maggio, and his wife, Catherine, were axed to death in their home.

The common thread in the 1911 and 1919 killings was the Axeman's method of breaking into homes through a door panel and leaving the bloody axe behind.

Further evidence that there was an axe-wielding maniac on the loose came two weeks later when a deliveryman discovered that grocery store owner Louis Besumer and his live-in lover, Anna Lowe, had been savagely attacked. Lowe had been battered with an axe. Besumer survived but was unable to identify the attacker.

August 1918 brought an attack on a pregnant woman, who survived and told police she had awakened to find a dark figure looming above her with an axe. Five days later a similar figure killed thirty-year-old Joseph Romano, setting off a wave of panic in New Orleans that resulted in several innocent men being chased down and beaten.

The next appearance of the Axeman occurred on August 10 when grocer Steve Boca was attacked in his home. The attacker had broken in through a panel in a door and the axe was left in the house. Boca recovered but was unable to identify the assailant. Two weeks later Sarah Laumann was struck once with an axe by a man who had climbed through her bedroom window. Laumann lived. The axe was found on her lawn.

After another hiatus, the Axeman resumed his bloody rampage by butchering another grocer, Mike Pepitone, in what was the last known attack by the unknown killer.

Recent cases include the very public axe murder of Roosevelt Tillotsen by Ronald Logan during an argument in Philadelphia in 1980. Logan axed him in front of horrified passengers on a city bus.

On the morning of May 29, 1993, Hilda Mae Herbert was found dead in a chair in her home in New York City with a blanket over her head. When her niece and a neighbor removed the blanket, they found a hatchet with a twelve-inch handle buried in her head. Police surmised that she had been killed after objecting to a romance between her stepdaughter and a young man of whom Herbert did not approve.

The suspect in the case was tracked to Philadelphia six months later and arrested. But when he offered an alibi, he was released on bail and promptly vanished. He remained at large until August 1999 when he was caught jumping a subway turnstile in New York City.

Realizing who the fare-beater was, police charged him with Hilda Herbert's murder.

In 1997 Heidi Challand and her four children, ages two through twelve, were hacked to death in a farming community on Vancouver Island, British Columbia, Canada.

In Auckland, New Zealand, in 1998, a twenty-one-year-old Vietnamese, Thanh Ngoc Vo, admitted the axe-murder of another Vietnamese refugee during a brawl outside a nightclub. Vo claimed to be acting in defense of a brother.

That year in Cornwall, England, the bodies of sixty-four-year-old Philip Heyward, a tree surgeon, and his wife, Phyliss, were found in their burning home, their heads battered by an axe, victims of a family dispute.

In Sylacauga, Alabama, thirty-nine-year-old Billy Jack Gaither was clubbed to death with an axe handle in February 1999 because two young men objected to Gaither's homosexuality.

What made these and each of the axe-murders detailed in this book so compelling? In a few cases there was a genuine mystery.

In others when there was no question who did it, motive fascinated. Was it simply an act of cold-blooded killing for profit? A moment of rage? Insanity?

Whatever the motive, the central lure of these crimes was described in 1841 by New York newspaper baron Horace Greeley. He wrote, "The imagination cannot avoid picturing to itself this terrible murder, nor can it dwell for a moment upon the scene without deep thrills of horror; that one human being, with the warm bright sunlight streaming alike upon him and his victim, at the corner of two of the most thronged streets in our Metropolis, with the bustle of business and the voices of men in his ears, should thus murder his fellow, with such aggravated atrocity."

No matter when and where such a crime has been committed, our minds reel in revulsion, knowing that to kill another human somebody took an axe.

One

Crocodile of Vices

"Life of the party."

Hardly anybody in the mountains and lowlands around the Toe River of Anson County, North Carolina, in 1831, could disagree that good-looking Charlie Silver, one of old John Silver's brood of strapping sons, was just that. In fact, all of John's sons were described as very agreeable sorts. If anyone should need a helping hand in raising a barn, throwing up a rail fence, or building a cabin from poles hacked out of the woods, it was Charlie Silver who could be counted on to be there. He'd be the first to show up bright and early, sunny grin on his face, and raring to get to it.

Hand Charlie an axe and he'd stride into a stand of trees and begin whacking off limbs from hickory trees to quickly produce a stack of fine wood for building a house or kindling for the hearth—whatever was needed. He practiced an axeman's skills so easily that he was the envy of the good people of Deyton's Bend. On top of that, you just couldn't find any more agreeable young man anywhere in those parts. Or a more talented one at singing after the work was done. At a dance he was also downright handy with a fiddle; that is, if he could by pried away from a bevy of admiring young ladies with minds set on finding a suitable husband.

Among that group none was counted prettier than Frances Stewart.

Known by family and friends as Frankie, she was, in the description of one admirer, "a mighty likely young woman." A blonde beauty, she had the makings of a fine wife, by all accounts. Though she was small, she was able to spin three yards of cotton a day. However, she had a strong mind of her own and if she felt provoked she had a tongue that could sting like a scorpion. But so did plenty of Deyton Bend women. Life in those parts was hard, and if a woman lacked the mettle to deal with it, that life could be even more difficult.

To survive in those rugged mountains the woman of the house had to be just as tough as the man, and often more so.

"Let him who thinks otherwise go to wrest a living from a corn patch laboriously tufted upon a high rocky slope," wrote North Carolina historian Manly Wade Wellman. "One must be vigorous if only to walk the steep, shivery-high trails between cabin and cabin. The breed tends naturally toward tall spareness of body and reserved dignity of manner."

In coping with a plain and poor existence, the axe and rifle were employed with a familiar skill that became almost instinct. Such folks struggled day in and day out in the region of the Toe River. The name is a short version of Estatoe, the daughter of a long-ago Indian chief. She had planned to elope with her lover from another tribe, only to learn that on his way to spirit her away he'd drowned when his canoe capsized. Inconsolable, Estatoe gave the region a romantic story to be told again and again around countless cabin hearths by killing herself.

Nor too far from the spot where Estatoe went into legend an explorer named Elisha Mitchell lost his life exploring the highest peak in North Carolina, which was promptly named after him.

But there were happier yarns to be spun on cold mountain nights in cabins tucked into the hills overlooking the tiny town that grew up at a bend of the Toe. On blustery nights many a tale was told of heroic mountaineers in the time of the Revolution who'd battled soldiers of the king of England on what was later named King's Mountain. Later, similar brave hearts would rally to the cause of the Confederacy to do battle with Yankees advancing toward Chickamauga.

Some of these stories were related in the words of songs accompanied by music played on fiddles, banjos, and guitars, which outsiders would call "hillbilly songs." Over the years the popular image of these apparently plain and evidently simple-living folk that took root in the minds of northerners produced characters that lampooned them in the form of denizens of Dogpatch, the fanciful home of Li'l Abner, Mammy and Pappy Yokum, buxom-but-brainless Daisy Mae, and General Cornpone.

Yet the real people of Deyton Bend in the bend of the Toe River were as human as any condescending northerner and the sophisticates of North Carolina towns and cities that were not in the mountains. Named for a settler whom no one could remember by 1831, Deyton Bend had—for reasons known only to Isaiah Stewart—caused Stewart to uproot his family from Anson County a few years earlier and build their cabin on a patch of hardscrabble land near the Silver farm.

Not long after the arrival of the Stewarts no one could recall exactly when Charlie and Frankie met; probably at a party after one of the barn raisings. That the two had hit it off was immediately apparent.

They'd made such an attractive and evidently well-matched pair that before long it was obvious that a wedding could not be long in the offing.

In preparation for the nuptials Charlie Silver used his

axe with consummate skill to hack out a spot across the river from his father's home and erect a snug pole cabin with a large fireplace, in which Frankie would soon be cooking all the simple food required by her handsome and hard-working husband. Nor were residents of Deyton Bend and the surrounding mountainside farms surprised to learn a few weeks after the wedding that Charlie and Frankie were well on their way to becoming parents.

For the women of town the news became the subject of countless quilting bees. Plans were made to knit and sew clothing for the child and the ladies of the region looked forward to a grand party to celebrate the blessed event.

Almost exactly a year after the couple had "tied the knot," they had a girl whom they named Nancy. Like all new fathers, Charlie Silver put up with a great deal of teasing from friends and found himself even more a center of attraction among the women at parties than he'd been as a bachelor. They seemed to enjoy peppering him with questions. Was he enjoying married life? Did he regret giving up being single? Always good-natured, he took the teasing well and even did some teasing in return, especially with the women.

Yet nothing pleased him more than to come home after a day's work than sitting by the fireplace after supper and cuddling the infant in his arms. He planned to do just that on the brutally cold night of December 22, 1831, because in the morning he intended to leave the child and Frankie to trek into the mountains with his friend George Young for a few days of hunting so that there would be plenty of meat on hand for the coming winter.

As he came into the cabin Frankie paused in the preparation of supper to point out that the supply of firewood was low. With an acknowledging nod of his head, Charlie got his axe from a corner and set out to remedy the situation.

After a filling meal and as Frankie cleared the table, he settled into a chair in the chimney corner with Nancy nestled lovingly in his strong arms and drifted to sleep.

After a bitterly cold night, the wind had died down and the sky had cleared, promising a warm day for getting the washing done and the likelihood that clothes hung on the line to dry would do so without freezing solid. Trudging over the ridge to the Silver farm just past dawn, Frankie found her mother-in-law and her two oldest daughters busy with that chore.

She told her relatives that she'd already completed the washing and hanging out the clothes because Charlie's plan to go hunting had gotten him and her up even earlier than usual.

After a few minutes' visit, Frankie left.

When she returned to the Silver farm at sundown, she reported that because Charlie had not returned she did not want to stay the night in the cabin alone with the baby. Announcing her intention to spend it at the home of her father, she asked if the Silvers would give Charlie's cow its evening feeding. The chore fell to seventeen-year-old Alfred, Charlie's brother.

When Charlie did not return the next day, nor on Christmas Day, Frankie again showed up at the Silver farm. Carrying Nancy, she told her mother-in-law, "As Charlie has stayed away this long, I don't care whether he comes back or not."

Her intention, she announced, was to return to the cabin, pick up some clothes, and move in with her father.

The day after the holiday, Charlie's friends were so alarmed by his failure to return that they met to organize a search. Dividing into small groups, they spread through the valley of the Toe and along the streams that fed it and ranged up the slopes of the mountains to no avail. That a man with Charlie's knowledge of the terrain and experience with guns could get lost or injure himself accidentally struck the men as highly improbable.

Yet good mountain men like Charlie Silver had been known to run into bad luck by stumbling and falling and finding themselves unable to move in a remote area where a cry for help was not likely to be heard. With snow piling up in the hills and temperatures at the freezing mark, chances of survival dwindled by the hour.

At this point Charlie's desperate father, John Silver, saw no recourse but to seek the help of a man who was said to have the power to find people. He did this by suspending a crystal ball attached to a string above a map or drawing. According to accounts of the conjure-man's use of the object, the ball would magically move to the spot where the item or person being sought would be found. He was a slave of a man named Williams who lived on the other side of the mountains, in the state of Tennessee.

After a perilous two-day, forty-mile trek on horseback along snowy trails and beside steep ravines, Silver arrived at Williams's door only to be told that the conjure-man was not at home. He was told that the man was not expected back soon.

Fortunately, Williams informed Silver that the conjure-man had not taken his magic crystal with him. Perhaps if they tried their luck with the object, Williams suggested, the talisman might provide them the answer to Charlie's whereabouts.

Figuring anything was worth a try, Silver agreed to the experiment.

When the ball dangled over a hastily drawn map of the area around Charlie's cabin, it showed no inclination to move. Nor did it animate itself during two subsequent attempts. With a shrug, Williams proposed that either the magical ball worked only in the hands of the absent conjure-man, or it was telling them that Charlie Silver would probably be found inside or around the cabin.

Determined to organize a search of his son's land, Silver returned to Deyton Bend only to be astounded to learn that the conjure-man's shiny trinket-on-a-string indeed had done its work. While Silver was in Tennessee, Charlie's whereabouts had been discovered—exactly where the crystal ball had indicated.

On the very day Silver and Williams had tried their luck with the object, Silver was told, a Deyton Bend man by the name of Jake Cullis had taken it upon himself to investigate. Silver knew Jake Cullis very well.

A savvy mountain man with a gray beard, discerning eyes, and a sterling reputation as a tracker, Cullis had been a familiar figure as he trudged in and around Deyton Bend with a long walking staff in his hand for as long as anyone could remember. Arriving at Charlie's cabin unannounced, he'd startled Frankie by wandering around the cabin and poking the end of his staff into the partially frozen ground.

Unbidden by Frankie, he abruptly barged into the cabin and went directly to the fireplace. After poking the stick into the ashes for a few minutes, he declared, "There's pieces of bones in there." Bending, he pulled out what looked like a pebble.

Turning to Frankie, he demanded, "Get me a bowl of water."

Shaken by the sharp command, Frankie promptly obeyed, then watched in silence as the elderly mountain man dropped the pebble into it. A moment later, the water bubbled.

Cullis exclaimed, "Grease bubbles!"

By this time a group of Frankie's curious neighbors had gathered. Fascinated but quiet, they watched as Cullis once again poked the ground. Near the spring from which Frankie had drawn the water, he found a soft spot. Furiously digging into it, he found more ashes.

Scooping up handfuls, he discovered a piece of metal that could only be either a buckle for a belt or a pair of shoes. Somebody exclaimed, "That's from Charlie's shoes."

This precipitated a flurry of digging, and as the work proceeded, more and more ashes were found. In the clumps of ashes were found shards of bone and several human teeth. Then someone went into the cabin and ripped up freshly washed wooden planking in front of the fireplace.

Despite an attempt at scrubbing, the planks bore a brownish stain, described by one onlooker as "big as a hog's liver."

No one doubted it was blood, or that it was Charlie Silver's.

Summoned to the cabin, Sheriff W. C. Butler promptly arrested Frankie.

After several days of questioning her, and reasoning that such a slight young woman could not have killed her husband and disposed of the body by herself, he issued arrest warrants for Frankie's mother, Margaret, and her brother Blackston. They were brought to the jail at Morgantown for questioning on January 9, 1832. Both denied complicity in the alleged murder.

Arraigned before two justices of the peace, J. C. Burgner and Thomas Hughes, mother and son were represented by lawyers hired by Isaiah Stewart. These attorneys whose names have not survived in the records of the proceedings succeeded in winning the release of Frankie's mother and brother on bonds of one hundred English pounds. They were ordered to return to court for the March term.

When a grand jury met on March 17, it indicted Frankie, but it declined to do so with her mother and brother.

Frankie pleaded not guilty and was remanded for trial on March 29 before Judge John R. Donnell. Jurors were chosen from a pool of 150, which was an exceptionally large number.

Little information remains concerning the one-day trial. Although it's recorded that the prosecutor was a William Alexander, the identity of Frankie's defense counsel is not known for sure. He was probably one of three noted members of the Burke County, North Carolina, bar: D. J. Caldwell, Joseph McDowell, or Isaac T. Avery.

The chief witness was Jake Cullis.

The physical evidence consisted of the buckle, the teeth, bits of charred bone, and the purported murder weapon. It was a dull axe with notches in the blade that had to have been made by something other than the hickory trees surrounding Charlie Silver's hand-hewn cabin.

Courtroom observers expected a quick conviction. But the jury deliberations lasted well into a candlelit night, then adjourned until morning.

When the jurors convened again, they promptly informed Judge Donnell that before they could reach a verdict, certain questions had to be answered. This meant bringing back witnesses.

While the judge permitted their recall, Frankie's defense counsel vehemently protested. He argued that throughout the trial the court had scrupulously kept all the witnesses apart. Since the end of testimony, the attorney pointed out, they had been allowed to talk to one another about the case.

Judge Donnell ruled that because "it could not have been anticipated that you [the jury] would wish to hear any of the witnesses examined again after the case had been put to you and you had retired" to deliberate, "the jury ought to hear the witnesses without prejudice arising from the circumstances of their having had an opportunity of being together since their former examination."

This was a serious setback for the defense, but it laid the basis for an appeal in the event that Frankie was convicted. When she was a few hours later, her lawyer moved for a new trial and was denied. Prosecutor Alexander moved for immediate sentencing.

Judge Donnell complied. He ordered Frankie "taken back to the prison from whence she came and there to remain until the last Friday of July . . . and then be taken from thence to the place of public execution, and then and there to be hung by the neck until she be dead."

Courtroom spectators gasped. No woman had ever been condemned to death in the state of North Carolina.

An immediate appeal by Frankie's lawyer to the state supreme court assured she would not hang on the designated date, pending a ruling on her appeal. It was based on the jury's having been allowed to hear re-questioning of witnesses whom the defense considered tainted.

When the high court found no judicial error, Frankie's execution was scheduled for the fall term of the Burke County court, beginning in September 1832. Its presiding judge was D. L. Swain. An especially brilliant young jurist, he had just been elected the youngest governor in the state's history. Consequently, hardly anyone was surprised or upset that he failed to assume the bench to open court and to sentence Frankie.

There was also a new sheriff. As one of the present sheriff's last acts before turning over his office to his successor, John Boone, who claimed kinship with Daniel Boone, adjourned court until the spring of 1833. This gave Frankie an unexpected extra six months of life.

During that time she would be permitted regular visits by her family, including a brother with a keenly observant set of eyes and a talent for whittling wood. Using the former, he studied the lock on Frankie's jail cell. Exercising the latter on a chunk of hardwood, he fashioned a key that was smuggled to Frankie.

Awaiting her outside the jail on the night she decided to use it to open her cell door and attempt to escape was an uncle with a suit of men's clothes and a broad-brimmed hat. He also had a scissors for cutting Frankie's long blond hair and a wagon loaded with hay. But with stunning audacity, Frankie chose not to burrow under it as planned. Instead, she preferred to walk behind it in the guise of an innocent farm boy.

When a jailor discovered Frankie was not where she was expected to be, Sheriff Boone organized a posse of deputies. Mounted on horses, they commenced a search that quickly caught up with the hay wagon and the farm boy walking beside it.

With no time to leap into the wagon and under the hay, Frankie had no choice but to put her trust in her disguise.

Whether Sheriff Boone saw through it, or simply took

a chance, is not known. What is certain is that he rode up to the figure beside the wagon and said, "Frances."

"Thank you, sir," Frankie replied with as low a voice as she could produce, "my name is Tommy."

"Yes," declared the uncle, "her name is Tommy."

Boone blurted, *"Her* name?"

Locked up again, Frankie once more awaited the convening of the next court and the setting of an execution date. It was to be June 28. But this was delayed until July 12. Despite the ill-fated escape, she was still allowed visitors.

One of those who came to see her was a woman from Deyton's Bend who had been a neighbor and stalwart friend. Convinced that she would soon swing from a gallows, Frankie asked the woman to promise that the story she was about to relate would remain her secret until after the hanging.

When the woman agreed, Frankie related what had happened in the cabin on that bitterly cold December 22, 1831.

While Charlie Silver dozed in the chair she slipped baby Nancy from his arms and placed the child on a bed. Taking Charlie's axe from its usual place in a corner, she carried it to the chair in which he slept, lifted it with both hands, and brought it crashing down upon Charlie's head.

Somehow he'd survived. Leaping to his feet, he cried, "God bless the child!"

Terrified, Frankie threw herself on the bed beside the baby and buried her head under the quilt in a vain attempt to block the horrible sounds of Charlie Silver thrashing around the room. When the noises continued, she leaped off the bed, retrieved the axe from where she'd dropped it, and delivered a crushing blow to Silver's head.

To get rid of the body she'd chopped it into pieces and then built a roaring fire. To keep it going as she fed it Charlie's body she used all the wood he had chopped that day, plus planks for the front steps and an old doghouse.

As the body burned she scrubbed the blood from the

floor. The accumulating ashes were carried into the yard
and buried in a shallow hole she dug next to the well. The
grisly task took her all night. Then it was simply a matter
of persuading everyone that Charlie had gone hunting and
for reasons she could not explain had not come back to
her.

Trusting that others would believe that Charlie Silver
had been unfaithful and finally run off with a woman, she
had not expected Charlie's friends to refuse to believe that
explanation for his disappearance.

Confident that her own friend would not renege on her
pledge to not reveal the confession till after the hanging,
Frankie kept her date with the gallows on the twelfth of
July. She offered the hangman and a huge crowd of spectators no last words. But as the gruesome drama unfolded,
souvenir hawkers went through the crowd selling a poem
they claimed Frankie had written:

> On one dark and dreary night
> I put his body out of sight.
> To see his soul and body part,
> It strikes with terror to my heart.
>
> I took his blooming days away,
> Left him no time to God to pray,
> And if sins fall on his head,
> Must I not bear them in his stead?
>
> The jealous thought that first gave strife
> To make me take my husband's life,
> For days and months I spent my time
> Thinking how to commit this crime.
>
> His feeble hands fell gently down,
> His chattering tongue soon lost its sound.
> My mind on solemn subjects rolls,
> My little child—God bless its soul;

And all that are of Adam's race,
Let not my faults this child disgrace.

 Farewell, good people, you all now see
What my bad conduct brought on me;
To die of shame and disgrace
Before this world of human race.

Awful, indeed, to think of death,
In perfect health to lose my breath;
Farewell, my friends, I bid adieu,
Vengeance on me must now pursue.

Great God! How shall I be forgiven?
Not fit for earth, not fit for Heaven,
But little time to pray to God,
For now I try that awful road.

Four years after Frankie paid the price for murder, the child of her marriage to Charlie Silver was placed under the guardianship of Frankie's mother. Nancy grew up to marry David W. Parker, who was killed in the Civil War's first battle of Bull Run, Virginia, known in the South as First Manassas. Nancy married again and lived into her nineties.

Tradition and a stone marker place Frankie's grave along North Carolina Highway 105, nine miles west of Morgantown. Whether her body was placed there is open to debate.

There is no question that she went to the gallows having misjudged Charlie Silver. In the words of an observer of the axe murder at Deyton's Bend, Frankie Silver had fallen prey to "that crocodile of vices," jealousy.

Therein was her tragedy.

According to Frankie's brother-in-law Alfred, "Nobody ever imagined she had a cause to be jealous, for Charlie was true to her."

Two

This Monstrous Affair

Saturday, April 9, 1836, was Richard P. Robinson's nineteenth birthday, and as he spent the day at his job as a clerk, he was looking forward to an evening visiting a beautiful prostitute named Helen Jewett.

Born in Durham, Connecticut, he was the first of eight sons and as a boy had proved to be both quite a good wrestler and a skilled debater. Attending the local academy, he'd learned Latin and was deemed by teachers to be one of their brightest students and a gifted writer. By every measure he appeared to be a fine young man with a promising future.

One of those who held that view was a cousin, Joseph Hoxie. A merchant known for benevolent, educational, and political activities, he owned a dry-goods emporium in Maiden Lane in New York City.

Engaged as a clerk in the store, Robinson quickly embraced the enticements of city life. His boyishly handsome face, set off by curling golden-brown hair, soon became one of the most familiar in the "fast set." Cutting a dashing figure in a jaunty cap and long Spanish cloak, he enjoyed attending the theater. Most of all, he loved spending time with beautiful young women. But if he found himself without the company of a respectable one, he had no qualms about seeking solace in one of the city's flourishing houses of prostitution.

The one at Number 41 Thomas Street was rented by Rosina Townsend. It stood not far from New York's City Hall and offices of the daily newspapers that stretched along Park Row. It was also an easy walk from Maiden Lane. While Mrs. Townsend contended that she ran a respectable boardinghouse for women, anyone the least bit observant and possessing but a modicum of common sense knew it was a fancy whorehouse. It offered elegant furnishings, discreet and efficient servants, and a cadre of the most attractive young women Mrs. Townsend's roster of customers could desire.

While Robinson could not hope to compete with the richest of this clientele in money and the social status it brought, nor in the power of the politicians and journalists who patronized the house, he fit in well with most of the men who were lawyers, merchants, and clerks.

Mrs. Townsend, the young women of the house, and the servants knew this attractive youth as Frank Rivers.

When he rang the doorbell shortly past nine o'clock, he was met by the young woman he had come to see.

"Oh, my dear Frank," exclaimed Helen Jewett, "how glad I am that you've come."

They had met the previous year, not by way of being introduced by Mrs. Townsend, but by chance in the lobby of a theater. In an exhibition of charmingly daring chivalry, Robinson had leaped in to rescue Jewett from the advances of a drunken ruffian.

Her reward to him was an invitation to call on her at an address on Duane Street. Robinson immediately recognized it as a house of prostitution. Run by Mrs. Mary Berry, it was known as the "Palais de la Duchessse Berri."

Robinson agreed to call. Using the name Frank Rivers, he soon learned that Helen's interest in him went beyond gratitude and an interest in developing a professional relationship. She expressed genuine affection, and to Robinson's surprise, he found himself returning it. He asked her to write to him.

"When I made you a promise that I would write you," she penned on June 17, 1835, "you, perhaps did not expect that I would, as the ladies are not apt to keep their promises when there is nothing in a tangible shape to make them binding."

The letter concluded, "You do not know how much I want to see you. Believe me, I think your acquaintance a very valuable acquisition, and should dispense with your visits with much reluctance and regret; and shall never voluntarily do anything which may render me unworthy of your confidence and esteem."

Three days later she wrote, "I know not my Dear Frank what your idea of this chequered life may be, but to me the current of existence would be but a black and sluggish stream, if love did not guild [*sic*] its surface and impel its tide. I anticipate a further acquaintance with you will throw an additional charm over my time, and make the sands of life run more gaily than before. There is so much sweetness in that voice, so much intelligence in that eye, and so much luxuriance in that form, I cannot fail to love you."

Robinson's letters, in which he called her Nell, were no less romantic.

On a Sunday less than a month after the relationship began, he wrote to her, "Here I sit, now almost noon, just out of bed, fresh from heavenly dreams of you. Nell, how pleasant it is to dream, be where you will and as hungry as you will, how supremely happy one is in a little world of our own creation. At best we live one little hour, strut at our own conceit and die. How unhappy must those persons be who cannot enjoy life *as it is,* seize pleasure as it comes floating on like a noble ship, bound for yon-der distant port with all sails set. Come will ye embark?—then on we go, gayly, hand in hand, scorning all petty and trivial troubles, eagerly gazing on *our rising* sun, till the warmth of its beams (i.e.love) causes our sparkling blood to o'er-flow and mingle in holy delight, as mind and soul per-chance some storms arise, but our good bark conscious of its valuable burden, labor and yields momentarily to the breezes of Heaven, but like a fond girl, after the storm is past, is ten times more fond of its lover and burthen."

He signed his letters, "Yours, Frank"

Presently, however, the "noble ship" of their love affair, both in words, in Jewett's room in Mrs. Berry's house, and in other houses to which Jewett moved early in 1836, ran into rough waters. She found that at times her lover could be aloof and even downright mean.

In a dark and brooding letter to her in mid-February, he admitted to "feelings over which I have no control, and which, if trifled with in any way, would make me unhappy and almost crazy."

In late January 1836 Richard Robinson provided an ex-planation for his moodiness. He found it painful to know that she made herself available to other men for money. He wrote, "I, *cannot,* I cannot sit with you in the presence of one who has, and may again purchase you as his."

He said he was never happier than when he was with her at the theater, then went on to tell her that on Saturday evening he would be seeing a new play entitled *Norman Leslie*. Based on a 1779 book by Theodore Ray, it was about a man awaiting trial for the murder of a young girl.

Throughout early spring the relationship between the clerk and the prostitute veered back and forth between breakups and reconciliations. But when Helen Jewett heard tales that her lover was seeing other women, her letters took on a bitter and threatening tone. She called him "un-kind, ungenerous Frank." It was in his power, she wrote, "to decide whether or not I longer remain this unhappy."

Told that Robinson was frequently visiting another pros-titute on Broome Street, Jewett went to the house and at-tacked the woman, then wrote to Robinson pleading for forgiveness. A reconciliation followed but didn't last. Furious at the discovery that Robinson was again seeing other women, Jewett threatened to spread a story that Robinson had caused the death of a young girl whom he had wronged and then deserted.

Terrified that she would carry out the threat, he tried to buy her silence by promising to marry her. Jewett then heard that he was in fact planning to marry a young woman with wealth and the social status that came with it.

Robinson received another letter. "I feel amazingly like blowing you up, if I dared," said Jewett, "but not with powder."

The implication was not lost on Robinson.

Evidently, Helen Jewett believed she knew enough about him that might at the very least cause him public embarrassment. Terrified, he sent word that he wished to see her.

On Thursday, April 7, she wrote complaining that he had failed to keep his word or send "a single line, even in the shape of an excuse." The letter continued, "Please, Frank, pause, ere you drive me to madness. Come to see me tonight or tomorrow night. Come and see me and tell me how we may renew the sweetness of our earlier acquaintance, and forget all our past unhappiness in future joy. Slight me no more. Trample on me no further. Even the worm will turn under the heel. You have known how I have loved, do not, oh do not provoke the experiment of seeing how I can hate."

Robinson replied by note, "Keep quiet until I come on Saturday night, and then we will see if we cannot be better friends hereafter. Do not tell any person I shall come."

That evening at nine o'clock he rang Mrs. Townsend's doorbell. Helen Jewett offered a warm greeting, curled a possessive arm around his slim waist, and led him upstairs.

About an hour later Mrs. Townsend heard Helen's voice calling down the stairs for a bottle of champagne.

When Jewett took it from her at the bedroom door, the madam had a glimpse of Frank Rivers in Helen's bed.

Returning to her room, Mrs. Townsend was content that

all her Saturday-night clients had been tended in the manner they expected and which she required. As the evening progressed there was an occasional ring of the doorbell announcing the arrival of a new patron and the closing of the front door signifying a departure. But as the hands of her mantel clock neared one in the morning and the house fell still, she went to bed.

Upstairs in a room opposite Jewett's, Marie Stevens had been asleep since midnight, but a noise woke her. It sounded like a thump. When this was followed immediately by a woman's low moan, she got out of bed and listened at her door. A moment later she heard the door to Jewett's room open and close and the sound of footsteps going down the hall.

Opening her door a crack, she observed a tall man in a long cloak and carrying a small lamp going down the stairs. Thinking nothing more of it, she returned to bed.

Two hours later, Mrs. Townsend awoke and took the opportunity to see if all was well. As she left her room she found a lamp burning on a hall table and recognized that it belonged in Helen Jewett's room. She then noticed that the back door was open. She closed and bolted it and took the lamp to Jewett's room.

Finding the door ajar, she smelled something burning. When she opened the door wider, she saw thick black smoke. As she tried to peer through it a draft of air flowing into the bedroom from the hallway caused a smoldering fire to erupt into flames that illuminated and licked at a woman's body on the floor.

The madam recoiled with horror and shrieked, "Fire, fire!"

Dashing downstairs, she repeated the cry of alarm, then opened a window and shouted it into Thomas Street. Hearing her at his nearby post, a watchman (the New York City Police Department was not created until 1845) came running. Moments later two others responded.

Rushing into the smoke-filled room, they set about extinguishing the flames. As the smoke cleared, they found the body of a woman facedown on the floor.

Clad in a nightgown, she had one arm raised over her head and the other across her breast. Her left side from the waist up was badly charred. Her left temple appeared to have been struck savagely three times with something heavy and sharp.

The man whom Mrs. Townsend had seen in Jewett's bed was gone. Asked to name him, she replied, "Frank Rivers." Queried about how he had been dressed, she replied that he'd been wearing a long dark cloth cloak.

Might any of the women happen to know Frank Rivers's address?

One of the women said she believed he was employed as a clerk by a Maiden Lane dry-goods merchant.

Officers Dennis Brink and George Noble rushed to the address and were told by a night watchman that the clerk's name was Richard P. Robinson and that he lived in a boardinghouse owned by Mrs. Rodman Moulton at 42 Dey Street.

A startled and nervous servant girl who opened the door to the insistent knocking of the two men confirmed that Richard Robinson was a boarder. She readily escorted the officers to the room that he shared with James Tew, a clerk for a Williams Street clothier.

Sleepy-eyed, Tew responded to the servant's rap on the door. When he opened it, Brink and Noble saw another man apparently sound asleep in the double bed.

Shaken awake by Tew, Robinson exclaimed, "This is an odd business."

When the two intruders identified themselves as police officers, he showed no emotion. Ordered to get dressed and come with them to the station house on Chambers Street, he offered no protest. Asked if he owned a dark cloth cloak, he replied that he did, but that it was made of a combination of wool and silk known as camblet. For the journey to the police station he put on a double-breasted frock coat.

The officers noticed that a leg of Robinson's dark trousers bore a white stain.

After leaving Dey Street, Robinson realized he was not being taken to the police station. He asked, "Where are we going?"

When Brink replied, "To a house on Thomas Street," the officer discerned a flicker of a change in Robinson's cool demeanor.

"A woman named Helen Jewett was murdered there," Brink said. "We have reason to believe you killed her."

Robinson exclaimed, "Well, I certainly did not."

On arriving at the house, Brink and Noble found seven additional watchmen in the parlor, along with the highest-ranking police magistrate, Oliver Lowends.

Also present was the city coroner, William Schureman. He looked at Robinson and said, "Come with me, young man."

Led upstairs to Jewett's room, Robinson was shown the body while the coroner and the accompanying police scrutinized him for any sign of emotion. But Robinson disappointed them by remaining passive.

He could not have done this horrible deed, he protested, because he had been at home all night. "Do you think I would blast my brilliant prospects by so ridiculous an act?" he demanded. "I am a young man of only nineteen years of age yesterday, with the most brilliant prospects."

Unmoved, the police arrested him.

While Brink and Noble were apprehending Robinson in the Dey Street boardinghouse, evidence had been discovered at Number 41 Thomas Street. Under a pillow on Helen Jewett's bed they found a man's handkerchief. It would be identified as belonging to another of Jewett's clients, George P. Marston.

The only man who'd been in Jewett's room, said Townsend, was Frank Rivers.

In the backyard lay the apparent murder weapon—a bloodstained hatchet. On the ground next to a whitewashed fence was a man's cloak. A woman who lived in the house beyond the fence said she had been awakened by the sound of a cellar door being forced open. She then observed a man emerge from the basement and dash into the street.

As the night wore on toward dawn, Robinson continued to deny having killed Helen Jewett.

At nine o'clock two doctors arrived to take charge of the body and to conduct an autopsy to learn the cause of death. They ruled that Jewett would have been killed instantly by any of the blows to the head. The attack had come as a surprise, they said, because they found no evidence that she had struggled. The fire had been set in a vain attempt to conceal the murder.

After randomly selecting twelve men from a crowd that had assembled outside the house, the coroner empaneled a jury and conducted an inquiry.

It ended with the men asserting, "It is the opinion of this jury from the evidence before them that the said Helen Jewett came to her death by a blow or blows inflicted on the head, with a hatchett [cq] by the hand of Richard P. Robinson."

He was immediately taken to Bridewell, a city jail on Broadway west of City Hall that was earmarked for demolition. In the Revolutionary War the British had used it to confine captured American rebels. It was being used currently as a debtors' prison.

A newspaper reporter who had learned of the horror on Thomas Street and rushed to the jail to observe Helen Jewett's accused killer described Richard Robinson's "countenance clear, calm and unruffled" and his demeanor so composed that he asked for "some segars [sic] to smoke."

Word of such a gruesome murder could not long remain unreported to James Gordon Bennett, the editor of the *New York Herald*. Arriving on Thomas Street in the afternoon, he pushed through a throng of curiosity-seekers and rapped on the door. A policeman admitted him immediately.

An angry onlooker demanded of the policeman, "Why did you let that man in?"

"He is an editor," came the reply. "He is on public duty."

Later, Bennett described what he found in the room. "I could scarcely look at it for a second or two," he wrote. "Shortly I began to discover the lineaments of the corpse, as one would the beauties of a statue of marble. It was the most remarkable sight I ever beheld—I never have, and never expect to see such another. 'My God,' exclaimed I, 'how like a statue! I can scarcely conceive that to be a corpse.' Not a vein to be seen. The body looked as white—as full—as polished as the pure Parisian marble. The perfect figure—the exquisite limbs—the fine face—the full arms—the beautiful bust—all—all surpassing in every respect the Venus de Medici [*sic*] . . . For a few moments I was lost in admiration at this extra-ordinary sight—a beautiful female corpse—that surpassed the finest statue of antiquity."

Helen Jewett had been a beauty, all right. But how and why had she come to lead the life of a prostitute and reach so ghastly a fate? As New Yorkers posed these questions to themselves, the city's newspapers rushed to provide answers, and none with more interest than James Gordon Bennett's *Herald*.

Recognizing a means to boost circulation, Bennett dictated a banner headline:

MOST ATROCIOUS MURDER

With the paper's steam-driven presses working overtime, the *Herald* was barely able to keep up with demand. Then, at the worst possible moment, the machinery broke down. Bennett complained, "We could have sold thirty thousand copies yesterday, if we could have got them to work."

In pouncing on Helen Jewett's murder and the plight of

the handsome youth who stood accused of it, Bennett revolutionized the institution of the press and defined a role for that institution in the American system of criminal justice that continues to this day. In events that were about to unfold following the murder of Helen Jewett and the subsequent trial of Richard P. Robinson, the newspapers of the era invented what a twentieth-century generation of journalists would call "investigative reporting."

The newspapers of New York City in April 1836 went beyond mere reporting of facts and took it upon themselves to dig into all aspects of the murderous drama and into the lives of victim and accused. Regarding the handsome young man in Bridewell jail, reporters provided readers sympathetic descriptions. One of Bennett's competitors, the *Transcript,* offered:

> It is not to be wondered at that such an excitement does exist as was manifested in every part of the city yesterday, in relation to this dreadful and almost unparalleled atrocity. The high respectability of the family and connexions [*sic*] of the unfortunate young man who is charged with the aggravated crime; his heretofore exemplary and excellent character and conduct; his youth; the superior accomplishments, beauty and attractions of the poor murdered girl, compared with those ordinarily possessed by the common herd of unfortunates; the deliberate, premeditated, ferocious character of the assassination; and the desperate means which were resorted to, to prevent exposure and detection; all combine to invest the catastrophe with an interest and a horror that have rarely, if ever, been connected with the occurrence of any homicide, however heart-rending and awful, in any country.

The New York Sun also offered a portrait of Robinson as an unlikely hatchet-wielder, citing "his general mildness of disposition and correct deportment."

Bennett continued his personal interest in the affair by visiting the murder scene again. As Hy Turner, the preeminent historian of the Park Row newspapers, noted in his 1999 book, *When Giants Ruled,* a change came over the editor.

"At first, he was convinced of Robinson's guilt," Turner wrote, "but he began an independent investigation of the killing and seemed to change his mind about the circumstances implicating the suspect."

Bennett asked in print, "Can there not be shown to be naturally growing out of some other person's guilt—of the deep conspiracy of female rivals—of the vengeance of female wickedness—of the burnings of female revenge? The cloak—the hatchet—the twine [found wrapped around the hatchet, it was the type used where Robinson was employed]—the whitewash on the pantaloons [Robinson's trousers]—the traces of blood—all the circumstances to cover the youth with guilt—may yet be explained on the trial."

Not everyone found Bennett's obsession with the murder to their liking. One Bennett critic said he was "like a vampire to a newly found graveyard—like the carrion bird to the rotten carcass—like any vile thing, to its congenital element."

This was not the view of a public who not only scooped up every edition of the *Herald* but every paper containing Jewett stories. But Bennett didn't limit himself to visits to the scene of the crime and speculations about a conspiracy to pin the crime on Robinson. The tireless editor invented the journalistic interview by questioning Rosina Townsend.

When all the queries had been posed and answered, Bennett saw in the madam a sinister figure. He declared, "She is the author and finisher of this mystery."

Caught off guard by this apparent scoop, the rival *Sun* interviewed Townsend and printed her claim that the interview with the *Herald* had not happened. Townsend denounced Bennett as a "depraved inventor."

Bennett responded by writing and publishing a poem with pornographic undertones about the madam, which began:

> Rosina's parts for all mankind,
> Were open, rare and unconfined,
>   Like some free port of trade;
> Merchants unloaded here their freights,
> And agents from each foreign state,
>   Here first their entry made.

In seizing the Jewett murder as a method to pump up *Herald* circulation, Bennett had declared full-scale war on New York's other leading newspapers, the *Sun* and the *Transcript*. The latter's editors at first had hoped to shun a lurid story they deemed "disgraceful." Soon they were forced to change their tune.

With the newspapers in agreement on the otherwise laudable nature of Richard Robinson, they turned their collective attention to the victim. On April 12 the *Sun* cited a "respectable source" in an article announcing that Helen Jewett's real name was Ellen Spaulding, daughter of Major General Spaulding in Maine.

The story went on to portray an intelligent girl who had attended a fine boarding school, where she had excelled in studies of French and Italian. The sad downfall of Ellen Spaulding began with her seduction by a bank cashier. As a result of the man's "heartless perfidy," said the newspaper, Ellen "abandoned herself to her late degraded course."

The *Transcript* produced a different version of Jewett's life, not on the basis of an unnamed source, but out of the newspaper's archives. It was a two-year-old story in which its police reporter, William Attree, had written an account of Jewett's life that had been provided by Helen herself. Published on June 30, 1834, the article titled "Fruits of Seduction" had stemmed from a complaint filed with the police by Jewett that she had been accosted and kicked in a theater by the son of a prosperous merchant.

To convince readers of the legitimacy of the story Attree included "a brief sketch of the history of this young girl" who in Attree's words had suffered "the misery resulting from the villainous artifices of those whose sole aim in life seems to be the seduction of a young and innocent girl, and then abandon her to the sneers and insults of the heartless and despicable."

Helen Jewett had told Attree a story similar to the one that ran in the *Sun*. She'd been born in Massachusetts, orphaned early, and placed in the care of a guardian who put her in a boarding school. Her seducer was the son of a merchant who took her to Boston "to live in sin." Rescued by the guardian but feeling shamed, and believing that regaining her former standing in society was "impossible," Attree wrote, Jewett had fled to New York City, "alone and unprotected."

On the same day that the *Transcript* and *Sun* ran their accounts of Helen Jewett's life, the correct version appeared in Bennett's *Herald*. Her actual name, declared the newspaper, was Dorcas Doyen.

She came to New York City from New England, but not from Massachusetts. She had been born in Augusta, Maine, and orphaned at an early age. Taken into the family of a judge by the name of Western, she was educated at the Cony Female Academy. She'd lost the "honor and ornament of the female character," said the *Herald* story, at age sixteen to a bank cashier, not as a result of seduction, but willingly. After a falling-out with the judge, she left Augusta for Portland and became "a regular Aspasia" [a fifth-century B.C. Greek courtesan and mistress of Pericles] by taking up prostitution as Maria B. Benson. Moving to Boston, she adopted the name Helen Mar.

As Helen Jewett in New York City, the *Herald* story continued, she delighted in wearing a green dress and strolling seductively along Broadway, catching the eyes of young brokers, and after seducing them claiming, "You have ruined me. I'll ruin you—I delight in your ruin."

The day after the *Herald* account of how Dorcas Doyen became Helen Jewett, only to be killed with a hatchet, James Gordon Bennett pointed an accusatory editorial finger, but not at Robinson. He faulted "a state of society" that produced many Helen Jewetts. Because of society's failings, he asserted, "We are guilty alike."

"Suppose Robinson is guilty," he wrote, "suppose he is carried out to Bellevue, and privately executed according to our bloody law. Will that take away the awful guilt of the present age—of this city—of our leaders in society—of our whole frame of morals and manners in permitting such a state of things to exist in a respectable, moral, and Christian city?"

The next edition of the *Transcript* assailed Bennett's proposition that Robinson might have been the victim of a conspiracy. The paper suggested that Bennett somehow had turned to bribery to underpin his surmise that the women in the Thomas Street bordello participated in a conspiracy in which Rosina Townsend planned to pin the murder on Robinson.

"The excitement in the public mind in reference to this monstrous affair," said the editorial of April 14, "and, notwithstanding the puny and purchased efforts of a ricketty [*sic*] print—notorious only for its easy access to petit bribery, and as being the most corrupt, profiligate, and contemptible concern that was ever palmed upon any community—to produce an impression that other persons than Robinson have been the perpetrators of the foul assassination; yet the general conviction from the evidence before the public, is, (and we record it with regret,) that he alone is the guilty individual."

Four days later the *Sun* also launched an attack on Bennett's conspiracy theory. It found one of its own in the form of "heartless and fiend-like attempts which are now in progress, made by the associates of the prisoner Robinson in his debaucheries and iniquities, through a supple tool [Bennett] whom they have found willing to prostrate his press [*Herald*] to their diabolical purpose, to create in the public mind a prejudice against the unfortunate inmates of the house at which the murder occurred, and particularly against Mrs. Townsend, its proprietor."

Had Rosina Townsend concocted a scheme to kill Jewett, direct suspicion upon Robinson and somehow gain by it, the madam certainly had reason to regret it. Due in no small measure to the Bennett conspiracy theory, she received death threats and turned to the police for protection. Notoriety, and now the presence of police watching the premises, instantly resulted in a lack of clients. With customers shunning the establishment, several of Rosina's girls decamped to other houses of prostitution. Effectively forced out of business and in need of funds, Rosina Townsend arranged to have the house's furnishings sold at auction.

The event drew the morbidly curious and a large contingent of young men who happily paid up to four times the value of the items on the selling block. When Helen Jewett's bed was sold, it was promptly smashed into pieces that were, according to an account of the auction in Bennett's *Herald,* carried away "as meekly, but joyously, as would a pilgrim a portion of the true cross."

Most if not all of the youths who scavenged Mrs. Townsend's belongings demonstrated their sympathy for the man in Bridewell jail by sporting "Robinson cloaks" and caps like those he had worn on his last visit with Jewett.

In addition to haberdashers and tailors seeing a nice profit in capitalizing on the murder, lithographers rushed to get out sketches, drawings, and paintings that depicted the murder in progress. Artists turned out romanticized images of Helen Jewett in her smartest attire or lounging on a couch in alluring poses. And there was a grisly picture by H. R. Robinson (no relation to Richard) of a dead Helen half naked and partially draped with a burned blanket—in vivid colors.

Of this gruesome souvenir the *Sun* said, "It is sufficiently indecent to render it attractive to persons of depraved tastes, but as to being a likeness of Ellen [*sic;* some
papers called her Ellen] those who have seen her say that
H. R. Robinson has murdered her far more barbarously
than Richard P. Robinson did." Of course, Richard was yet
to be convicted of the murder.

In 1836, as today, the press and public opinion far out-
distanced the legal system in rendering judgment on someone accused of a crime, especially a sensational one. But
the wheels of justice were turning in the *People* v. *Richard
P. Robinson.* The first proceeding had been the hastily convened coroner's inquest with its dragooned jurors finding
that Helen Jewett had been bludgeoned to death with a
hatchet in the hand of Richard Robinson.

Next on the calendar would be a grand jury. After it
returned a true bill of indictment Robinson was taken from
the dilapidated Bridewell jail and confined in a cell at
Bellevue, a facility at Twenty-ninth Street. Overlooking the
East River, it served as a hospital, a place for the insane,
and a lockup for those awaiting criminal trials.

As the government moved inexorably toward putting Robinson in the dock, Richard's employer, Joseph Hoxie, was
engaged in hiring lawyers to defend him. He chose some of
the best in the city: Ogden Hoffman, William Price, and Hugh
Maxwell. But as they conferred with their client and portrayed
him in public statements as "this innocent boy," they and avid
readers of the newspapers were hit with a shocking revelation,
in Robinson's own hand, that he hadn't been such a fine,
upstanding, and respectable young man.

Evidence of this was found in pages of a diary discovered
by police magistrate Lowends in Robinson's room in the
Dey Street boardinghouse. A hint of what might be found
within its pages appeared on its cover: "Whoever shall pry
unbidden into the secrets of this book, will violate the
whole of the ten commandments."

Editors of the *Sun* and *Transcript* who obtained one of

the diary's two volumes were not intimidated. The latter described the contents as "appalling and astounding." Both papers deluged their eager readers with excerpts.

"Most youths of seventeen or eighteen years of age take pride in boasting of their amours, of their dissipations, and of their wild exploits," Robinson wrote. "I have, however, no taste for such exposures. If I had, I could mention things that would make my old granny, and even wiser folks, stare, notwithstanding that I am young, and look very innocent."

While the diary omitted details of Robinson's liaisons with women, the portrait that emerged was that of such a morally corrupt young man that even Mr. Bennett of the *Herald* was shaken. He declared, "Robinson's private life appears to have been, so far as the female sex was concerned, licentious in the extreme." But Bennett noted that so were the lives of "hundreds of his age and sex, still moving in respectable society, smiled upon by the virtuous; adorned by the beautiful and desired by the witty and accomplished."

Furthermore, Bennett asserted, as dismal as the diary was, it was not evidence that Robinson had become so morally bankrupt that he was capable of murder.

Proof of that had to be presented at trial by the prosecutors—and accepted by a jury beyond a reasonable doubt.

New Yorkers interested in gaining glimpses into the mind and soul of Richard Robinson were not limited to reading excerpts of the diary in newspapers. A pamphlet containing longer portions of it was being peddled on the streets. The preface to this document noted that there seemed to be "nothing in nature destitute of interest to him" and "little in his appearance or conversation of strong character."

Publishing the diary, the printer high-mindedly asserted, "will do more to guard the footsteps of the young than all the fictions of the stage, or the homilies of the pulpit."

While depicting Robinson in the vilest terms as a "consummate scoundrel," the pamphlet portrayed Helen Jewett as a beautiful girl tragically seduced and set on the path to a "career of guilt" and ultimate perdition. Like Bennett, the publisher found Robinson's history "very much like the history of thousands of other young men, similarly educated, who have left behind them the restraints of home, and waded in the dissipation of cities."

Copied into the diary by Robinson was a letter from his father that expressed concerns about Richard's decision to move to New York. "I fear that your moral character may suffer," he wrote to his son. "You will there be ensnared by a thousand temptations which I fear you have not the strength of principle to resist. I know your self-confidence; but I also know your weaknesses, my son. I tremble for you. Indeed, you are, I fear, a child of the devil."

While his diary was bared for all who cared to read it, Robinson sat in a Bellevue cell awaiting trial. A visitor found him smoking and reading. "As his trial approaches," he went on, "his great flow of good spirits decreases, but his firmness remains unshaken."

When the trial opened on a Thursday in early June, in a courtroom on the second floor of City Hall, a crowd of six thousand gathered in the rain in City Hall Park in vain hopes of getting seats. To cope with the throng fifty extra marshals were ordered to duty by the sheriff. The plan they devised to rotate spectators allowed a thousand at a time into the chamber.

Presiding in the Court of Oyer and Terminer would be Judge Ogden Edwards.

At age fifty-five he had been a member of the New York State Legislature and a judge for two decades. A seventeenth-century ancestor had been John Ogden, who was also a distant relative and namesake of Robinson's chief attorney. Forty-three-year-old Ogden Hoffman came to the trial with a sterling reputation as both a criminal defense lawyer and spellbinding speaker with a voice described as ranging from the note of a lute to the blast of a bugle. A graduate of Columbia University and a veteran of the War of 1812, he was a master debater and universally regarded as superior to any member of the bar and unparalleled in his command of criminal law. Part of that expertise had been garnered during a six-year term as district attorney. A year earlier he had been the D.A. who'd handled the complaint brought by Helen Jewett that had prompted William Attree of the *Transcript* to write her life story. He'd left the D.A.'s office to return to private practice six months before her murder.

Assisting Hoffman were his partner, Hugh Maxwell, a forty-nine-year-old former district attorney, and fifty-year-old William Price, an English-born Columbia graduate.

Presenting the case against Robinson was Hoffman's successor as the district attorney, Thomas Phoenix. He was not in the best of health. Assisting him was Robert H. Morris. About these two men's previous lives little is known. As they came to court, the consensus of the New York law community was that they were greatly outmatched by Hoffman and his associates.

Out of fifty-nine prospective jurors summoned to the court, only twenty-one appeared. An explanation for this demonstration of poor citizenship offered by author Patricia Cline Cohen in her celebrated 1998 book, *The Murder of Helen Jewett,* was that the absentees preferred paying a $25 fine "rather than risking prying questions about their acquaintance with brothel life and clerks like Robinson."

Required to stand throughout a five-hour jury-selection process, Richard appeared calm and composed and wore a blue suit. Because his hair had been closely cropped in jail, he wore a brown wig. With a jury picked, he stood for the reading of the indictment charging him with one count of willful and deliberate murder.

After District Attorney Phoenix's brief opening statement, Rosina Townsend was called to testify to admitting Robinson to the house between nine and ten o'clock, taking champagne to Helen Jewett's room at eleven, observing Robinson on the bed, the noise that awakened her, the burning lamp on the hallway table, the unlocked door, going to

Jewett's room, seeing the smoke and fire, and finding Jewett's dead body.

However, testimony about a thump and moans coming from Helen Jewett's room and about a man seen leaving the room carrying a lamp immediately thereafter did not come from Maria Stevens. The young woman had left Townsend's foundering establishment for another house and had died there only a few days before the trial opened.

Next came police testimony concerning the layout of the house, the backyard, the hatchet, and the cloak.

"Could someone who lived in the house have put the hatchet there?" Hoffman asked. Watchman Richard Eldridge said it was possible. But improbable.

A porter employed in Joseph Hoxie's store identified the hatchet as one he always used for chopping wood. When he'd looked for it the Monday after the murder, he'd been unable to find it.

A pair of public porters told of carrying letters back and forth between Robinson and Jewett. This testimony set off a squabble over admitting any of the letters into evidence. The fray ended with only one being accepted.

Robinson's roommate testified that Richard had been out late on the night of the murder and had returned to Dey Street after one or two o'clock.

The clerk in an apothecary on nearby Broadway told the jury that a week or so before the murder a man calling himself Douglas had wanted to buy arsenic to kill rats. The clerk had refused. Now he identified Douglas as Robinson.

All this was perhaps very interesting, said Hoffman, but Robinson was accused of killing Helen Jewett with a hatchet, not poison. Whether Robinson attempted "to obtain poison for the purpose of killing Ellen [sic] Jewett, or any other woman, was not proper evidence."

The judge agreed.

He also ruled Robinson's diaries were inadmissible because all its pages could not be certified as being in Robinson's handwriting.

To undermine a case of impressive circumstantial evidence Hoffman questioned the evidence that Robinson had been the only man in Jewett's room that night by introducing into evidence a handkerchief of another man that had been found under her pillow. A grocer named Furlong took the witness stand to swear that at the time of the murder Robinson was in his shop smoking cigars and reading newspapers.

The white stain on Robinson's trousers was explained by a nephew of Joseph Hoxie. He told of Hoxie's shop having just been painted and how he and Robinson had gotten white paint on their clothes. The manufacturer of the hatchet said that since 1834 he had sold 2,500 such tools in New York.

After five days of testimony, the time had come for summations. Following an opening skirmish between William Price for the defense and Robert Morris for the prosecution, the jury, spectators, and the press settled back in anticipation of the oratory of Ogden Hoffman.

They were not disappointed. Hoffman launched an attack on the credibility of the star witness for the state. Like James Gordon Bennett, Hoffman pointed to Rosina Townsend as the architect of a conspiracy against Robinson.

"It is her [*sic*] who has sworn against him; it is she who would erect a gallows for that man; it is she who would send him to an early grave," he said. "There is a foul conspiracy in this matter, and the whole in that house have combined . . . God knows who he had offended in that house."

District Attorney Phoenix took two hours to recapitulate a case that he believed he had shown to be overwhelmingly convincing for a verdict of guilty. He called Richard Robinson a monster and a vampire who was afraid Helen Jewett would expose some horrible secret.

When Phoenix took his seat, the hour was late—close to 11 P.M. Rather than adjourn court, Judge Edwards launched into his charge to the jury. When he finished a few minutes past midnight, he had all but directed the jurors to find the prosecution had failed to prove "beyond all reasonable doubt" that Robinson was guilty.

Testimony of prostitutes was not be believed, unless corroborated. Robinson could have left his cloak at some other time. Perhaps Robinson took the hatchet with him for self-protection while on his way to the brothel. If the jurors felt there was reasonable doubt, they must acquit and not "immolate an innocent victim."

The jury retired to deliberate around twelve-thirty. They returned well before 1 A.M. with a verdict of not guilty.

Spectators roared approval. Robinson burst into tears.

With the exception of James Gordon Bennet's *Herald,* the press assailed the verdict as a mockery of justice.

A free man, Richard Robinson left New York for Texas, which had declared freedom from Mexico as the Republic of Texas. He settled in Nacogdoches, opened a saloon a year later, and in 1838 became clerk of the county court, serving throughout the 1840s. During a trip east in 1855 he contracted a fever and died on August 8 in a hotel in Louisville, Kentucky.

An elderly black woman who had been hired by the hotel proprietor to attend to him as he lay dying reported that in his delirious state he kept saying the name of a woman she supposed was his wife—Helen Jewett.

Returned to Texas three months later, Robinson's body was buried in Nacogdoches by members of his Masonic lodge. They eulogized him as a "valiant soldier of the Republic" and a man admired by friends for a "character noble and firm of purpose."

Helen Jewett's body was dug up by medical students, reduced to a skeleton, and hung in a cabinet. A representation of her in wax, along with a figure of Robinson, became a central attraction of a chamber of horrors that traveled from city to city on the East Coast offering what one observer described as "an awful warning," especially to young men.

Three

Such a Man as That

The idea for a gun with a revolving ammunition chamber that popped into the inquisitive mind of a sixteen-year-old sailor aboard the brig *Corvo* en route to India in 1830 would affect the history of the United States like no other device. In the lore of firearms it's said that young man got the inspiration while observing the turning and locking of the ship's wheel. Having had an interest in guns since early childhood, the youth spent his spare time at sea carving a piece of wood to craft a pistol with a drum that automatically fed one bullet after another into the breech, allowing it to be fired several times without reloading.

When the young man returned to the United States in 1831, he showed his father and a friend who was commissioner of the U.S. Patent Office the prototype of a pistol that would be in the hands of soldiers and sailors on both sides of the Civil War and toted by the rugged men who took the West. The "revolver" would make Samuel Colt famous and rich.

Unfortunately, wealth was not in the cards for Sam Colt's older brother.

When Sam had his brainstorm on the *Corvo*, twenty-year-old John C. Colt already had a reputation as a rake and petty thief. By the time John was thirty, and Sam was manufacturing his firearms, John had perjured himself to join the Marines and committed forgery to get out of the service. He then become a professional gambler on river-boats.

While in the South he'd had a love affair with the mistress of a wealthy planter and barely escaped the man's fury with his life. Living in New York City in the autumn of 1841 with a woman he had not bothered to marry, he was barely earning a living as a teacher of bookkeeping and penman-ship in an office on the second floor of the Granite Build-ing. An office bloc on Chambers Street behind City Hall, its tenants were mostly picture-framers, bookkeepers, pub-lic stenographers, and scribes.

As an aid in teaching accounting and penmanship, Colt had published several books that had been printed by Sam-uel Adams on a press with which Adams also turned out the *Missionary Herald.* Concerned that Colt had fallen in arrears in paying for the work, Adams left his office on the damp afternoon of Friday, September 17, 1841, to see if he could collect at least part of the debt. Miserable weather notwithstanding, he found Broadway thronged by the com-merce of the largest city in the country, with a thriving seaport crowded by tall ships, which were bringing in so many immigrants that from 1835 to 1850 the city's popu-lation would double.

Along Park Row adjacent to City Hall stood the build-ings of James Gordon Bennett's *Herald* and its chief com-petitor, the *Sun* (the nettlesome *Transcript* had gone belly up in 1839), which five years earlier had pounced on the murder of Helen Jewett by Richard Robinson to wage a fierce circulation war. Now there was a fresh Park Row contender for readership.

Founded by Horace Greeley, the *New York Daily Trib-une* had issued its first edition on April 10. Nine days later Greeley asserted that his newspaper would be dif-ferent. Claiming a high moral ground and eschewing the kind of lurid coverage given the Jewett case, Greeley blasted the established Park Row penny-a-copy papers in general and Bennett in particular for their zest in poisoning "the fountains of public intelligence" and fanning "into destroying flames the hellish passions which now slumber in the bosom of Society."

Bennett lost no time in retorting, likening newcomer Greeley to a large, galvanized New England squash. That sensationalism paid off was evidenced by Bennett's new presses. No longer would he have to fret about broken-down printing machinery denying him even greater sales. In the cellar of the *Herald* hummed two brand-new presses capable of spewing out 6,000 copies of the paper an hour—vastly more than the output of the press used by Samuel Adams to print the *Missionary Herald* and the bookkeeping texts ordered by slow-to-pay John C. Colt.

Eager to reach his home and the enjoyment of a dinner prepared by his wife, Emeline, Adams scaled the stairs to the second floor, paused to catch his breath and steel himself for the unpleasant task of debt-collecting, and knocked on Colt's door. Admitted, he found himself in a one-room office whose most noticeable furnishings were a desk and a large wooden crate.

Eager to get the ugly business done, he demanded payment of the funds.

Colt replied that the amount demanded was incorrect.

As the disagreement quickly escalated into a shouting match, Adams grabbed Colt by his necktie and twisted it tightly. Gasping for breath, Colt reeled against his desk and searched for anything with which to fend off the irate bill-collector. The object he grabbed and smashed onto Adams's head with killing force was a short-handled combination hammer and hatchet.

Sinking into a chair, Colt gazed in horror at a widening red pool on the bare wood floor. Gripped by panic and fearing that the spreading puddle might seep into the gaps in the planks and through the ceiling of the room below, he lurched out of the chair, grabbed a towel, and began mopping it up. When he was done, the blood filled a third of a scrub bucket. Seated again and feeling sick in the stomach, he confronted the dilemma of a killer—what to do with the body.

Were he to go to the police and explain that he had acted in self-defense, Colt reasoned, they were bound to discover the misdeeds and perjuries in his past. Once the newspapers got hold of the story, he would undoubtedly face a terrible ordeal of further probing that could only result in disgrace for his family.

Overwhelmed by the horror of what had happened and unable to think clearly with the body sprawled before him, he left the office, locked the door, walked to City Hall Park, and sat on a bench. Having decided against reporting the deed to the police, he pondered again the problem of the body.

After a while he became too agitated to remain seated. He paced the small park for nearly an hour. Part of the time was spent weighing a plan to dispose of the corpse by setting fire to his room. But this plan was no guarantee that the body would be consumed by the flames. If it was not destroyed, he would be called upon to explain the presence of a dead man in his office.

Another way to solve his problem by fire, he speculated, was to burn down the *building*. But if the fire department arrived in time to put out the blaze before the flames consumed the office, he would still have to explain the bludgeoned corpse in his room.

Feeling more and more desperate, he returned to the office. With the door locked, he sat at his desk and stared despondently at the apparently insoluble predicament on the floor. It was not a large body. It could be easily shouldered and carried out, but that required wrapping it in something. A carpet would do nicely. Men were often seen entering and leaving buildings with carpets over their shoulders. Unfortunately, his office floor had no carpeting.

Looking around the room, he discovered the answer to his problem in the wooden crate. It had been there for days, yet for some reason he hadn't gotten rid of it. Was it big enough to hold the body? Estimating that it was, he removed his coat and set about the gruesome task. First he had to place the box next to the corpse. Lifting the body, he discovered the meaning of the term "deadweight." He also discovered to his dismay that it did not quite fit. Realizing that the dead man's clothes were the cause of the difficulty, he removed them and tried again. Finding it still did not fit, he trussed it tightly with rope and pieces of cloth. Then he found that the dead man's protruding knees kept the lid from closing. Exasperated, he stood on the lid and used the weight of his body to force it closed. Using the very tool that had killed Adams, he nailed the lid shut.

In the following minutes he bundled up the clothing, threw it down an outside privy, and made several trips carrying several buckets of water with which to scrub the floor. Satisfied with his work, he again left the office, this time to go to a bathhouse on Pearl Street. There he washed himself, along with his bloodstained shirt and trousers.

Returning to the Chambers Street building the next morning (Saturday), he hired a burly man for two-and-six-pence to help him carry the crate to the Maiden Lane wharf, where he paid the cost of having the box shipped aboard the freighter *Kalamazoo*, bound for New Orleans.

Satisfied that he had concealed his bloody deed, he evidently gave no thought to the likelihood that somewhere in the millions of people in the sprawling city of New York someone might wonder about the mysterious disappearance of the printer Samuel Adams.

Adams's wife, Emeline, certainly did. Never during their marriage had Samuel gone anywhere without informing her of his plans and where he would be. Her husband was not the sort of man who took an interest in other women. He was not a drinker or gambler. Consequently, she had expected him home at his customary hour on the night of Friday, September 17. That he didn't appear, and did not show up the next day and the next, could only be explained in terms of his having been the victim of an accident or having fallen prey to one of the gangs of ruffians and robbers from slum areas, such as the notorious Dead Rabbits and other packs of hoodlums who thrived in the Five Points area north of City Hall. They were the plague of the city.

Desperate for any information regarding her husband, she resorted to the common practice of placing notices regarding missing persons in newspapers. She sought to hear from anyone who had seen him on September 17, or had witnessed anything out of the ordinary that day.

As it happened, Henry Wheeler, who also taught bookkeeping and penmanship in an office next to Colt's, read the ad. He recalled hearing from the next room strange noises that sounded like the clash of fencing swords, followed by a thud. He'd been so concerned that he'd gone into the hallway to investigate. Finding nothing untoward, but fearing something might have happened to his fellow teacher, he peered through the keyhole of Colt's door and saw a man bending over something on the floor.

When Wheeler reported this series of events to Mrs. Adams, she went to the police.

After their investigation led to a man who on Saturday morning had observed two men carrying a heavy crate from the building, Mrs. Adams placed a new ad in newspapers in the hope of finding anyone who might provide further information regarding the mysterious box. This resulted in a wagoneer coming forward to report having transported the crate in question to a ship named *Kalamazoo* moored at the foot of Maiden Lane.

By now a week had passed since Adams had gone missing.

In that time, circumstances had arisen to delay the ship's departure for New Orleans.

Rushing aboard, police joined a team of stevedores in a

search of the hold. Approaching a particular crate, they smelled the foul odor of rotting flesh. Prying open the lid, they found the decomposing body of a nude man whose head had been savagely battered.

Identification of the ghastly remains as those of Samuel Adams was made by a gold pinkie ring and a scar on a leg. Horrified and outraged to learn that a brutal murder had been committed in a Chamber Street building within sight of his office at City Hall, Mayor Robert Hunter Morris appointed himself to lead a contingent of police to place John Colt under arrest.

When word of the murder swept across another street to editorial rooms of newspapers of Park Row, an even greater number of reporters rushed to cover the event.

Despite having expressed a policy for his new paper of not following others in dwelling on lurid crimes, Horace Greeley of the *Tribune* found himself with no choice but to cover the most sensational murder since the Jewett case. But this did not mean he couldn't find in such a sordid affair a moral message to preach to his readers. After inspecting the room where Adams met his death, he wrote on September 28:

> The imagination cannot avoid picturing to itself this terrible murder, nor can it dwell for a moment upon the scene without deep thrills of horror; that one human being, with the warm, bright sunlight streaming alike upon him and his victim, at the corner of two of the most thronged streets in our Metropolis, with the bustle of business and the voices of men sounding in his ears, should murder his fellow with such aggravated atrocity, and then proceed with such cool, heartless indifference to remove the corpse and to stifle the terrible voice which cried aloud, and all around him, for swift vengeance upon his most unholy act, seems impossible, and the mind half dreams—and rejoices

at the delusion—that some fiend from the realm of guilt and woe has wrought this awful ruin.

As he had done in covering the Jewett murder, James Gordon Bennett reveled in day-to-day reporting of the killing of Samuel Adams and a young man who, like Richard Robinson, was the scion of a respectable family but had somehow gone astray. *Herald* reporters were quickly unleashed to learn more about the hapless brother of the inventor of the Colt revolver.

An artist was sent to make a woodcut of Colt in jail. It showed him seated with upraised left arm resting on the arm of a chair, the hand with curled fingers at his temple, and wearing a stylish frock coat, white shirt, and large bow tie. On the same date on which Greeley offered his moralizing, Bennett's paper provided a word portrait of John Colt as "well made, but very slim, although full of nerve and sinew. He is about 5 feet 9 inches high. His hair is dark brown and curly, and he has largish whiskers. He would be good-looking but for his eye, which is one of those brown colored class of eyes that cannot be easily read, and that are generally found in the faces of all scoundrels, schemers and plotters."

Alarmed at such portrayals, Colt's lawyers—retained by his brother Sam—rushed to see Judge William Kent and demanded that he issue a judicial edict banning press coverage of the case. In response to this early attempt in the history of American journalism (if not the first) to impose what is now called a "gag order," Kent showed himself to be a jurist with a realistic grasp of the nature of New Yorkers.

"It would have been strange," he said, "if, in the city of New York, the public mind would have been shocked by the murder, but I have no doubt that every justice has been done to the prisoner."

To defend his brother, Samuel Colt and another brother, James Colt, a prominent lawyer in St. Louis, had enlisted the services of two outstanding lawyers. Dudley Selden was a former one-term congressman and a cousin of the Colts'. John A. Morrill was a veteran of the criminal bar whose most recent task had been a vain attempt to defend a notorious abortionist, Madame Restell, after the death of one of her clients.

The third member of this 1841 team of lawyers was Robert Emmett, described by journalistic historian Andie Tucher as "a smooth-tongued Irishman" with "a family tree studded with both lawyers and martyred patriots."

Mounting a defense was complicated by the fact that John Colt had confessed to killing Adams. Shortly after being arrested, he told a friend who visited him in jail that he had acted in self-defense. In his statement he recounted the argument with Adams, striking him with the tool, mopping up the blood, pacing City Hall Park and considering arson as his only way out, stuffing Adams into the crate, hiring a man to help him remove it, and his feeling of relief after he had placed the box on the *Kalamazoo*.

Bennett's *Herald* headlined: TRADESMAN BLUDGEONED FOR A PICAYUNE DEBT.

With the confession in the hands of the police and its details provided by Colt's friends to the newspapers, the only question in the mind of a fascinated public was whether John Colt would be found guilty of murder or the lesser crime of manslaughter, based on a plea of self-defense. But after Greeley's *Tribune* ran an article quoting Colt as saying mental illness was "hereditary in the family," the public and the prosecution expected an insanity defense. In the article Colt cited a sister who in "a fit of madness" had poisoned herself. He also asserted that he (Colt) had "several times become insane."

As the newspapers provided their avid readers with each new development in the case, John Colt railed against what he considered unfair treatment.

He complained to a visitor to his cell, "The newspapers!

They are the true mischief-breeders; *they* are the really un-principled and re-morseless murderers."

Compared to the coverage afforded Richard Robinson in the Jewett case, Colt's killing of Samuel Adams was presented in the papers as devoid of any aspect of romance. Helen Jewett had been a beautiful young woman. Both the hapless girl who'd been fated to become a prostitute and the young man with a promising future had fallen victim to a love-turned-to-hate. John C. Colt had bashed Samuel Adams's head with a hatchet in a tussle over a "picayune debt."

In the Jewett affair there had been ample room to specu-late upon a sinister conspiracy of jealous prostitutes led by a vindictive madam. Jewett's death had been premedi-tated—Robinson brought an axe into her room with the intention of using it to kill. The death of Samuel Adams had been impulsive—a hatchet grabbed off a desk in the midst of a struggle.

"Indeed, the facts of the Colt affair displayed none of the theatricality, the panache, the poetic potential of the prostitute's murder," wrote Andie Tucher in his book on journalistic coverage of both murders (*Froth and Scum: Truth, Beauty, Goodness, and the Ax Murder in America's First Mass Medium;* University of North Carolina Press, 1994). Tucher continued:

> It was petty and sordid, a crime more of petulance than of passion, with overtones of perjury rather than of privilege. The chief players of the drama were, by and large, humdrum characters. The suspect in the case had influential friends but no claque of like-minded supporters to whoop and cheer him in court. As the undistinguished teacher of an unlovely art, he never garnered much public interest, and his hard sullenness while on trial invited no sympathy. Nor were his attorneys either brilliant or provocative; their personal lives were unremarkable, their political and professional histories commonplace.

The murder victim, too, was no exotic being charged with myth and meaning, but rather an ordinary tradesman; character witnesses at the trial painted him as soft of voice, permissive toward his apprentices, and so mild-mannered that sharp words from a clergyman once drove him to tears. The scene of the crime was no elegant, fascinating haunt of the demimonde.

Yet there was a tantalizing bit of sex in John Colt's story to which newspapers were able to treat their readers. In digging into Colt's life they learned of the woman with whom he shared a bed without the formality of marriage. Their abode was a furnished room on the third floor of Number 42 Thomas Street, only a few doors away from Helen Jewett's elegant bedroom in Rosina Townsend's former whorehouse.

Her name was Caroline Henshaw and she was pregnant. But in the minds of press and public alike, a woman who lived in sin was not viewed with sympathy. At the trial, prosecutor James Whiting used Henshaw's involvement with Colt to warn women "not to put their earthly and eternal happiness in the keeping of such a man as that."

The wronged woman, shouted Bennett's *Herald,* was the widow—Emeline Adams. So carried away with her plight was Bennett that he was not satisfied with merely reporting facts. On October 6, 1841, he published an account of a drama in the courthouse where Colt was on trial in which Emeline Adams and John Colt found themselves face to face. Adams gave Colt a look, Bennett wrote, "as few ever received from a mortal" and in return Colt had "glared upon her like Macbeth upon the ghost of Banquo."

It was vivid writing, but the highly charged scene had not transpired. Bennett made it up, then went on to falsely state that the murder of her husband had turned Emeline Adams into a maniac. "Her reason is a shattered wreck," he declared, "and it is probable that she will soon lie peacefully beside her husband in the quiet grave." In fact, Adams was fine and looking forward to testifying at Colt's trial in January.

In preparing John Colt's defense the team of lawyers rejected the option of portraying Colt as a victim of hereditary insanity. They chose to persuade the jury that contrary to Adams's reputation as a mild-mannered man, the printer was a hothead who had attacked the startled bookkeeping-teacher. In a desperate act of self-defense Colt had grabbed the hatchet off the desk. This wasn't a case of murder. This was homicide in the heat of passion; by legal definition, manslaughter.

In this seemingly plausible defense the prosecutor, James Whiting, discerned flaws. If the killing of Samuel Adams had been an impulsive act of self-defense, why had Colt gone to such extraordinary lengths to conceal the act? Why pack the body in a crate and cart it off to a ship bound for New Orleans? Was the convenient presence of that crate in the room happenstance? Why hadn't Colt gone straight to the police? These were not the acts expected of a man who'd simply defended himself. But they were perfectly in keeping with the actions of a man who had *premeditated* murder.

As in the Robinson case, the trial convened in a large room on the second floor of City Hall. Although crowds gathered around the building, unlike Robinson's trial, according to a *Herald* reporter, "excellent regulations prevented any confusion or uproar." Only persons who'd been "authorized and required to attend the trial were admitted."

John Colt entered the courtroom wearing a dark blue frock coat and black satin vest, black trousers and boots, and a black silk kerchief looped loosely around his neck. A reporter noted that he appeared "uncommonly calm" but "evidently somewhat nervous, though he suppressed all traces of emotion." Awaiting him were his father, "a venerable, fine, benevolent looking man," and brother Samuel.

On the opposite side of the room sat Emeline Adams, looking "pale and agitated" with a black veil down. She was accompanied by her father. A reporter noted that she gazed toward John Colt "earnestly" and exhibited no signs of the "mania" and shattered reason, which were attributed to her by Bennett. Indeed, the editor of the *Herald* criticized her in print on January 22 for her "cold, unfeeling, and flippant manner."

A jury, which would find itself sequestered in the Knickerbocker Hotel on nearby Park Row, consisted of twelve men who despite their familiarity with the case, and in a few instances had expressed opposition to the death penalty, had sworn to render a verdict based solely upon the evidence presented in court. With the jury accepted by both sides, Judge Kent called on the clerk to present the indictment.

Standing with arms folded and gazing "earnestly" at the jury during the reading, Colt "looked tolerably calm, but his lips moved as if in the act of chewing all the while."

After an opening statement by the prosecutor, the first witness called was Henry Wheeler to relate hearing noises like fencing foils and a thud. He then told of peering through a keyhole and seeing a man bent over something on the floor in the room next to his on the second floor of the Granite Building, located directly behind City Hall.

Next came the man who had helped Colt carry a heavy crate from that building and then carted it to the ship *Kalamazoo* moored at the Maiden Lane wharf. To the witness stand came the mayor of New York to relate how he had supervised the arrest of John C. Colt, and in so doing, although he did not say so on the witness stand, he had reaped political benefit from the act.

The coroner and other medical experts testified concerning the condition of Adams's body and to the mortal wounds to the head.

Seizing the opportunity, Colt's chief defense lawyer, Dudley Selden, questioned whether such blows could have been struck in self-defense. To the astonishment of Selden, his client, and everyone else in the court, the prosecution asserted that doctors who had examined the head had been mistaken in attributing them to blows from a hatchet. They now said the holes could have been made by shots from a "six-shooter," which John Colt was known to possess. If so—if Adams had not been killed with a hatchet in an act of self-defense, but with a pistol—then there could be no doubt that Adams had died as the result of cold-blooded, deliberate murder.

Might the head wounds have been inflicted with a gun? Could such wounds have been made by pistol balls? Who was more qualified to answer these questions than the man seated in the courtroom—the inventor of the revolver?

In a scene described as "one of the rowdiest, most startling, and most bizarre the city had yet seen," Samuel Colt was called as a witness to demonstrate for the first time, and possibly the only time, the effect of bullets at various distances by firing a gun in a courtroom. To do so, he used a book as the target.

Now the question was whether the damage inflicted on the book matched the damage done to Samuel Adams's head. But how could such a comparison be made without examining the wounds to the head? Samuel Adams was long-buried. Producing the head as evidence required not only exhumation of Adams's body but its decapitation. Ordered to carry out the grisly task, the coroner delivered the head to the court and sat with it in his lap while the lawyers argued about actually showing it to the jury.

"However painful it is," declared Judge Kent, "justice must be administered and the head produced, if the jury think it necessary."

The jury said it was.

As the coroner held the head for all to see and demonstrated that the blade of the hatchet perfectly fit the wounds, John Colt covered his eyes with a hand.

Although the prosecution's theory that Colt shot Adams

to death had been disproved, the defense still had to persuade the jury that killing Adams with the hatchet had not been a coldly planned act. Selden argued that no one who intended to murder would plan to do so in daytime, in a building filled with people, in the very heart of the city—and choose an axe as a weapon. But there was no way for Selden to explain away Colt's actions and demeanor after the killing.

To underscore Colt's behavior following the brutal death of the printer, the prosecutor introduced Colt's confession to paint a picture of Colt's utter callousness in mopping up blood, stripping the corpse to make it fit into the crate, standing on the trunk to force the lid shut, disposing of clothing, hiring a man to haul away the crate—then going about his business as usual.

There was no question that John Colt had killed Samuel Adams, Judge Kent reminded the jurors as he gave the charge. The decision facing them was not guilt or innocence, but whether Colt had committed a premeditated homicide—murder—or acted in self-defense—manslaughter. Having completed an explanation of the law, he launched into a summation of evidence and what conclusions the jurors might draw from it.

If they believed that John Colt had acted in self-defense, they must find him guilty of manslaughter. But if "the coolness of character," "careless" and "gay air," and "intrepidity and coolness such as rarely can be met" which Colt "displayed" after the death of Samuel Adams were deemed by the jurors "sufficient to believe him capable of premeditation," they must "bring him in guilty of murder."

The case went to the jury on the night of Saturday, January 29, 1842.

It returned at four o'clock Sunday morning with a verdict of murder.

Dudley Selden sprang to his feet immediately to demand a new trial and was denied. He promptly informed Judge Kent of intent to appeal. Colt was taken back to his cell, confident that his conviction would be overturned outright, or that a new trial would be ordered. Should he lose on appeal, he believed that efforts of his family and friends in the state capital of Albany would result in a life-sparing order of clemency from Governor William H. Seward.

Newspapers that had found him guilty from the outset of the case hailed the verdict and built on the sorry affair a platform from which to preach public and private morality. Only eleven days after the murder of Samuel Adams, and within hours of John Colt's arrest, Horace Greeley shaped the story into a morality lesson. Colt's slide into "a depth of horrid guilt and blasting infamy," he wrote, showed that crime was a vital, growing power that "thrusts downward deep into the heart of its mighty roots, and overshadows the whole inner being with its death-distilling shade." On that same day James Gordon Bennett's *Herald* saw in Colt's brown eyes the look of "all scoundrels, schemers and plotters."

The *Sun* declared the murder "one of the most coldblooded and atrocious ever perpetrated" and found the verdict fitting. "Had the result been different," it editorialized, "the moral atmosphere would have seemed tainted."

Looking ahead, Bennett wrote on the day Colt was found guilty, "Now comes, then, the most exciting part of the drama; will he be hung—or will a new trial be granted? Will the Governor dare to pardon him? We think not. The verdict seems to give general satisfaction. The public have had their eye on Colt from the time of his arrest till this hour; and had the verdict not been 'murder,' we don't know what would have been the consequence."

When John Colt's appeal was rejected, the papers welcomed the decision, although when the date for Colt's execution by hanging was set for November 18, 1842, the *Sun* and Mr. Greeley's *Tribune* expressed opposition to the imposition of the death penalty on principle. But that was hardly the end of press interest in the condemned man. The papers scrambled to publish all the information about Colt that came their way, either gathered by their own reporters or purchased from Colt's friends. Leading the pack was the *Sun,* which put out a pamphlet containing letters purportedly written by Colt as he awaited execution.

"Death hath no terrors for me," one declared. "There is a world above this, and I believe a just one. Man, at the worst, can only destroy the body."

This fatalism, however, did not dissuade John Colt from seeking to avoid the noose. Family and friends were working hard to persuade Governor Seward to commute the death sentence. A stream of letters and petitioners themselves flowed into Albany. All proved unavailing.

Other sensations were not long in coming. Rumors circulated that friends of John Colt had tried to bribe guards to let him escape disguised in women's clothing smuggled into his cell by his lover, Caroline Henshaw. Then, hours before Colt was to go to the gallows, he and Caroline were married in his cell by the Reverend Henry Anthon, rector of one of the city's most prestigious churches, St. Mark's in the Bowery. Witnesses to the ceremony were Samuel Colt; family friend John Howard Payne, a dramatist who'd written the words to "Home, Sweet Home"; and a handful of other friends.

As the hour for the hanging neared, a crowd that had gathered outside the prison smelled smoke. Inside, guards discovered a small fire and quickly doused the flames. Meanwhile, a rumor swept through the crowd that the fire had been set, using a kind of gunpowder invented by Samuel Colt, in order to create sufficient panic and confusion to allow John Colt's confederates in the jail to spirit him away. Minutes later a guard assigned to escort Colt to the gallows found him, in the guard's words, "stretched out at full length on the bed, quite dead, but not cold. A clasp knife, like a small dirk knife, with a broken handle, was sticking in his heart."

James Gordon Bennett provided this scene around and in the prison to *Herald* readers:

In Colt's cell all seemed still as death! Three o'clock
came—the suspense was terrible—half past three—
the excitement was of a frenzied character—quarter
to four, and the mob seemed about to break into the
jail—the sheriffs put on their death livery—five minutes to four—the time's up—bring him out—how's
he coming—where's the cap and rope?—the cell door
is slowly unfastened and opened—in stepped the par-
son, and, merciful Providence, what a sight met his
glazed vision—there lay Colt, stretched out on his
back on his cot, weltering in his blood—warm, but
dead! The excitement resembled madness.

John Colt was quietly buried at St. Mark's. But many
New Yorkers believed this was also a ruse in which another
body was placed in the coffin and interred while John Colt,
his new bride, and their child, a boy born just before Colt's
trial, escaped to California.

What no one who celebrated the death of John C. Colt
knew was that the woman he had married in his cell was
not legally his wife, and that he was not the father of her
child. Caroline was, in fact, the wife of the inventor of the
revolving pistol. Samuel Colt had married her some years
earlier in Europe and had brought her to America without
acknowledging Caroline as his wife, nor that the child was
his. Knowing this, John had taken Caroline in.

Although the truth can never be determined, it's likely
that just as John Colt planned to cheat the hangman by
committing suicide, he also—in the final hour in the life
of a man who'd been excoriated as a cad and a scoundrel
in the newspapers, and then been found guilty of murder
by them and a jury in what may, indeed, have been a case
of self-defense and a panic-induced coverup to protect the
family name—chose to restore everyone's reputation but
his own with a noble act.

Four

Who Killed Jess?

In the twenty-fifth year of the reign of Victoria, Queen of England, Ireland, Wales, and Scotland, Counsel for the Crown Mr. Adam Gifford rose in a courtroom in Glasgow, Scotland, to summarize for the twelve men in the jury box the evidence he had presented to prove a charge of murder brought against a household servant, Mrs. Jessie M'Lachlan.

"Gentlemen," said Gifford, "this case stands, perhaps, unprecedented among the many crimes that have ever taken place. It is encompassed with mystery, which is not uncommon. But this crime is encompassed with a mystery of a darker kind and deeper shade than any other. In the present case you have the fact that a defense has been stated that the murder was committed by another person *who is named.*"

The murder had been committed on the night of Friday, July 4, 1862. The victim, also a house servant, was Jess M'Pherson.

"There seems to be no difficulty as to whether a murder was committed," continued the prosecutor. "I need address you only on whether the prisoner was or was not the murderer. You are not on a roving commission, asking who did

the deed? You are only asked—Did the prisoner at the bar
do it?"

With these words Gifford brought to a climax the greatest murder drama set in Scotland since English playwright
William Shakespeare had placed a dagger in the hand of
Lady Macbeth. But M'Pherson hadn't gone to her death
in a remote castle in craggy Scottish highlands. Jess had
been slain in a house at Number 17 Sandyford Place, Glasgow. Nor was she stabbed. The weapon, the doctors who
conducted an autopsy surmised, was most likely an axe or
a meat cleaver. The indictment of Mrs. M'Lachlan described "a cleaver or chopper, or some similar instrument."

The body had been discovered in her locked bedroom
on Monday, July 7. Entering the room with assistant su-
perintendent of the Glasgow police, Alexander M'Call, detective officer Donald Campbell and Dr. Joseph Fleming
found her facedown on the floor in front of the bed. She
was naked from the waist down. Torso and head were covered by a dark cloth.

A short time later Robert Jeffrey, another police officer,
arrived, accompanied by another doctor, George MacLeod.
The doctors agreed that the woman had been murdered
with extreme ferocity. Wounds to hands and arms left no
doubt the young woman had struggled against her attacker.
She lay on her face near the foot of the bed. Her dressing
gown and chemise had been pulled over her head and shoulders. The physicians counted forty wounds, inflicted before
or immediately after death by either a woman or a weak
man. All the wounds on the neck and head, with the exception of those on the nose and forehead, had been made
by an attacker standing over her as she lay on her face.

Examining the bloody room, the police found three
prints of a bare left foot in blood by the window. They also
found the maid's clothes closet empty. A survey of the entire house indicated that the murder had been committed
in the kitchen and the corpse had been dragged facedown
by way of a lobby to the bedroom in the front of the house.

On a counter in the scrubbed kitchen they found a meat cleaver, also scrubbed.

The only other person known to be in the house on Friday night was eighty-seven-year-old James Fleming. A retired handloom weaver and father of John, a prosperous accountant, the old man had been living with his son and his family for several years. On Friday afternoon John had taken his family for a weekend at their summer place on the coast, leaving the old man alone with the maid, Jess M'Pherson.

Looking into the bloody room on Monday, he threw up his hands and exclaimed, "She's been lying there all this time, and me in the house."

Questioned by the police, James Fleming said he had gone to bed early Friday night, but around four o'clock Saturday morning he was awakened by "a squeal."

He thought the sound had come from the street. Hearing two more squeals, he supposed someone was spending the night with the maid in her downstairs room and went back to sleep. He awoke early, as usual, and expected to have his breakfast of porridge and milk brought to him in bed. When Jess did not appear, he got up, put on a robe, and went down to the kitchen. In the kitchen he found a few articles of women's clothing drying on a screen, but no maid.

Thinking she had overslept, he went to her room and found the door closed. He knocked three times. Unanswered, he tried to open the door but found it locked. Deciding that the maid had gone out for some reason, he returned to the kitchen and prepared his breakfast.

When M'Pherson did not return that day or the next, he told the police, "I assumed she'd cut," meaning she'd abandoned her employment and ran off with whoever had been in her room early Saturday morning. Satisfied that this is what had happened, he gave the matter no more thought and fended for himself. He'd been to church on Sunday twice. On Monday morning he'd gone about his own work of collecting rents at nearby small tenements, where one of the residents very kindly gave him breakfast.

This is what he told his son when John and family returned on Monday afternoon. Finding it out of character for a woman of steady habits who had been an excellent and loyal servant for quite a long time, John doubted his father's explanation. In view of the old man's account of hearing squeals during the night, and Jess not serving him breakfast on Saturday morning, a more reasonable explanation, John Fleming decided, was that she had been taken ill and the squeals had been a call for help. Fearing the worst, he rushed to the maid's locked room. Breaking in, he found her lying dead on the floor.

The obvious conclusion to be drawn from these facts, John Fleming proposed to police, was that the woman had been killed by someone she'd invited to spend Friday night with her. But aspects of his story rang hollow. For two days James had made no effort to get into M'Pherson's room. Nor had he told anyone when he'd gone to church twice on Sunday that he believed M'Pherson had "cut." Neither did he make note of an absconding servant to a tenant who gave him breakfast on Monday.

Suspicious of this story and finding no evidence that anyone else had been in the house Friday night, and believing sex was the motive, the police suspected that James Fleming, his age notwithstanding, had killed the maid. As they questioned persons outside the Fleming house about him, their suspicion was deepened. The individual who emerged from these interviews was not a venerable gentleman, but an obnoxious, prying, gossipy, lewd-minded man who drank and spent most of his time bothering female servants. Police heard him described as "a nasty body" and "that auld deevil."

Consequently, eighty-seven-year-old James Fleming found himself arrested on a charge of murdering Jess M'Pherson. But after detaining him for a few days, the police found themselves regretting their haste. Informed by John Fleming that several objects of silver plate and articles of M'Pherson's clothing had gone missing, there appeared to be a different motive—robbery. If so, the proceeds of the theft might show up for sale. In that hope they canvassed pawnbrokers. On July 9 they interviewed Robert Lundie and learned that he had received articles of plate that the police described from a woman the police knew as a friend of the dead maid and a former servant of the Flemings'. Named Jessie M'Lachlan, she was married to a sailor and had one child. She gave a story of her whereabouts on Friday night that had her nowhere near Sandyford Place.

How did she come into possession of the silver plate she'd pawned?

"It was given to me by old man Fleming."

"When?"

"The night before the murder. He came to my house about a quarter-past eight and I let him in and took him into our parlor. He carried a parcel wrapped tightly up in a white cloth, and laid it down on the table. He asked me if I would pawn some silver plate which was in the parcel. I said the pawnbroker would know the plate did not belong to me. He said I was to give the name of Mary M'Kay and that I was to seek three pounds ten for the plate, or as much as I could get."

Had anyone else been present during this conversation?

"No, we were alone."

"So you went to the pawn?"

"It was between twelve and one o'clock on the Saturday. The pawnbroker's young man who attended me offered me more than three pounds ten. I gave the name of Mary M'Kay, got the money and a pawn ticket and left the silver plate in the same cover which old Fleming had brought the articles in."

As Jessie was telling this story her questioners observed a cut and what appeared to be bite marks on her left hand. At some point in the interview they measured her feet and found they were larger than M'Pherson's feet but the same size as the footprints in blood in M'Pherson's room. Asked about clothing in her possession, she became evasive.

Convinced that she had committed the murder, the police arrested her and released James Fleming, with apologies.

In weighing the police case against his client, M'Lachlan's lawyer, Andrew Rutherfurd Clark, felt it was based on circumstantial evidence that would not persuade a jury that M'Lachlan had wielded the cleaver. While jurors were expected to render a verdict on the basis of evidence presented in court, few, if any, people in the Glasgow juror pool believed M'Lachlan had killed M'Pherson. The consensus of the public, and that of the newspapers, save one, was that Jess M'Pherson had been slaughtered by the old man.

Jessie M'Lachlan went to trial on September 7, 1862, at Old Court, Jail Square, Glasgow, before the Honorable Lord Deas. One of the Lords Commissioners of Justiciary, he was fifty-eight years of age and described as a man of dry looks and air and the most striking personality in Scotland. He now found himself presiding over the most sensational case in anyone's memory.

Jail Square was mobbed with people hoping to get seats into the courtroom. Those who managed to enter the galleries were described by one observer as "a preponderance of the fair sex" representing the "inevitable fashionably dressed women inseparable from any newspaper account of a sensational trial . . . and the few gentlemen present are there possibly less from curiosity than from the need to protect their ladies."

The trial also attracted more newspaper reporters than had ever before covered a criminal case in Scotland. The dramatic opening of the trial was described by Christiana Brand, author of the definitive book on the case, *Heaven Knows Who*, published in 1960. "As the clock struck ten," she wrote, "a blare of trumpets echoing through corridors and ante-rooms, heralded the approach of Lord Deas. In the floor of the dock, a trap door opened and the prisoner appeared, as though rising out of some tomb to which, in too hasty anticipation of an adverse decision, she had been prematurely confined."

Jessie M'Lachlan was wearing a lilac gown and little black shawl, a straw bonnet trimmed with white ribbons, and a short black veil covering her face.

Reporters described her as pale and thin, haggard and anxious, yet marvelously controlled, showing "a rare fortitude," "magnificent resolution," and "an iron strength."

A clerk read an indictment accusing M'Lachlan that "albeit by the laws of this and of every other well-governed realm, murder, as also theft, are crimes of an heinous nature and severely punishable; yet it is true, and of verity, that you, the said Jessie M'Lachlan are guilty of the said crime of murder, of the said crime of theft, or one or the other of the said crimes, inasmuch as she did wickedly and feloniously attack the said Jessie [*sic*] M'Pherson. . . ."

M'Lachlan would maintain that the killer was not her, but old James Fleming.

Jurors heard that the old man had been a creature of peculiar habits—with great curiosity, inquisitive—to the annoyance and distress of everyone, including his family. He was constantly in the kitchen inquiring about the affairs there. He looked to see who was going in and out of the house. The doorbell could not ring without him going out to see who it was. And he was a man with a lewd turn of mind.

Rather than attempting to refute this portrait of James Fleming, the prosecution agreed that he was not an exemplary person. But he was eighty-seven years old!

Contrast Fleming with the accused woman! M'Lachlan was an intimate friend of the deceased. They had been fellow servants in the Fleming household for two years. The prisoner knew M'Pherson well. She knew what she had, she knew her habits, she knew her ways, and more than that, she knew Number 17 Sandyford Place well—its entrances and exits, all its rooms and facilities. She had been in that house on the night of Friday, July 4. She had pawned the stolen plate. She had M'Pherson's clothing.

The fact is, said queen's counsel, James Fleming is not on trial.

"It is possible in crimes of this kind that one or more person has connection with it," said Mr. Gifford in his summation. "If there were more murderers than one, if the prisoner were one of them, you must find a verdict of guilty against her. For the question always is, and the only question is, Is the prisoner guilty or is she not guilty?—not that she had confederates, not was she alone. These are not the questions, and your verdict will not find anybody else concerned in the crime. All that your verdict can find is whether or not the prisoner was concerned."

After deliberating only fifteen minutes, the jury found Jessie M'Lachlan guilty.

A newspaper recorded her reaction:

> The deathly pallor of her countenance seemed to increase, but the same strength of will she had heretofore displayed was again shown. Nervous sweat covered her face; and she now and again lifted up her hands from under the black shawl beneath which during the day she kept them folded together, and pressed them over her face, wiping away the sweat. She for an instant leaned forward and covered her face with a handkerchief as if crying, but sitting upright again, she folded her arms together under her shawl, drawing it close around her.

The advocate deputy said to the judge, "My lord, I move for sentence."

Jessie M'Lachlan signaled her lawyer, Rutherfurd Clark. After a brief discussion with him she gave him a sheet of paper. Clark turned to the judge. "My lord, I understand that the prisoner desires to make a statement before sentence is passed, whether by her own lips or to be read by someone for her."

Lord Deas replied, "She is at liberty to do so in any way she prefers."

M'Lachlan said, "My lord, I desire to have it read. I am as innocent as my child who is only three years of age at this date."

Clark read the statement.

On that fateful Friday night she had been in the Fleming house. She'd sat in the kitchen drinking with her good friend Jess and the old man. At some point Jess said she had "a tongue that would frighten somebody if it were to break loose on them." M'Lachlan took this to be either a teasing jibe intimating M'Pherson knew things about the old man that could cause him trouble, or an actual threat.

At this point Fleming gave M'Lachlan a shilling and twopence to go out and buy a pint of whisky. By the time she reached the spirits shop, it was closed. Upon returning to the Fleming house, she found no one in the kitchen. When the old man appeared a few moments later, she asked, "Where's Jess?"

Fleming did not answer but turned and left the room. Following him, M'Lachlan heard a moan from the front bedroom. When she tried to go in, Fleming stopped her. Pushing past him, she looked into the room and saw Jess lying on the floor, supported on an elbow, her head down, the hair soaked with blood. Rushing to her friend, she cried to the old man, "What have you done?"

"I didn't mean to. It was an accident."

"Bring cold water and a handkerchief."

Fleming did so and stood back, watching M'Lachlan tend to Jess's bleeding head.

"How could you do such a thing to her?" she demanded.

"I don't know," muttered Fleming. "I don't know."

"We must have a doctor. Go and get one. If you won't, I will."

Suddenly, M'Pherson spoke, but weakly. "No, Jessie. Stay with me."

The old man left the room.

In a weak voice M'Pherson told what had happened while M'Lachlan had gone to buy whisky. The old man had demanded an explanation of her remark about a tongue that would frighten somebody if it broke loose. She refused to reply and went to her room. He followed her and they argued. He rushed at her and struck her, knocking her down.

M'Pherson asked Jessie, "Am I badly cut?"

"Yes, badly, very badly."

"Then I'll have to see a doctor, and I'll have to account to him for these injuries."

Fleming entered the room. He was sorry. He would make everything right for Jess. And he'd make everything right for Jessie, too, if she held her tongue and said nothing about this.

Presently, M'Pherson seemed stronger and expressed a desire to make water. With the help of Jennings, M'Lachlan took her through the hallway to the kitchen. Still promising to make everything right, Fleming went upstairs to his room.

As M'Pherson dozed by the fire, M'Lachlan left the kitchen to fetch a blanket from the bedroom. On the way she met Fleming coming down the stairs. "Jess is worse," she said. "I think she's very ill. I'd better get a doctor right away."

Saying nothing, the old man wandered into the kitchen.

Determined to find a doctor, M'Lachlan found the front door locked. Going into the kitchen to ask Fleming for the key, she discovered him bending over M'Pherson. Then she saw the cleaver in his bloody hand and Jess's battered head.

He couldn't let her go wagging her tongue, he said. And he couldn't let her tell any of this to a doctor. "The thing is done. They'll think we both had a hand in it. You see—my life's in your power; and so is your life in my power. We must pretend there was a burglary."

All she had to do was take things from the house—some plate and some of M'Pherson's things.

"I'll look after you," he said. "I'll set you up in a shop. You'll never want again."

Faced with the choice of going along with the scheme or being charged with murder, she elected the first option.

"I never had any quarrel with Jess," the statement concluded as those in the courtroom sat in silence. "On every occasion we were most affectionate and friendly."

"Sound and movement returned to the courtroom," said one account of that extraordinary moment. "The jury, hitherto so cocksure, now looked ill at ease, some shaken, some unconvinced, but all utterly taken aback." A policeman was in tears. M'Lachlan, who had wept during much of the reading, pulled herself together and "returned to her former outward calm."

All eyes turned anxiously toward the judge.

After declaring from the bench that he did not believe "the old gentleman" had anything to do with the murder of Jess M'Pherson, Lord Deas raised a triangular black cloth above his head. The sentence of the court, he said, was that Jessie M'Lachlan "be removed from the bar to the prison of Glasgow, therein to be detained and fed upon bread and water only, until the eleventh day of October next, and upon that day, between the hours of eight and ten o'clock in the forenoon, to be taken from the said prison to the common place of execution in the burgh of Glasgow and there by the hands of the common executioner to be hanged upon the gibbet till you be dead; and ordains your body to be thereafter buried within the precincts of the said prison; and ordains your moveable goods and gear ti the escheat and inbrought for Her Majesty's use."

He then observed the custom of declaring, "And may God Almighty have mercy on your soul." In reply to which

Jessie whispered, "Mercy! Aye, He'll have mercy, for I'm innocent."

Few Scots agreed with the verdict. Many who were outraged by the severity of the penalty caustically referred to Lord Deas as "Lord Death." Dismay was even voiced in far-off London by Scottish members of Parliament. So great was the uproar that official inquiries were ordered, resulting in commutation of M'Lachlan's death sentence to life in prison. Even that was denounced as an injustice.

After serving fifteen years in Perth General Prison as a "model prisoner" who'd shown "exemplary conduct," Jessie M'Lachlan sailed with her son to the United States. Still protesting innocence in 1899, she died in Port Huron, Michigan, according to a letter to a cousin in Scotland from her son, of "pleurisy of the heart on New Year's morning, at 10:20."

Five

The Smutty Nose
Horror

In March 1873 a living could be made out of the sea around the nine outcroppings of rocky land known as the Isles of Shoals. About ten miles south and east of Portsmouth, New Hampshire, they were first spotted by European eyes when explorer Captain John Smith plied waters of the New World for England. He was followed soon by seafarers from other nations with designs on the riches of America. When dreams of finding gold and other mineral treasure were disappointed, they settled for dragging riches from the sea in the form of swarms of fish, called shoals, around the nine islands. They did so at great peril. Across the centuries since Captain Smith chartered the islands, countless numbers of ships were driven to destruction on shores of islands that had come to be named Appledore, Duck, Malaga, Cedar, Star, Lunging, Seavy's, White, and Smutty Nose.

So called because of a black "smutch" of seaweed on the nose of the small flat formation of quartz rock, it found its way into ocean folklore as the site of the honeymoon of the dreaded pirate Blackbeard and as one of many spots where the notorious marauder was believed to have buried loot in the form of silver and gold coin and bullion. Whether four silver bars found under a flat stone by a latter-day resident, a lobsterman named Samuel Haley, was part of Blackbeard's trove is a matter of conjecture. A practical man, Haley used the proceeds of the sale of the find to build a breakwater connecting Smutty Nose with Malaga.

Digging up treasure and building the breakwater were not Haley's only claim to a place in the history of Smutty Nose. After the Spanish ship *Sagunto* wrecked against the island's rocks, he'd buried the bodies of fourteen sailors on his land. When he died in 1811 at the age of eighty-four he was buried beside them, praised on his tombstone as "a man of great ingenuity, industry and honor, true to his country & a man who did a great publik good in building a dock & receiving many a poor distressed seaman & fisherman in distress of weather."

Sixty-two years after Haley went to his heavenly reward for his good deeds, the only residents of Smutty Nose were John Hontvet, a Norwegian fisherman and owner of a small schooner, the *Clara Bella;* his wife, Maren, and her small dog, named Ringe; John's brother Matthew and Maren's sister Karen; Maren's brother Ivan Christensen and his wife, Anethe. The nearest neighbors lived on Appledore Island: another Norwegian-born fisherman, Emil Inger-bretson; Oscar and Cedric Laighton; their invalid mother, Eliza; and a sister, Celia Thaxter.

A gifted writer, Celia admired the Norwegians as gentle, intelligent, faithful, God-fearing folk who "daily use such courtesy toward each other and all who come in contact with them, as puts our ruder Yankee manners to shame." When the Hontvets settled on Smutty Nose, she had taken an immediate liking to them.

They'd come from the small town of Laurvig, near Christiana, Norway, in 1868. Since then John Hontvet had acquired the *Clara Bella* and for a time had employed a tall, dark, powerful man named Louis H. F. Wagner. Quiet and moody, he had come to the Shoals from Ueckermunde, a town of lower Pomeranie in Northern Prussia.

At the age of twenty-eight, Wagner had been in America seven years. Five of them had been spent shipping out as a seaman from New York. After that he'd tried his luck in Boston and then made his way to Portsmouth. Told that a man could prosper at the Isles of Shoals, he'd gotten a small boat but never managed to make a decent living. Then he'd met John Hontvet. Finding employment with the young Norwegian, he moved in with him and his wife. That Hontvet was doing well was evidenced by his telling Wagner that he had already saved most of the $600 he needed to buy a new schooner. He was also able to afford to invite Maren's sister, Karen Christensen, to leave Norway and live with them. A rather sad-looking figure, Karen was thirty-nine years old. Mourning a lost lover, she had a pensive way of letting her head droop a little to the side and hummed sad Norwegian tunes as she turned a spinning wheel.

A year after Karen moved into the Hontvet house she was followed by John's brother, Matthew, whom she later married, and the next year by her own brother, Ivan Christensen, and his brand-new wife, Anethe. Celia Thaxter described Ivan as "tall, light haired, rather quiet and grave," while Anethe was "young, fair and merry, with thick, bright, sunny hair, which was so long it reached, when unbraided, nearly to her knees; blue-eyed, with brilliant teeth, and clear fresh complexion."

With a brother and brother-in-law working beside him on the *Clara Bella,* John Hontvet informed Wagner he no longer needed hired help. Moving to Star Island, Wagner again tried fishing alone, but when that effort proved insufficient he gave it up and moved to Portsmouth and signed on as a member of the crew of the schooner *Addison Gilbert.* But hopes for making a decent living were soon dashed when the ship was caught in a storm and wrecked.

Unable to find employment, Wagner was frequently seen

with a brooding look on his face, arms crossed on his chest, wandering around Portsmouth docks, picking up occasional work baiting trawls, and muttering he would have money even if he must murder for it.

On March 5, 1873, unshaved, looking ragged, and behind in the amount of $12 to his landlady, he made his way to the waterfront in hopes of getting work. Finding no ships in port, he grumbled to a passerby, "What's the use?"

Early that day, Celia Thaxter had stepped out onto the piazza of a house on Appledore to watch the boat of Emil Ingerbretson leaving Appledore Island and the *Clara Bella* setting out from Smutty Nose to reap the rich harvests of the trawling nets they had set some miles to the northwest. The day was so still, so bright, Thaxter thought as she looked at a clear sky grown less hard than it had been for weeks, that surely the hope and light of spring would soon dispel a long winter weariness.

As John and Matthew Hontvet and their brother-in-law Ivan Christensen left the house that morning they told Maren, Karen, and Anethe to expect them back around noon. After a lunch they would sail to Portsmouth with the day's catch and restock their trawls with bait coming in by train. But rough weather forced them to change their plan. When pulling in their trawls took much longer than anticipated, they asked Ingerbretson to inform the women at Smutty Nose that they intended to go directly to Portsmouth and to expect them home in time for dinner.

When the *Clara Bella* sailed up the Piscataqua River and docked at Portsmouth late in the afternoon, the three men on board saw the familiar figure of Louis Wagner. If he wanted work, John Hontvet told him, he could lend a hand baiting the trawls. Wagner accepted. Expecting to begin work immediately, Hontvet learned to his dismay that the train bringing the bait had not arrived. Another was not due until eleven o'clock. So much for dinner on Smutty Nose!

When the train pulled in, Wagner was nowhere in sight.

The last time he had been seen, Hontvet was told, he was having a mug of ale in a Congress Street pub around seven o'clock.

Indeed he had. And he'd been doing a good deal of thinking about his plight and about the good fortune of his former employer. Fortified with strong drink and resolve, he had left the pub and wandered to a wharf at the foot of Pickering Street and spotted a tied-up dory belonging to James Bourke. No one was around. The tide was high and going out so swiftly that the only rowing a man would have to do to reach the sea would be for the purpose of navigating. But to reach the destination Wagner had in mind would be quite another matter. Portsmouth stood twelve miles from the Isles of Shoals. To get to Smutty Nose he must travel in moonlight three miles past Eliot, Newcastle, Kittery, and lighthouses at Fort Point and Whales Back. Then came nine miles of open ocean.

As Wagner employed all the skills he had learned in his fruitless efforts to earn a living by fishing alone, Celia Thaxter slept in her room in a large house on Appledore Island. Years later the woman who would be known as the "island poet," and do much to attract tourists to the isles, would take up her pen at the request of the *Atlantic Monthly* to imagine the scene. She wrote, "Slowly the coast-lights fade, and now the rote of the sea among the lonely edges of the Shoals salutes his attentive ear. A little longer and he nears Appledore, the first island, and now he passes by the snow-covered, ice-bound rock, with the long buildings showing clear in the moonlight. He must have looked at them as he went past. I wonder how we who slept beneath the roofs that glimmered to his eyes in the uncertain light did not feel, through the thick veil of sleep, what fearful thing passed by! But we slumbered peacefully as the unhappy women whose doom every click of oars in the rowlocks, like the ticking of some dreadful clock, was bringing nearer and nearer."

Snug in their house, Maren, Karen, and Anethe, with the

dog Ringe for company, had been informed by Emil Inger-bretson not to expect their men back until late in the eve-ning. For them the hours were passed cheerfully chatting by the fire. When John, Matthew, and Ivan had not returned by ten o'clock, they decided to go to bed. Rather than feel "lonesome" in the bedroom she shared with her husband, Matthew, Karen slept on a mattress laid across chairs. Maren and Anethe slept in the adjoining room.

Not far away, Louis Wagner guided his stolen little boat silently ashore at Haley's cove. Stepping onto snow-covered ground, he crept past the graves of Haley and the hapless Spanish sailors of the ill-fated *Sagunto* toward the moonlit red house where he'd been a welcome guest. He knew the layout, and he knew that when John Hontvet had cash he kept it in a cabinet in the kitchen. He also knew the room he had occupied on the north side would be un-occupied because it was now a workshop. The Hontvets' bedroom was on the second floor. Ivan and Anethe had a bed on the ground floor next to the kitchen, where Matthew had slept on a mattress when he first arrived.

Peering toward the darkened house, Wagner saw the win-dow shades were not drawn. This was a stroke of luck that allowed him to look into the room adjoining the kitchen and to discern a large bed with at least two of the women asleep in it.

Because the door between this room and the kitchen was open, he recognized that if he were to search the kitchen for money he would have to shut and bar the door. The answer to the problem, he decided, was to jam the door latch with a stick. Finding a suitable one on the ground, he moved silently to the outside door to the kitchen and found it unlocked. Standing beside it, as usual, was an axe used by John Hontvet to chop firewood. Quickly entering the kitchen, he tiptoed toward the open door of the adjoining room without noticing as he shut the door that there was a makeshift bed of chairs and mattress in the kitchen. As he slipped the stick into the latch, it made a slight sound—not so loud as to disturb the sleeping figures in the next room, but enough to set the dog Ringe barking.

Jolted awake in the makeshift bed, Karen asked, "Who is it? John, is that you?"

From behind the closed and latched door, Maren shouted, "What's the matter?"

Believing that John had returned, Karen replied, "John scared me."

Gripped with panic, Wagner lunged through the darkness toward the sound of the voice and slammed into the chairs supporting the bed. Grabbing one, he raised it high and brought it crashing down on Karen's head. In doing so, Wagner also smashed the chair against a shelf on which stood a clock. It crashed to the floor with such force that it stopped with its hands frozen at the exact time of the attack—seven minutes past one. (And thereby providing inspiration for planting a clue in the stories of countless mystery writers for generations to come.)

"John kills me," screamed Karen as Wagner battered her. "John kills me!"

Managing to get out of bed, she made her way to the closed door before collapsing. As she fell, her body dislodged the stick that had been immobilizing the latch. On the other side of the door, Maren screamed at Anethe to put on clothes and run for help. Gripped by fear, Anethe was unable to move.

Trying the door again, Maren felt it swing open. She found Karen at her feet, and in the dim moonlight through a window, she saw the figure of a tall man lunging toward her with a chair in hand. Dragging Karen into the bedroom, she felt the chair smash her three times before she managed to slam the door shut. Leaning against the door and holding down the latch, she shouted to Anethe to open the window and run for help.

Finally alert to the horror of what was happening and wearing only a nightgown, Anethe got the window open and scrambled through it. Landing barefoot in the snow, she found herself face to face with a man wielding an axe.

Recognizing him, she screamed, "Oh, Louis, Louis, Louis."

Flailing the axe as Maren watched through the window, Wagner was so close she might have touched his shoulder as he smashed Anethe's head again, and again, and again. Maren was certain he would come after Karen and herself; a moment later he was pounding on the door.

Maren tugged at Karen's limp body and pleaded with her to follow her through the window.

"I cannot," gasped Karen. "I cannot."

Recognizing she could not save her sister, Maren grabbed a skirt, wrapped her shoulders in it, and scrambled out the window. Stumbling over Anethe's battered body, she fell onto the bloodred snow, pushed herself up, and ran with the dog Ringe keeping pace and barking, but not so loud as to drown out hideous sounds from the house.

Having smashed his way into the room, Wagner had discovered the stunned and bleeding Karen struggling to climb through the window. In attacking her with the axe he swung it so hard that a blow missed her and splintered the windowsill. The savage assault stopped only when the handle broke. Fearing that the crushing chops of the heavy axe had not killed her, he made certain she was dead by strangling her with a scarf. Leaving Karen, he went outside again to ensure Anethe was dead by also choking her. He then dragged the body into the kitchen.

Now he went looking for Maren.

With Ringe at her side, she'd first made a dash for a henhouse. Afraid the dog's barking would betray her, she abandoned that idea and the possibility of hiding in one of several vacant houses on the island for the same reason. In desperate hope of finding the boat that had brought Louis Wagner to Smutty Nose, she fled to the cove and found nothing. Her only chance of surviving, she decided, was to get as far from the house as possible, find a sheltered spot among the rocks, and pray that Wagner would give up looking for her—and that she wouldn't freeze to death. She found such a place on the eastern end of the island, a half mile from the house. Curled up with Ringe, she knew there was a possibility he might betray her by barking, but the dog's body helped to blunt the cold. Although she did not realize it, time was also an ally.

It was well past two o'clock and Louis Wagner had no way of knowing whether the men of the *Clara Bella* had finished with their trawls and were on their way to Smutty Nose. He had come to the lonely red house to get money. Bad luck had made him a murderer. The money that might have settled his rent arrears with more than enough left over to provide a fresh start in his life, perhaps in Boston or New York, was needed now to finance an escape. If bad luck changed to good, the woman who'd gotten away would freeze to death, or not come out of hiding until he was long gone.

Acutely conscious of fleeting time and anxious to get away from the island before dawn, he began looking for John Hontvet's $600.

Twenty-two years later, the woman who'd slept through the night on Appledore Island gave readers of the *Atlantic Monthly* an account, based on the subsequent investigation of the murders, of Louis Wagner's frantic activity in the early-morning hours of March 5, 1873. Celia Thaxter wrote:

> All about the house he searches, in bureau drawers, in trunks and boxes: he finds fifteen dollars for his night's work! Several hundreds were lying between some sheets folded at the bottom of a drawer in which he looked. But he cannot stop for more thorough investigation; a dreadful haste pursues him like a thousand fiends . . . But how cool a monster is he! After all this hard work he must have refreshment to support him in the long row back to the land; knife and fork,

cup and plate, were found next morning on the table near which Anethe lay; fragments of food which was not cooked in the house, but brought from Portsmouth, were scattered about . . . Can the human mind conceive of such hideous nonchalance? It is almost beyond belief! Then he went to the well to wash with a basin and towels, tried to wash off the blood, and left towels and basin in the well. He knows he must be gone! It is certain death to linger. He takes his boat and rows away toward the dark coast and the twinkling lights; it is for dear life now!

He landed near New Castle, at a place known as the Devil's Den. From there he took a familiar road for a two-mile hike to Mrs. Johnson's boardinghouse. Rent arrears notwithstanding, the landlady gave him tea and informed him that John Hontvet had been looking for him last night. He replied that he'd been up most of the night baiting trawls. He then asked Johnson if she'd heard him come in. No, she hadn't, she said.

To Johnson's daughter he said, "Mary, I have got into trouble. I feel as if someone will be after me."

He told Mrs. Johnson, "I feel queer, as if I had been tight last night."

"If so," said the landlady, "you had better go to bed."

"No, I must be going," said Wagner.

In his room he exchanged the bloodstained shirt for a clean one, but the coverall he had on was the only one he owned. However, he felt confident that until he could obtain a new suit the stains on it could be easily explained away as the result of handling fish bait. Ripped into three pieces, the bloody shirt was thrown down a privy.

After stopping at a bakery to buy a roll, he boarded the nine o'clock train for Boston. On his arrival he got a shave and haircut and bought the suit. Stopping at the Fleet Street cobbler shop of Jacob Todtman, whom he knew, he shed the coveralls and donned the new outfit. He then went to a boardinghouse he had patronized during his previous visit to Boston. Greeted by the wife of the owner, Katherine Brown, he asked for a room until he could find a job on a ship. Exhausted, he collapsed into a chair and fell asleep.

Meanwhile, Maren Hontvet had emerged from hiding. Half-frozen, she heard hammering coming from Star Island where work was proceeding on the building of a hotel. Waving the skirt that had served as a blanket during the long night, she hoped to catch the attention of workers. They stopped hammering, but only briefly. Apparently believing the woman on Smutty Nose was greeting them, they waved back and resumed working. Avoiding going near her house, she made her way across to Haley breakwater. Beyond it on Malaga, the Ingerbretson children were at play. Hearing her shouts for help, they dashed into the house to inform their father.

Recognizing Maren Hontvet, Ingerbretson climbed into his dory and paddled toward her. When he saw her bruised condition, he demanded, "Who did this to you?"

"Louis," she cried as she fell into his arms. "It was Louis Wagner."

Rowing her to Malaga, Ingerbretson listened in horror to her nearly hysterical account of the bloody night in the red house on Smutty Nose. Leaving Maren in the care of his wife, he rowed to Appledore to enlist the help of anyone he could find.

Seated at her writing desk by a window, Celia Thaxter saw him hurrying past the house and called to him, "What has happened?"

Ingerbretson replied, "Trouble at Smutty Nose."

Assuming there'd been a drunken brawl among sailors, Thaxter resumed writing. But half an hour later she saw Ingerbretson again, accompanied by several men, including workers from the hotel. Rushing outside, she again asked what had happened.

"Karen is dead. Anethe is dead," someone replied. "Louis Wagner has murdered them."

As the men, many of them toting rifles, set out to search Appledore for Wagner, Celia Thaxter rushed to the Ingerbretson house on Malaga. Writing in the present tense, she recalled in her later account of the murders, "I find the women and children with frightened faces at the little cottage; as I go into the room where Maren lies, she catches my hands, crying, 'Oh, I so glad to see you! I so glad I save my life!' Poor little creature, holding me with those wild, glittering, dilated eyes, she cannot tell me rapidly enough the whole horrible tale."

Presently, the *Clara Bella* sailed into view, and Celia Thaxter recalled watching her sail out the previous morning: "Oh brightly shines the morning sun and glitters on the white sails of the little vessel that comes dancing back from Portsmouth before the favoring wind, with the two husbands on board!"

A signal from Appledore brought the fishermen ashore.

"Ivan and Matthew, landing, hear a confused rumor of trouble from tongues that hardly can frame the words that must tell the dreadful truth," Celia Thaxter recorded. "Ivan only understands that something is wrong. His one thought is for Anethe; he flies to the Ingebretson's cottage, she may be there; he rushed in like a maniac, crying, 'Anethe, Anethe! Where is Anethe?' "

Maren answered, "She is—at home."

Bolting from the cottage, Ivan dashed for the boat.

When he, John, Matthew, and the men recruited by Ingerbretson reached Smutty Nose, they found bloody footprints everywhere in the snow around the red house. Bursting through the door, they found the butchered women and evidence of Wagner's rampage in search of money.

Presently, John Hontvet sailed *Clara Bella* back to Portsmouth to inform the authorities of what Louis Wagner had done. City Marshal Frank B. Johnson issued an order for his arrest. Told Wagner had been seen boarding the Boston train at nine o'clock, Johnson telegraphed the Boston police requesting that Wagner be seized and held on a charge of double-murder. He gave them a description of Wagner and advised that because Wagner had once lived in Boston it was likely he would seek out old acquaintances.

Accompanied by an Officer Entwistle, the marshall caught the next train to Boston. By the time he arrived, two Boston police patrolmen, William Gallagher and William Currier, had seen Wagner in the doorway of the Hamburg House and arrested him without a struggle. Plans were made to return him to Portsmouth by train at ten o'clock the next morning.

In the interim, sketchy accounts of the horror at Smutty Nose reached newspapers up and down the east coast. These stories, combined with word-of-mouth accounts of Wagner's arrest, resulted in the gathering at ten o'clock of what one paper described as "a hooting mob" to see him put on the train. News that this brutal murderer of two women was en route to Portsmouth drew similar mobs along the route. But none was as immense or threatening as the club-wielding crowd that waited the train's arrival at Portsmouth's Eastern Depot. In response, a contingent of Marines was rushed to the station.

When it became known that the train would stop a quarter of a mile short of Portsmouth, a mob that had gathered there was prevented from dragging him off the train by police with guns drawn. Described by a reporter as "shaking like a leaf," Wagner was carried from the train and shielded from a cascade of hurled stones accompanied by a chorus of shouts: "Kill him! Lynch him! String him up! Tear him to pieces!"

At noon the next day, a Saturday, Maren Hontvet was brought to the Portsmouth jail to identify Wagner as the killer. So weak that she had to be assisted by her husband, John, to a couch, she sat silently staring.

Wagner said, "I'm glad Jesus loves me."

John Hontvet shouted, "The Devil loves you!"

All that had to be done now was assure that Wagner

received a fair trial. But where? In the long history of the Isles of Shoals there had been a legal wrangle over whether Smutty Nose belonged to New Hampshire or Maine. At the moment the prevailing claim was Maine's. This meant that Wagner would not be confined in Portsmouth but in the town of Saco, York County, Maine. The problem for the police of Portsmouth and the sheriff of York County was transferring him safely. The plan they devised called for the sheriff and three deputies to join a posse of Portsmouth police and Marine officers.

When they took Wagner from jail at 9:45 Saturday night, they found themselves surrounded by a mob, which was both angry at Wagner and with the state of Maine for depriving them of the opportunity to hold the trial, and then hang him. Weathering a storm of stones, bricks, chunks of ice, and everything else within reach of the furious crowd, the force of deputies, police, and Marines delivered Wagner to the railway depot with only a badly cut head, the result of a rock.

Ensconced in a jail in Saco, Wagner was described by a reporter as "a tall, dark and powerful man, with a very mild expression of countenance, and easy, assured manner." His was a face to which you would naturally take a liking, the report continued, "though there is about it a weak appearance, which grows upon you the more you look at him."

One of many women who were allowed to visit him in cell 49 said, "I hope you put your trust in the Lord."

Wagner answered, "I always did, ma'am, and I always will."

While he proclaimed innocence and pointed out that the only evidence against him was the word of Maren Hontvet, a coroner's jury was convened by the York County attorney to investigate the murders. The panel consisted of doctors (W. Hoskins Rogers, John W. Parsons, D. W. Jones, C. L. Hayes) and a U.S. Navy Surgeon named Buell.

They and a large number of naval officers and citizens

left the Portsmouth Navy Yard on the steamer *Mayflower* on the evening of March 6. They arrived at Smutty Nose at 8 P.M. After inspecting the scene of the crimes and the bodies of the slain women, they retired to the hotel on Appledore to discuss their findings.

Their report noted Anethe's head had been "terribly hacked to pieces; both ears nearly severed; one ear ring cut out and tangled in her hair; left temple bone above the eye completely crushed; other numerous scratches and bruises." Karen was in a similar condition. A bloody axe with a broken handle was found near the door.

On the Saturday after the murders, the bodies were moved to Woodbury, Gerish and Co., undertakers, in Portsmouth. A double funeral was held following the regular Sunday service at St. John's Church.

Two hearses followed by a large crowd conveyed them to the South cemetery and the coffins were buried side by side.

A single marble stone would be engraved with:

> A sudden death, a striking call,
> A warning voice which speaks to all,
> To all to be prepared to die.

Arraigned on Tuesday, March 12, 1873, at the South Berwick court, Wagner was ordered held for trial on June 9. Two prominent lawyers were appointed by the court to assist him in his defense. Rufus P. Tapley of Saco, Maine, was a former judge. Up from Boston came Max Fischacher, chosen not only because he was a distinguished defense attorney, but because he was of German extraction.

While these lawyers worked to devise a defense to present in court, based on Wagner's insistence that he could produce alibi witnesses, Wagner waged a defense aimed at the public by making himself appear to visitors, including reporters, to be the victim of either Maren's mistaken identification or a deliberate plan by someone to frame

him, possibly Maren herself or her husband, John Hontvet.
All the evidence against him, he told all who would listen,
was purely circumstantial.

This insistence that he was a wronged man struck such
sympathetic chords in many who visited him that it
prompted the Portsmouth *Chronicle* to state on March 13,
"Wagner still retains his amazing sang-froid, which is wonderful, even in a strong-nerved German. The sympathy of
most of the visitors to his jail had certainly been won by
his calmness and his general appearance, which is quite
prepossessing."

In a 1927 book dealing with the Smutty Nose murders,
Edmund Pearson attributed the phenomenon of growing
public doubts that Wagner was guilty to "extraordinary
powers" as an actor, which he exercised from the moment
he found himself arrested. "Continued professions of
innocence," Pearson explained, "if accompanied by a
good personal appearance, and backed by sanctimonious
phrases, will convince many persons that an accused man
is suffering grievous wrong. If in addition, the words 'circumstantial evidence' enter into any part of the case, some
of the public will vote immediately to acquit a man of all
charges, and give him a certificate of high moral character."

Another student of the case, Lyman P. Rutledge, wrote
in his 1958 pamphlet *Moonlight Murder at Smuttynose* that
it was during the three months between Wagner's arraignment and the trial date that the public proceeded to try the
case in its own way. "No one seemed to doubt the sincerity
of Maren Hontvet, but after all she could be mistaken in
her identification. How could she tell in the dim light of a
low-hanging moon? On the other hand the prisoner was
putting on so convincing a show of innocence that even
the best newspaper men came away from his cell deeply
moved and wondering. His sympathizers grew in number
and in determination, saying among themselves that this
innocent man must be defended! By the time of the trial

there was much more general sentiment for him than against him."

Facing mounting public doubts that the man accused of the two terrible murders had done them, the attorney general of Maine, Harris M. Plaistead, took over the prosecution of the case himself. He was assisted by York County attorney George C. Yeaton. The trial would be held before Judge William G. Barrows of the supreme judicial court in Alfred, Maine.

Heralded by the press as "the trial of the century," it attracted throngs of people. Hoping to gain a scarce seat in the court, they flooded into the town off trains from Portsmouth and many points south. Those who succeeded in being admitted heard a parade of prosecution witnesses paint a portrait of Louis Wagner as a man desperate for money. Emil Ingerbretson quoted Wagner as saying, "I must have money in three months if I have to murder to do it." Ivan Christensen testified about money taken from the pocketbook he had left in a drawer in the red house that day, an amount of coins and bills that matched the money found on Wagner in Boston. Three five-dollar bills had been taken from the house. Wagner had paid for his suit with five-dollar bills. Karen had a silver half-dollar, a silver five-cent piece, silver three-cent piece, and "a lot of coppers." Three such coins and thirteen coppers were found in Wagner's pockets.

A group of witnesses swore they saw Wagner on the morning of the sixth making his way from Newcastle to Portsmouth. Mrs. Johnson spoke of Wagner's haggard appearance when he'd arrived at her boardinghouse that morning. A police officer related finding a torn, bloodstained man's shirt in the privy behind the boardinghouse. The stolen dory was discussed, along with its discovery miles away on the seacoast. The owner, James Bourke, came to the stand to aver that he had installed new pins in the oarlocks, and that when he retrieved his boat, its pins and oarlocks had been so roughly used by a rower they were ruined. A Boston police officer told of Wagner's blistered hands.

But it was testimony by Maren Hontvet concerning the contents of Karen's purse that startled the crowded courtroom. She said that Karen had been planning to go to Portsmouth and that she and Anethe had asked Karen to purchase some items for them. Anethe gave her three-quarters of a dollar and Maren gave her a dime to buy her a hair braid. Karen put the money in her purse.

"Beside the money," asked the prosecutor, "did you see her put anything else in her pocketbook that afternoon?"

"Yes."

"What was it?"

In her uncertain English, Maren replied, "A button, white button like."

"Have you any articles of clothing with similar buttons upon it?"

"Yes, have got some."

"Where was the button taken from, if you know?"

"From my sewing basket."

"State what was done with the button, how did it come from there?"

"She [Anethe] wanted a button. She took the sewing basket and looked for a button, and took a button there and handed it to Karen and Karen put it in her purse."

Later testimony elicited that when the Boston police arrested Wagner and had him empty his pockets, they found among a few coins a small white agate button. Offered in evidence, it was compared to buttons Maren Hontvet had brought to court. They matched.

When Rufus Tapley adopted the daring strategy of putting Louis Wagner on the stand, Wagner offered a detailed account of his movements on the night in question. After being invited by John Hontvet to assist in baiting trawl nets, he said, he ate supper and went to Pier Wharf and helped a man whose name he did not know to put boxes of fish in a cart. For another man he could not name he'd baited more hooks on a schooner, name not recalled, until ten o'clock. He then drank ale in a saloon, name not recalled, and later became sick. Walking down Court Street toward a water pump so as to wash his face, he slipped on a patch of ice, fell, and went to sleep. He awoke around three in the morning, staggered to Mrs. Johnson's boardinghouse and, rather than go up to his room, slept on a couch. He stayed there until five and then walked to the wharves again. He returned to Mrs. Johnson's around seven. Then he decided to catch a train to Boston in the hope of finding work. As to the money on him, he earned it, along with the blistered hands. He swore he hadn't been to Smutty Nose since December and that he'd borne no ill will against the Hontvets or anyone else on Smutty Nose Island.

Although Rufus Tapley in his summation attacked most of the evidence and testimony presented by the state, he glossed over Maren Hontvet's tale of the button that matched the one found in his client's pocket.

Attorney General Plaistead took three and a half hours to summarize his case, claiming to have "overthrown" Wagner's alibi and asserting that an alibi overthrown was a conviction.

After a nine-day trial, the case passed into the hands of the jury on June 18. They needed only fifty-five minutes to find Louis Wagner guilty of first-degree murder.

Pending sentencing, Wagner was taken to nearby Alfred Jail. Brand-new, it was deemed by experts in methods and facilities of incarceration to be state-of-the-art. The word most often used to describe it was "safe." Perhaps it was safe, said Wagner in a tone that a guard took to be jesting, but he intended to break out of it.

Within the week, no one was laughing. In place of Louis Wagner, in his cot was a dummy. The state-of-the-art lock on his cell door had been deftly picked, along with the locks on cells of two other prisoners. How long they and Wagner had been gone, no one could say. The only thing to do was sound the alarm to every town and city on the

East Coast that a convicted axe murderer was on the loose, and to send out search parties.

Ironically, the man who had demonstrated masterful seamanship by rowing a small boat twelve miles to Smutty Nose Island and back again in the dead of night turned out to be hopelessly inept on land. A man who had crafted a wooden key to open cell doors in a "safe" jail and made an escape that astonished those who had intently followed his trial, many of whom still believed he was innocent, had no idea what to do with his freedom. After subsisting on a diet of wild berries and nearly being run over by the carriage of one of the sheriff's deputies who was looking for him, he was spotted by a man named William Cheney near Farmington, New Hampshire. Four days after his escape he was back in custody.

After an appeal to the entire bench of the supreme judicial court was rejected, Wagner was sentenced to be hanged, but under Maine law not until he completed one year's confinement in the state prison at Thomaston. The delay was a concession to a strong anti-death penalty sentiment in the state. Taking advantage of it, Wagner resumed his personal campaign to persuade the public he was innocent.

At the end of the mandatory year Governor Nelson Dingley Jr. had three options: grant a pardon, commute the sentence to life in prison, allow the execution to proceed. Ruling out the first choice, the governor sought advice on the second from his council. Its members voted five to two against. The council agreed unanimously to set January 29, 1875, as the date of execution.

Resolved never to send a man to his death without having seen him, Dingley paid a call on Wagner at Thomaston Prison. Wagner asked him, "Do I look like a man who would commit such a crime?"

The governor replied, "You look to me like a man that got himself into a corner and murdered his way out."

But two weeks before Wagner was to hang, he learned

that his date with the scaffold was to be postponed pending a decision on whether to commute the death sentence of triple-murderer John True Gordon. He'd used an axe to butcher three members of his brother's family at Thorndike, near Belfast, Maine. It was a case with no mystery, no conflicting testimony, no doubt in anyone's mind that Gordon had wielded the axe.

Wagner was reprieved until February.

However, this target date was pushed back to March 26. Two days before, the governor's council reprieved both Wagner and Gordon until June 25, 1875.

It was the last respite. With no further shilly-shallying by the council when it met next, the governor signed warrants for both men, to be carried out simultaneously.

On the night before Wagner's date with death, the editor of the Lewiston, Maine, *Journal,* Edward P. Mitchell, visited him. Having followed the case and studied the testimony again, he entered Wagner's cell convinced of his guilt. His impression of Wagner was that he was an ignorant and even stupid man. Yet when Wagner spoke of his faith in God, and professed confidence that God would intervene to save him, Mitchell thought he sounded sincere.

After listening to Wagner's slow, deliberate, heavily accented but well-chosen English, and studying a round face that was "good-natured," Mitchell found himself beginning to doubt his belief that Wagner had actually carried out the "marvelous performance with oars" that had been a cornerstone of the case against him.

When the time came for Mitchell to leave, he did so, he wrote later, "after seeing how the condemned bore himself and hearing his simple forcible discussion of the case." As the cell door closed, Mitchell said, "there was doubt and not certainty in my mind."

As the hour of execution neared, the man who was scheduled to accompany Wagner to the gallows, John True Gordon, very nearly cheated the hangman. Using a shoemaker's knife that had been smuggled in to him, he stabbed himself in the leg and side. The wounds were serious enough that he was likely to bleed to death before he could be hanged.

This presented a problem. The death warrant required both Gordon and Wagner to be hanged between eleven o'clock and noon.

The dilemma facing the warden of the prison was described by Mitchell. Gordon was unconscious and rapidly sinking. "What was to be done? Proceed with Wagner, disregarding the warrant in Gordon's case, or hang them together before noon, one of them insensible and dying?"

The decision was to go ahead.

Wagner walked while Gordon was carried to the scaffold set up in an old, disused lime quarry. As guards held Gordon up and the noose was looped around his neck, Wagner looked at him and said, "Poor Gordon, poor Gordon, you are almost gone."

Wagner was asked if he had any last words.

He replied calmly in heavily accented English, "What I have to say I have recorded in *mein* true story. I hope in the help of God. I believe in His Holy Word and His Commandments. That is all I have to say."

A moment later he was dead.

In 1927 crime historian Edmund Pearson wrote that if ever a case were proved to the hilt of the law, it was the one against Louis Wagner. The jury observed him for nine days. They'd heard him talk for hours. The jury made a prompt decision against him and the courts upheld their verdict.

"Even without the direct testimony of the eyewitness, a woman whose character was unimpeached, the case was strong," Pearson continued. "Combined with Maren's story, the mass of circumstances led to an inescapable conclusion."

While Wagner's execution was "a shocking spectacle," Pearson wrote, "far more pitiful, and a thousand times more wicked was the scene on that lonely island, under a wintry moon, when the terror-stricken woman paused in her flight to listen to the screams of her sister as she met her death at the hands of her slow and remorseless murderer."

In the article published by the *Atlantic Monthly* one week before Wagner was hanged, Celia Thaxter took up her pen again. She imagined a winter midnight on Smutty Nose as Louis Wagner's ghost still searched for the woman who'd gotten away and whose testimony had sent him to the gallows.

Thaxter pictured "two dim, reproachful shades," the murdered women, "who watch while an agonized ghost prowls eternally about the dilapidated houses at the beach's edge, close by the black, whispering water, seeking for the woman who has escaped him—escaped to bring upon him the death he deserves, whom he never, never, never can find."

Six

A Terrible Murder

When General Joseph E. Johnson of the Confederate army surrendered himself and 37,000 men to the Union army's General William Tecumseh Sherman at Raleigh, North Carolina; nine days after Robert E. Lee handed his sword to Ulysses S. Grant; and four days after John Wilkes Booth assassinated President Abraham Lincoln, twenty-nine-year-old Thomas Baxter Gunter was free to return to the concerns of farming and caring for his seventeen-year-old wife, Mary, and his sixty-two-year-old widowed mother, Olive. But Baxter knew that his life, his family's and everyone else's in and around the hamlet of Chatham Church, six miles southeast of Pittsboro, could never be the same as before the war. Most noticeable among the changes was the absence of a few relatives and many friends who'd been killed during the fighting. And there was the revised state of the negroes, freed from slavery by the provisions of a proclamation by a president now dead and the might of Union armies.

While Baxter's family had never been wealthy enough to own negroes, he found himself competing in the hard-scrabble business of farming with blacks who had gone from being chattel to sharecroppers, a condition that seemed to Baxter to be not much better than slavery. But as much as he and other whites around Chatham Church resented the new state of affairs, there was nothing he nor anyone else could do but get on with their lives as best they could. For Baxter this meant providing the needs of both a burgeoning family of his own and those of his aging mother and two sisters.

When census-taker Jonathan W. Jackson counted the Gunters on May 16, 1880, he tallied ten souls. The tally included Baxter's son, Simon, daughters Martha, age eight, Cornelia Jane, six, and Henrietta, four. Also in residence was sixteen-year-old Joseph Farren, a black employed by Baxter as a laborer.

Sometime after the census Baxter's mother, Olive, moved into a house of her own on McQueen Road. Shared with Baxter's spinster sister Jane, age sixty-four, it stood about a mile from Baxter's house. Because of Olive's advanced age and his sister's frail health, Baxter made a habit of stopping by to see how they were doing. When he did so on his way home from a prayer meeting in the local schoolhouse in the company of his neighbor William Womble at half past eight the night of Saturday, December 22, 1883, he found the older women in good spirits, due in large measure to the fact that Baxter's youngest daughter, Henrietta, now eight years old, was spending the night with them. As he left them, he told Olive and Jane he would return early in the morning to tend to the fire in the hearth and take Henrietta with him to Sunday church services.

Always the dutiful and caring son, he arrived at the crack of dawn to find the door to the small house ajar, but he thought nothing of it. Upon entering the one-room house and finding his mother, sister, and little Henrietta apparently still asleep, he went straight to the fireplace and began removing the ashes of a dwindling fire in order to stack fresh logs. When he heard a very slight moan, he said, "Mother, you are sleeping late this morning."

Unanswered, he turned to look at her and noticed an arm

dangling limply from the bed. Gripped with worry that she might be ill, he strode to the bed and touched her arm. It felt cold. He looked at her closely and gasped in horror at gray hair caked with blood.

Turning toward the bed in which his sister lay with Henrietta, he said, "Mother is dead." When Jane did not respond, he went to the bed and found her also lifeless. Pulling back the bedcovers, he saw Henrietta's little body stir. Bending over her, he found her hair matted with blood.

Summoned to the house, Dr. L. A. Hanks, the coroner, determined that the women had been dead for several hours. Olive Gunter's death had been caused by two severe blows to the head, struck as she slept on her left side, evidently by an axe she had normally kept beside the door. The bloodied tool was found some distance away lying beside a gate. One of the wounds was a little above and behind her right ear. The other was to the neck. Jane's skull had been crushed, apparently with the axe handle. Little Henrietta had been given two similar blows on the top of the head, leaving her unconscious but alive. Whether she could survive was doubtful.

Following a tradition as old as murder itself, Dr. Hanks immediately suspected the person who'd discovered the bodies. He arrested Baxter. The motive attributed to him was a desire to claim money bequeathed to him in his mother's will.

This dramatic turn of events so outraged Baxter's three brothers and six neighbors that they signed and issued a public statement to "positively contradict the report and hereby declare it is utterly false." To back up their insistence that Baxter was innocent and underscoring their belief that more than one person had committed the killings, they offered a reward of $100 for the arrest of "the murderers."

However, the grieving son, brother, and father quickly proved that he had been at his own house at the time of the murders. In the face of this alibi, Hanks cleared him of the murder, with an apology. A jury hastily convened to review the facts declared, "We find that Mrs. Oliver Gunter and Miss J. B. Gunter came to their death by the use of an axe in the hands of some person or persons to the jurors unknown."

Undaunted, Hanks pursued the investigation by questioning Olive Gunter's employee. He reported having told three black men that the old lady kept a lot of money in the house. Asked who these men were, he named Louis Ferrer, Fred Johnson, and Frank McClenehan. They were arrested and detained in jail, but the coroner's jury found insufficient evidence to charge them. A search of the house located Olive's treasure—$100.

This left Hanks convinced that the only hope of learning who'd killed the women rested with Henrietta. Unfortunately, the girl was in a deep coma. In hopes of bringing her out of it, a team of doctors operated and removed several pieces of crushed bone. Although she remained unconscious, the doctors informed Hanks they expected her to recover sufficiently to speak.

Indeed she did, but to the disappointment of the coroner. The *Fayetteville Observer* noted on January 2, 1884, "She has no recollection whatever about it [the attack], not even remembering that she spent the night at her grandmother's house. All the circumstances connected with it seem a blank in her mind, but may yet be revived and the murderer thus known."

Some memory did come back to Henrietta. On February 12, 1884, the *Chatham Record* informed its readers that she had testified before a new jury assembled by Coroner Hanks. The paper reported that she must have been asleep when wounded, because she knows nothing about receiving the wound. The article continued, "She says that on the night of the murder, her grandmother went to bed first, then she next, and her aunt last. She remembers her aunt covering up the fire in the fireplace and saying her prayers, and that is the last occurrence of that night that she remembers."

The newspaper concluded in a burst of optimism, predicting, "But 'murder will out' and we confidently predict that the murderer of these old women will yet be brought to punishment."

On Christmas, 1884, a year and three days after the killings, the *Record* lamented that "no one had yet been arrested, nor do we know that there is any clue likely to lead to the murderer's conviction."

Whether the details of the Gunter murders and the *Record*'s gloomy prediction regarding prospects for their being solved were of interest to a young mulatto woman named Mary Neal, who lived six miles from Chatham Church in the village of Moncure, is not known. Like most residents of the rural regions of Chatham County in central North Carolina, Mary did not know how to read. But neither did she have to. Living on a small farm with her brother, Jerry Finch, she helped with the chores on her brother's place and went every morning to prepare breakfast for other relatives, seventy-nine-year-old bachelor Ned Finch and his spinster sister Sallie. They lived nearby with a seventeen-year-old negro hand by the name of Ephraim Ellington. In return for her work in the kitchen, Mary Neal was allowed to have the milk of Ned Finch's cow.

On Sunday, July 4, 1885, she arrived at the Finch place to do just that. When no one answered her knocking on the door, she shouted for Ellington. Unanswered, she went ahead and milked the cow. Returning to the house, she again called out for Ellington and got no response. Noticing the door ajar and feeling nervous about venturing inside, she raced half a mile to the home of W. H. White, Ned's natural but officially unrecognized son. He and White's young son Tom accompanied Mary Neal to the Finch house. Tom went in alone.

A moment later he bolted from the house and shouted, "They all dead!"

Rather than go into the house, White rushed a quarter of a mile to the house of a neighbor, J. H. Poe; with him was a neighbor, Nathan Gilmore. Ordering his own farm-hands to cease work and come along, Poe, Gilmore, White, and the others ran to the Finch property. Fearing what he might find in the house, and not wishing to see his dead father, White waited outside as Poe and Gilmore went in.

Before them lay Ephraim Ellington in a large puddle of blood and his head almost cut off. In bed a few feet away was Sallie Finch, her head a mass of red pulp. Going into the adjoining room, the men found the old man, also in bed, throat slit wide, the head also savagely beaten. Coming out of the house a few moments later, Poe sent one of his men to fetch the coroner. Turning to White, he shook his head gravely and said, "They're all murdered. Old Ned, Miss Sallie, and the black boy. Looks to me like they were all hit many times with an axe."

Details of the second case of multiple axe-murder in the county in a year and a half would be published by the *Raleigh News and Observer:*

Mr. Finch was an old bachelor and much respected by his neighbors, and did not have an enemy in the world, as was supposed. His sister had always lived with him, and no one could have imagined that this good brother and sister would have met with so horrible an end, living, as they did, so quietly, peaceably and simply. With them lived the colored boy Ephraim, whose mother on her death-bed had given him to Mr. Finch, and who faithfully waited on this good old couple and shared their fate.

The wounds were all inflicted with Mr. Finch's own axe, which was found lying in the room covered with blood and gray hairs. Each victim had received more than one blow, showing that the murderers were determined to make sure of their bloody work. Ephraim's neck was almost cut in two, and his skull badly fractured. The old lady's face was a most ghastly sight, one side being crushed to a jelly, while Mr.

Finch's face and head were horribly mangled with seven blows of the axe. It is supposed that more than one person committed the murders.

After speculating on robbery as motive, the newspaper found "a most striking and suspicious coincidence between this murder and the Gunter murder" in December 1883. "Both occurred on Saturday night," the article recalled, "and the fatal instrument of death used at both was the axe that belonged to the victim; both occurred in the same neighborhood; and there was the same number of victims (three) at each, two being old and one being young."

To pursue the possibility that the Gunter and Finch murders might have been committed by the same person or persons, the Chatham authorities brought in a private detective, Jack Wren, from Richmond, Virginia. He confidently predicted he would "unearth both murders at once."

He agreed that motive in the Finch murder had been robbery. Ned Finch was a prosperous man who earned even more money by lending it. This, and a need to pay farmhands, meant he always kept plenty of cash around. With bureau drawers opened and the floor strewn with papers, including a mortgage document and a deed to the property, it seemed obvious that the motive was robbery. Yet untouched during the ransacking of the house was a secretary in which there was a compartment containing $365.

Outside the Finch house investigators had also discovered three sets of footprints, two made by shoes and one by someone who was barefoot. The path led from the house to a fence. Caught on it was a small thread, evidently torn from the clothing of one of the persons who had scaled the fence. Noticing mule tracks on the other side of the fence, the investigators followed them for a mile to the house of Jerry Finch, from which Mary Neal had set out that morning for Ned Finch's place. On a clothesline behind the house hung a pair of working pants of the same material as the thread found on the fence. The legs were still wet from a washing.

Asked about them, Jerry Finch's wife, Harriet, said they were her husband's and had been washed on Wednesday. Confiscated, they were sent to Philadelphia to be examined by a chemist who was a specialist in bloodstains employed by the state of Pennsylvania. Convinced that Jerry Finch had been involved in the murder of his rich relative and that Harriet was an accomplice, the Chatham County coroner ordered them arrested. When Jerry Finch insisted he could not have committed the murders because he had been in Pittsboro on Saturday night with a friend, Lee Tyson, the coroner ordered that Tyson be questioned. After the two men gave conflicting stories about their activities on the night of the murder, Tyson was also arrested. They were taken to the jail in Pittsboro.

Two days later, a black man, Jerry Faucet, walking in Haywood, a town about a mile from the town of Moncure, spotted what appeared to be a note that had been dropped on the path.

Addressed to the mayor of Raleigh, it said:

William Bryant, Sir

I sent dis her note by Eafron neal you and him must see bout dat ar thing de old man Peater Harris myself and de other boys have ours pistols and guns you felows must have de metins to de church and git all we was talking bout days got dem two felows up to day never will own nuffin when we goes to start we go whar we nose dar is money to git guns and pistols den we can son weed de whit folks out don never own nuffin I speekt Ras Cotton has got nuff of his start him caise he say he was goin to do it now we must stop dis thing Rite and not let whit folks se into dis I will meet you whar we sayd.

       William
       Harris

The "Eafron neal" in the note was Jerry Finch's brother and Peater Harris, Ras Cotton, and the signatory of the note were all well-known black men living in the vicinity of Haywood.

The meaning of the note was clear to Moncure's mayor, W. H. Dodd. A group of blacks, sympathetic to Jerry and Harriet Finch and Lee Tyson, were hatching a plan to free them from the jail in Pittsboro. On July 9 he telegraphed the governor, "There is a threatened insurrection of negroes, on the account of the arrest and incarceration of the negroes on a charge of murder in jail in Pittsboro. Send fifty armed men."

The governor responded by ordering a company of the Durham Light Infantry, a unit of black troops, to the Pittsboro jail under the command of a white officer, Captain E. J. Parrish. They were not needed. A telegram from Moncure on July 10 informed the governor that an investigation had proven the alarming note to have been a hoax.

Four days later, a public meeting of citizens of Chatham County approved a resolution "indignantly" denouncing the hoax "as an insult to, and a libel upon all the people of the county, both black and white." It declared that "there is the kindliest feeling existing between the two races in this county" and that there "has been no danger whatsoever of an insurrection of negroes in this county."

Although suspects were in custody in the Finch case, the detective who had been brought in from Richmond and continued to look into the Gunter murders believed he'd made a breakthrough in the form of reports that a twenty-one-year-old black man not only had been seen in the vicinity of both the Gunter house before the murders, but had known a great deal about them. His name was John Pattishall. The most likely place to find him was Raleigh. And, indeed, he was found there. Placed under arrest, he was transported to Pittsboro. Charged with the Gunter killings and suspected of being somehow involved in the Finch murders, he was placed in the same jail as Jerry and Harriet Finch and Lee Tyson.

Brought into court for a preliminary hearing on Thursday, August 27, 1885, Pattishall pleaded not guilty and found himself confronted with a dozen witnesses testifying or affirming in affidavits that they had seen him before, on the night of, and after the Gunter murders. A few stated that he'd told them of the murders long before the news of them had spread around the town. The court decreed "after hearing all the evidence" that "John Pattishall be committed to the common jail of Chatham County to answer the charge of murder of Mrs. Olive Gunter."

For the Finches and Tyson the constitutional guarantee of a speedy trial was slow in being realized. However, they received a bit of encouraging news from Philadelphia concerning the first clue in the Finch case—Jerry Finch's freshly washed pants. Stains had been detected that might have been blood, but the examining expert was unable to say so with certainty. But it was not until Monday, September 9, 1885, two months and four days after the murders of Ned and Sallie Finch and Ephraim Ellington, that a coroner's jury finally completed its work. It issued a verdict charging that the three had been killed by "blows on the head, inflicted by an axe, in the hands of Jerry Finch, Harriet Finch and Lee Tyson, and other party or parties to the Jurors unknown."

Before they could go to trial, however, they had to wait for the next convening of court. This meant six more weeks in the Pittsboro jail. They were under the watchful eyes during the day of the jailor, Thomas Cross, an elderly man who lived next door to the jail, and were locked up without supervision during the night.

Secure in their cells in the first hour of Tuesday, September 29, 1885, the four accused murderers and another prisoner, also black, being held on a charge of arson, slept peacefully. So did Cross, until awakened by pounding on his front door. He looked at his clock and noted the time—

ten minutes before one. The banging continued. Worried that a fire had broken out in the jail, he opened the door and found himself facing men in masks. They demanded the keys to the jail. Cross initially refused, but threats of harm frightened him into complying. Nor did he resist demands that he accompany the men to the jail and take them to the cells of the four accused murderers. Leaving his house, he found a silent mob of disguised men he estimated at between 75 and 100 in number. Moments later, a handful of the men followed him into the jail and to the cells. Ignoring the accused arsonist, they dragged out the terrified Finches, Tyson, and Pattishall.

Still moving in silence, the mob and their prisoners surged out of town by way of McQueen Road. About a mile from the jail at a spot where a road branched off to a pair of farms stood a large red oak tree. As a later observer noted, its limbs were "spreading and convenient."

Choosing one limb per man and one for Harriet Finch, masked men looped ropes around them and the four necks. Pattishall's arms were tied at the wrists; Finch's and Tyson's were not. In an apparent concession to decency, only Harriet's feet were tied. No blindfolds were provided. A moment later, the strongest men yanked the ends of the ropes dangling from the limbs and lifted their victims barely off the ground. Had the four been tried, convicted, and sentenced to hang by a court, they would have died of broken necks. Swinging from the old oak, they died by slow strangulation. Were Jerry and Harriet Finch and Lee Tyson guilty of the murders of Ned and Sallie Finch and Ephraim Ellington? Did John Pattishall killed the Gunters? The evidence against them was circumstantial but not so compelling that a fair juror might not express a reasonable doubt.

On October 8, the *Star* of Wilmington, North Carolina, declared in an editorial, "Some one or more may have been innocent. If so, what a tremendous crime has been perpetrated."

Seven

The Barnes Mystery

In March 1879 twice-widowed, sixty-year-old Julia Martha Thomas was regarded by her neighbors and congregants of the Presbyterian Church in Richmond, a few miles upstream on the Thames River from London, England, as reclusive. But in a country whose long history was replete with eccentrics of all varieties, an elderly woman who preferred to keep to herself was hardly noteworthy. Enjoying what class-conscious subjects of Queen Victoria called "a little independence of her own," she rented one of two small houses known as "Vine Cottages" from Miss Ives. For a time she had supplemented her finances by taking in lodgers, but in January 1879 she was living alone, except for a thirty-year-old maidservant named Kate Webster.

In sharp contrast to Mrs. Thomas's reserve, Webster's personality was viewed by patrons of Mrs. Hayhoe's pub, The Hole in the Wall, as typically Irish, and never more so than when she drank. Some of those who observed her night after night found her mood dark and morose, but so seemed many Irish to the English.

A few of Mrs. Hayhoe's regulars who looked into Kate Webster's dark, gleaming, and slightly oblique eyes discerned a chilling primitiveness, sharpness, cunning, and a pent-up fury. She also exhibited a fondness for finery and made no secret of an avarice for a far better style of living. But this, too, seemed to be in keeping with someone who had obviously experienced the crushing poverty of growing up in Ireland.

Born in 1849 into a poor but respectable family in Killane County, Wexford, she was not Kate Webster, but Catherine Lawler.

Almost from the start, she had been a problem for her parents. No matter how often the parish priest was called in to talk to her about being the good girl that the Blessed Virgin Mary, Mother of Christ, expected her to be, Kate continued to show more interest in helping herself to someone else's fine lace and bits of cheap jewelry than in her future standing in the eyes of the Holy Virgin and the Roman Catholic Church. When caught stealing, she sobbed and tearfully promised repentance, then went right back to her ways.

It surprised no one that at age sixteen she stole enough money to book a passage across the Irish Sea to explore the riches of England.

Arriving in Liverpool and calling herself Kate Webster, she managed to sustain herself for two years by thievery. One day when she was eighteen, an alert constable watched her dip a hand into a man's pocket and hauled her off to court. Unswayed by her tears and a vow to never do it again, a magistrate gave her a four-year sentence.

When she emerged from prison, she was a powerfully built twenty-two-year-old woman. Within hours of her release she departed Liverpool for London.

Perhaps chastened by having been locked up, she found employment as a charwoman, but when wages proved insufficient, she found an easy way to bolster her earnings by joining a vast number of women who survived by becoming prostitutes.

Contrary to the consensus of well-off Londoners that

women who became prostitutes had been seduced at an early age, a survey by a prison chaplain taken the year before Kate Webster got out of prison found only four percent of sixteen thousand prostitutes interviewed claiming to have been "ruined" by a man. The eleven thousand others stated that they had chosen to "sail along on their bottoms" to keep from drowning in poverty.

Such a means of earning a living carried risks, as five prostitutes in the Whitechapel section of London's East End would prove in 1888 as victims of Jack the Ripper. And there was always a chance of becoming pregnant, which is what happened to Webster.

Unmarried and living with her son in Kingston-on-Thames, she augmented her income as a prostitute and pickpocket by taking up the trade of boardinghouse thief. This involved taking a room in a lodging house for a few days, then absconding with whatever objects she might sell to pawnbrokers. Unfortunately for her, she proved as fallible in this enterprise as she'd been as a fledgling pickpocket in Liverpool. Between 1871 and 1875 Webster found herself charged with thirty-six counts of larceny.

The last of her incarcerations for these was for eighteen months, spent in the grim confines of Wandsworth Prison. Released in 1877, she returned to robbery and was quickly back in jail.

Freed the following year, she and her son moved in with a charitable friend, Mrs. Crease, in Richmond. Deeply concerned about Kate Webster and the boy, Crease informed her that an elderly widow by the name of Julia Thomas was seeking the services of a maid.

Dressed in her finest clothes, Webster applied for the job and on the recommendation of Mrs. Crease was hired. Leaving the child in Crease's keeping, Kate moved into Number 2 Vine Cottages in February 1879.

Within weeks Kate Webster and Julia Thomas regretted the arrangement. Webster found Thomas to be a tyrannical employer and Thomas discovered Webster was a sloppy worker with a surly demeanor. Webster also spent a lot of time lounging in Mrs. Hayhoe's pub. This was especially vexing for Mrs. Thomas because she was not on speaking terms with Hayhoe.

Despite being warned by Mrs. Thomas that unless she mended her ways she was in jeopardy of forfeiting her position, Kate Webster continued patronizing The Hole in the Wall. She was there on Shrove Tuesday, February 25, when another of Mrs. Hayhoe's loyal customers asked how she was getting along in her new job.

Webster replied that she expected to leave Richmond soon for Birmingham. An ailing aunt, she explained, was not expected to live long and had made arrangements for her to inherit a gold watch and chain, articles of jewelry, and all her furniture. Webster's intention was to sell it. Once that was accomplished, she would be well-off enough to not need to work.

Exactly what happened in the next five days to worsen relations between Mrs. Thomas and her maid is not known, except that on Sunday, March 2, the women argued and Thomas told Webster to pack up and go.

With that, Thomas left the cottage for evening church services. She spoke briefly to two congregants who noticed her hands trembling and redness around the eyes as though she had been crying. Respecting her privacy, they did not ask why.

Having participated in Communion, Thomas left the church appearing more composed. At home she found that the troublesome maid had evidently departed. Relieved, she went up to her bedroom to get out of her church clothes. As she did so, she heard footsteps outside the room and turned to see Webster rushing toward her with upraised arm and a hand clutching an axe.

It struck the side of Thomas's head a glancing blow. Struggling with the larger and heavier woman into the hall-way, Thomas lost her balance and tumbled down the stairs.

Whether Thomas was conscious as Webster reached her and drove the axe blade into her skull is not known.

What happened next elevated the murder of one woman by another to a level of infamy unique in the bloody criminal annals of a nation whose history even in 1879 was crammed with bizarre and gruesome *multiple* homicides.

Confident that Thomas was dead, Webster dragged the body to the kitchen, where water was boiling in a large copper pot. Arrayed on a table were a meat cleaver and an assortment of long-bladed knives. Beside them lay a large ladle. Nearby stood two empty jars. Carefully placed on the seat of a chair was a commodious black leather bag. On the floor was a wooden box containing several cloth sacks, each lined with thick brown paper.

After carefully removing the dead woman's clothing and placing the fine garments neatly folded on another table, Kate Webster picked up the cleaver, hacked off Julia Thomas's head, and placed it in the leather bag. Then she commenced the grisly task of chopping the corpse into small chunks.

How long a time she spent cutting and stuffing the flesh into the pot isn't known. It is a matter of record that at some point that evening she arrived at The Hole in the Wall and then spent an hour or so drinking and talking with Mrs. Hayhoe. Days later when all of Britain knew of the horror that had been perpetrated in Mrs. Thomas's kitchen, the colorful pub keeper quipped, "I little thought when Kate came in and I chatted with her that she had left her mistress boiling in the copper."

Fortified with Mrs. Hayhoe's liquor, Webster returned to Vine Cottages and resumed work. This involved removing boiled pieces of Thomas's flesh from the pot, stuffing them in the sacks in the box, skimming floating fat and ladling it into the jars, putting fresh chunks into the pot, and cleaning blood from the floor. In an attempt to dispose of bones, she built a roaring fire. Portions of the body that proved too big for the pot were placed in the box.

This laborious work continued through the night and most of Monday. In describing the task in *Victorian Studies in Scarlet,* British historian Richard D. Altick wryly noted, "It was quite a job to clean the utensils and set the house to rights after the rendering was complete; probably Kate, now liberated from the dictatorial presence of her employer, did a more thorough job than she had ever accomplished when Mrs. Thomas was still in health."

But Kate Webster did not labor without interruption, and not without moments of alarm. At noon on Monday she was startled by knocking on the front door. Opening it, she found the coal agent, Mr. Deane, come to collect a bill. When Webster told him Thomas was not at home, Deane said, "Will you be good enough to say that Mr. Deane called and wanted to see her?" Kate assured him she would.

Early Tuesday a girl named Roberts arrived at the door with a message from the owner of the cottage, Miss Ives. Webster was asked to inform Mrs. Thomas that repairmen would be coming the next day to fix a leak in the roof. Webster told the girl to tell Miss Ives that the leaking had been snow melting on the roof and that repairs were not required.

Next came an event, according to a story that breezed through England at the time, that assured Kate Webster immortality in murder history and a life-size representation of herself in wax in the Chamber of Horrors of Madame Tussaud's museum. It was said that she went from door to door in the neighborhood seeking to sell two jars of "the best fat dripping."

While that story's veracity may be questioned, there is no doubt that she appeared at the shop of a pawnbroker saying she was Mrs. Thomas and sold the dead woman's gold bridgework with several false teeth attached. She garnered six shillings and squandered them that afternoon at Hayhoe's pub.

Once again bolstered by drink, she went back to the cottage and helped herself to one of Julia Thomas's finer outfits in order to call on old acquaintance Henry Porter of Hammersmith.

Leaving a house that had never been so immaculately cleaned, she carried with her the black leather bag containing Mrs. Thomas's head.

Surprised to see her after several years, Porter remarked that she was better dressed now and appeared to have acquired some means. This was true, Webster explained, because she was now Mrs. Thomas, the widow of a prosperous gentleman. Furthermore, she continued as she had tea, she'd inherited "a small villa" from a well-to-do aunt in Richmond. Indeed, this was the purpose of her call. "Even though it's a cozy place," she said, "I'm eager to sell the furniture."

Might Henry Porter know someone who was in a position to broker some furniture and a few other objects of value?

Porter mentioned a friend, John Church, landlord of the nearby Rising Sun tavern, who might be just the man to handle such an undertaking. He would arrange for Webster to meet the man as soon as possible. With that settled, Webster announced that although she was thoroughly enjoying tea with her old friend, she had an appointment with a friend at Barnes, a nearby community. She got up to leave, black bag in hand.

Evidently enjoying their reunion, Porter suggested he and his sixteen-year-old son, Robert, accompany her as far as a nearby pub, the Oxford and Cambridge. Never one to pass a public house without going in, and black bag notwithstanding, Kate Webster decided to joint the Porters for a drink.

Presently, she told them she really had to keep the appointment at Barnes. Once again, Henry Porter offered the company of himself and Robert, at least as far as a bridge that connected Hammersmith and Barnes. Webster acceded, but when Porter volunteered to carry the bag, she retorted, "I'll carry it myself."

Father and son left her at the bridge and returned to the pub, but about twenty minutes later Kate Webster was back without the bag and eager to have another drink. One led to another before Webster asserted that she must make her way back to Richmond.

Concerned about a woman making the train journey alone at night, Henry volunteered Robert as a traveling companion, assuming the boy could catch a return train in time to go to work in the morning. Assuring Porter of this, Webster left with the young man.

Arriving at Number 2 Vine Cottages, she asked Robert to assist her in carrying a large box tied shut with a thick cord that she wanted to take to a friend. The boy agreed and between them they carried it to Richmond Bridge. At midpoint Webster said, "Leave me with it. You go back the way we came and I'll catch up after I've talked to my friend."

A few moments later as Robert Porter walked toward the station, he heard a splash.

When Webster met him at the station, she said, "Well, that's done."

They then learned that the last train from Richmond had already departed, so the youth stayed the night at Vine Cottages. He left early in the morning of Wednesday, March 5.

Among early risers that day were fishermen hoping to pluck a living from the waters near the bridge between Hammersmith and Barnes. When one spied a tied-up box on the muddy bank, he cut the cord. Opening the lid, he reeled back in horror at the contents. Believing the chopped-up body had been dumped by medical students at a nearby hospital, probably as a prank, he and the other fishermen stayed with the terrible find while one of the group summoned a constable.

When the headless corpse was examined by a doctor, he was aghast to find that portions of the body had been boiled.

The next day a newspaper trumpeted the horrible discovery with the headline:

THE BARNES MYSTERY

When the paper appeared, Kate Webster was in the Thomas cottage with Henry Porter discussing arrangements for her to meet John Church. Hearing a passing newsboy yelling, "Supposed murder! Shocking discovery of human remains in a box in the Thames," Webster looked calmly at Porter and said, "We might as well have a paper," and went out and bought one. Showing not a bit of concern, she resumed talking with Porter.

In proceeding with her plan to cash in on the contents of Number 2 Vine Cottages, she bargained with John Church over the price he was willing to pay for the furniture and other items. He gave her eighteen pounds against the agreed price of fifty pounds, withdrawn from the princely sum of four hundred pounds in Church's bank account.

Accompanied by a couple of burly helpers and two vans, he arrived at the house of the woman he knew as Mrs. Thomas on March 18 and the transferral of the goods from house to vans commenced. While the men loaded the furniture, Kate Webster carried a few articles of Julia Thomas's clothing she did not care to keep from the house and tossed them into the van.

This activity next door attracted the attention of the owner of the cottage, Miss Ives. She inquired of Church as to where the furniture was going, but for some reason known only to her, she did not put the question to Mrs. Thomas herself. Instead, she went to see the estate agent who handled the business of renting Number 2 to ask what to do about her evidently departing tenant.

Meanwhile, Church was feeling decidedly uneasy.

Unsettled by Miss Ives's inquiry, he feared that he might have been made an unwitting accomplice in a scheme to defraud the property owner. He ordered his helpers to return all the furniture to the cottage.

Confronting "Mrs. Thomas," he declared, "You've deceived me. I will have nothing to do with your goods."

As the vans departed, Kate Webster hurriedly collected her son and boarded the next train out of Richmond. Her ultimate destination was Enniscorthy, Ireland.

While she was en route, Church discovered the clothing in the van and found in a pocket of a dress a letter to Mrs. Thomas from a friend in Finsbury Park. Still upset about the attempt to deceive him, Church called at Number 45 Ambler Road, Finsbury Park. He learned that the woman who'd agreed to sell him the furniture could not have been Mrs. Julia Thomas.

Together with Henry Porter, Church went to the police.

When they investigated Thomas's cottage and discerned evidence that attempts had been made to dispose of a body, it appeared that the "Barnes Mystery" had been solved.

The question now was: Where was the woman who'd passed herself off as Mrs. Thomas? A possible answer was discovered in the pocket of a black silk dress belonging to Thomas that Kate Webster had decided not to sell. It contained another letter, this one sent to Kate Webster from an uncle in Ireland.

Alerted by the Richmond police that Webster was suspected of murder, the Royal Irish Constabulary located her on March 28, 1879.

Audaciously wearing one of Thomas's dresses and several of Thomas's rings, Webster asked the police, "Is anyone in custody for the murder? If there isn't, there ought to be. It's very hard that the innocent should suffer for the guilty."

Insisting she'd had nothing to do with killing Thomas, she was returned to Richmond. Brought face to face with John Church, she exclaimed, "There's your murderer."

When Church proved that on the night of March 2 he had been in his home, Webster pointed an accusing finger at Henry Porter. This brazen attempt to blame someone else for the murder also failed. Charged with the crime, she was ordered held for trial at London's famed criminal court, the Old Bailey.

In opening the case for the Crown on July 2, 1879, Sir Hardinge Giffard declared, "The facts are quite reconcilable with her having done the whole thing herself. She was quite capable of putting Mrs. Thomas to death, being a tall, strong woman; and having put her to death, to have done all else. It may be a question whether a woman, not a very old one, but not a very young one, could have contrived such a ghastly plan as this; but in the end you will come to the conclusion that it was a planned murder."

Through seven days of trial, witnesses called to testify supported Giffard's claim. Human remains belonging to a female were found in a box. The box was traced to Julia Thomas's house. In the kitchen grate were found charred bones. No one could be so silly as to suppose they were not remnants of Mrs. Thomas. Save for the accused, no one had seen the woman since she'd taken Communion on the evening of March 2. Nor, sadly, had anyone missed the reclusive soul.

The box containing body parts had been taken from the house on the following Tuesday. Kate Webster had been seen by the Porters carrying a black bag onto the Richmond Bridge, only to return to the Oxford and Cambridge pub twenty minutes later without it. Though the bag had not been found, could there be any doubt that it contained Mrs. Thomas's head?

Then came Kate Webster's unavailing attempt to sell Mrs. Thomas's furniture.

When Webster was located in Ireland, she was wearing Thomas's dress and jewelry.

The jury quickly found Webster guilty.

She screamed, "I never done it."

With a black cloth on his head the judge sentenced her to hang at Wandsworth Prison on July 28, 1879.

In an attempt to delay the event, Kate Webster said she was pregnant. Physical examination proved the claim a fraud. Undaunted, she continued to deny guilt, frequently with such obscenities that prison-hardened inmates and jaded jailors blushed.

While Webster awaited her date with the gallows, the furnishings of Number 2 Vine Cottages, which she had hoped to sell, went on the auction block. A major purchaser was the landlord of Rising Sun Tavern. Among items carried away by John Church: a carving knife.

On the evening of July 27 Kate Webster dispensed with salty phrases long enough to confide to the prison chaplain, Father McEnrey, and Wandsworth's governor, Captain Colville, that she had indeed struck Julia Thomas with an axe, dragged her into the kitchen, butchered, and boiled her. But she steadfastly refused to tell what she'd done with the black bag.

After watching Kate Webster go to the gallows, the mayor of Wandsworth, Arthur Griffiths, said she was "a defiant, brutal creature who showed no remorse and who broke out into the most appalling language."

Eight

When She Saw What She Had Done

A little after nine in the morning on June 6, 1893, the district attorney of the eastern district of Massachusetts, forty-year-old William H. Moody, Esq., rose in a courtroom in the seaside town of New Bedford to address twelve men in the jury box.

"Upon the fourth day of August of the last year," he began, "an old man and woman, husband and wife, each without a known enemy in the world, in their own home, upon a frequented street in the most populous city in this County, under the light of day and in the midst of its activities, were, first one, then after an interval of an hour, another severally killed by an unlawful agency. Today, a woman of good social position, of hitherto unquestioned character, a member of a Christian church and active in its good works, the own daughter of one of the victims, is at the bar of this Court, accused by the Grand Jury of this County of these crimes."

Thus commenced what the newspapers of the Gilded Age and Gay Nineties heralded all across the country as "the trial of the century." If anyone in the courtroom doubted this claim, he had only to look at the large assemblage of journalists crowded into the seats allotted to them. There on behalf of the *Boston Globe* and the *New York Recorder* sat curmudgeonly Joseph Howard Jr., famed—or was he notorious?—for perpetrating a hoax during the Civil War that President Lincoln was about to call for an enormous conscription, thereby sending shudders through countless households and the stock market. So renowned was Howard that the two newspapers hired a stenographer to assist him.

Near Howard but unaided in working for the *New York Sun* and the *Herald* of Boston was the most distinguished correspondent in America—Julian Ralph. A specialist in focusing his dispatches less on the facts of a case than on the mood and atmospherics, he invariably pursued what the universe of journalists call "color" and the "human-interest angle." By every measure the case that Moody and the district attorney for the southern district, Hosea M. Knowlton, had prepared to present for the People of the Commonwealth of Massachusetts offered plenty of that commodity. Already some wiseacre had composed a blood-curdling rhyme that was not only an indictment against the woman in the dock, but a verdict:

> Lizzie Borden took an axe
> And gave her mother forty whacks;
> When she saw what she had done,
> She gave her father forty-one.

The poem was wrong in every aspect. First, the victims had not been whacked with an axe; it was a hatchet. Second, there had not been a total of eighty-one blows, but only twenty-nine. Third, the woman victim was Lizzie's *stepmother.* Fourth, the killing of Lizzie's father did not occur immediately after the first, as suggested. The elapsed time between the two murders was between an hour and an hour and a half. Finally, under American law

Lizzie Borden was to be deemed innocent until proven guilty beyond a reasonable doubt. That a police officer had found probable cause to arrest her for the double-murder did not mean she'd committed them. Neither could she be considered guilty because a grand jury had weighed certain evidence and found it sufficient to return a true bill.

On December 2, 1892, a panel that had been convened and sworn as grand jurors for the Commonwealth of Massachusetts in the town of Taunton handed up in the precise language required by law the following indictment:

That Lizzie Andrew Borden of Fall River in the County of Bristol, at Fall River in the County of Bristol, on the fourth day of August in the year eighteen hundred and ninety-two, in and upon one Abby Durfee Borden, feloniously, wilfully and of her malice aforethought an assault did make, and with a certain weapon, to wit, a sharp cutting instrument, the name and a more particular description of which is to the Jurors unknown, her, the said Abby Durfee Borden, feloniously, wilfully and of her malice aforethought did strike, beat and bruise, in and upon the head of her, the said Abby Durfee Borden, giving to her, the said Abby Durfee Borden, by the said striking, cutting, beating and bruising, in and upon the head of her, the said Abby Derfee Borden, divers, to wit, twenty mortal wounds, of which said mortal wounds the said Abby Durfee Borden then and there instantly died.

And so the Jurors aforesaid, upon their oath aforesaid, do say that Lizzie Andrew Borden, the said Abby Durfee Borden in manner and form aforesaid, then and there, feloniously, wilfully and of her malice aforethought did kill and murder; against the peace of said Commonwealth, and contrary to the form of the statute in such case made and provided.

As to the second count of murder, that of Andrew Jackson Borden, the indictment used the same terminology to charge that Lizzie gave her father "ten mortal wounds, of which said mortal wounds the said Andrew Jackson Borden then and there instantly died."

But a murder indictment was nothing more than allegations. A jury would ultimately be assembled to decide whether a cold-blooded parricide had been committed by the diminutive thirty-two-year-old, fair-skinned, red-haired, gray-eyed Lizzie Borden, or whether Andrew and Abby Borden had been slaughtered by a mysterious intruder.

Whoever killed them on that sultry Thursday morning had acted so assuredly that the Bordens' maid heard nothing to disturb her as she took a breather by catnapping in her third-floor room until Lizzie shouted up the stairs, "Maggie! Maggie! Come down!"

The maid responded, "What's the matter?"

"Come down here! Father's dead. Someone came in and killed him!"

Finding Lizzie standing near a side door, the young maid moved toward the sitting room.

"No, Maggie, don't go in there," said Lizzie. "Go over and get the doctor. I must have him. Run!"

Learning that Dr. Seabury Bowen was not at home, the frantic maid rushed back to the Borden house. After reporting to Lizzie, she suddenly wondered how Lizzie had been spared.

"I was out in the yard and heard a groan," Lizzie replied, "and came in and the screen door was wide open." Later she would explain that she had gone to the barn to look for sinkers for fishing line.

Help was summoned in the form of two women neighbors, one of whom asked Lizzie the whereabouts of Lizzie's stepmother.

"I don't now," Lizzie Borden said. "She had a note to

go see somebody who is sick, but I don't know but that she is killed, too, for I thought I heard her come in."

Presently, Dr. Bowen arrived, followed by City Marshal Rufus B. Hilliard. He happened to be one of the few members of the Fall River police department on duty. Two-thirds of the men were attending the force's annual picnic and clambake at Rocky Point. What they found on a sofa in the sitting room was published the next day by Fall River's newspaper, the *Daily Globe,* in Bowen's words:

> Mr. Borden lay partly on his right side, with his coat thrown over the arm of the sofa. . . . His feet rested on the carpet. . . . I am satisfied that he was asleep when he received the first blow, which was necessarily fatal. . . . His clothing was not disarranged, and his pockets had apparently not been touched. . . . The cuts extended from the eye and nose around the ear. In a small space there were at least eleven distinct cuts. . . . Physician that I am and accustomed to all kinds of horrible sights, it sickened me to look upon the dead man's face. I am inclined to think an ax was the instrument. The cuts were about four and a half inches in length, and one of them had severed the eyeball and socket. There was some blood on the floor and spatters on the wall, but nothing to indicate the slaughter that had taken place.

Wearing a spotless dress and being tended by the neighbors, Lizzie Borden suggested that someone look for her stepmother. Accompanied by the maid, Mrs. Adelaide Churchill climbed the stairs to the second floor. In the guest room they found Abby's savagely hacked body lying between the bed and a dressing table. By all appearances she had been attacked from behind while she was bent over straightening up the room.

During the next hour, as Borden case historian Edmund Pearson wrote in his book *The Trial of Lizzie Borden,* friends, neighbors, physicians, policemen, and reporters tried to enter the house. This sloppiness in protecting a crime scene would come back to haunt Hilliard and remain a stain on his reputation and that of the Fall River police. They would be criticized for being either incompetent or stupid. But the crimes were, as Pearson noted, "astounding and practically outside the experience of any policemen" of the time.

These deaths had not occurred in a saloon or on a street and the victims were not ordinary people. They were the Bordens, steeped in the respectable atmosphere of the Central Congregational Church. Pearson rightly recorded, "Policemen cannot rush into such a place and conduct investigations in the ordinary way. Public Opinion demands that they step softly. It does not mean that there were no interrogations or no search. It does mean that there was no prompt examination, properly conducted by the police matrons of the persons and clothing of the two women left alive in the house."

The relatively new police procedure of fingerprinting was not yet in use in Fall River.

Hilliard and his investigators recognized that they were not confronted with a situation in which the victims had been killed in the course of a robbery. Mr. Borden's watch and money had not been taken. There'd been no struggle. Furthermore, the two murders had been committed at least an hour apart. This presented the police with the astonishing problem of a murderer who'd been able to conceal himself in the house for that time, unseen and unheard by both Lizzie and the maid. He then would have had to escape unseen, evidently carrying the murder weapon, because an initial search of the house had not found one.

The next day in the cellar, Police Officers Michael Mullally and John Devine were shown two axes and two hatchets by the maid. One appeared promising as a possible murder weapon, but all four were left in the cellar. On the following day another hatchet was found in a box. It had a broken handle. It appeared to have been washed and then coated with ashes. It, too, was left in the cellar. When shown to Acting Captain Dennis Desmond on Monday, five days after the murders, it was wrapped in newspaper and taken to police headquarters.

On Saturday, August 6, newspapers published a notice placed by Lizzie and Emma Borden offering a $5,000 reward for the arrest and conviction "of the person or persons who occasioned the death of Mr. Andrew J. Borden & his wife." That same day, funerals were held at Oak Grove Cemetery. In the evening the mayor of Fall River, Dr. John W. Coughlin, called at the Borden house in the company of Marshal Hilliard. The mayor requested the family to remain at home for a few days and offered police protection if the Borden sisters were annoyed by crowds of the curious. As the mayor was about to leave, Lizzie asked him if she was under suspicion. Caught unawares and looking embarrassed, Coughlin said, "Yes."

Five days later Lizzie Borden found herself arrested and on December 2 she learned she had been indicted on two counts of murder.

The trial was scheduled for June 1893 and would be presided over by three judges of the Superior Court for the County of Bristol. They were Honorable Albert Mason, Chief Justice, and Honorable Caleb Blodgett and Honorable Justin Dewey, Associate Justices.

Out of a panel of 148 prospective jurors, 108 were examined as to suitability. Of the twelve men chosen, none was a resident of Fall River and none professed personal knowledge of the woman they were required to judge, or the woman and man she was accused of murdering.

In keeping with the tradition of prosecutors before him, then and since, William Moody sought in his opening to the jury to present the victims as more than names on an indictment, while being careful to omit anything that seemed unfavorable, including Andrew's illegitimate son,

William. There was, in fact, much about Andrew Borden that was less than admirable.

Born in Fall River on September 13, 1822, he had one sibling, Lauanna. Tall and spare of frame with a beard but no mustache, he made his first money in an undertaking business, Borden & Almy, by overcharging for services. He'd also profited by buying the property of the grieving relatives at a bargain price. Shrewdly investing his money, he acquired ownership of one bank and interests in three others. He was also a landlord with large holdings in downtown Fall River, one of which was a huge commercial building he named for himself. He also owned farms and houses, the rent from which he personally collected. Shares of stock in a horse-car line were sold at a considerable profit. Claiming that he had achieved wealth without borrowing or ever signing a promissory note, he had a fortune at the time of his death estimated at a half-million dollars.

Prosecutor Moody said he got it "by earning and saving, and he retained the habit of saving up to the time of his death."

The day after the murders the *Fall River Daily Globe*'s obituary noted that Borden had been "a peculiar man in many respects. While his tall, neatly clothed figure was familiar to the older citizens, he had few intimates and was reticent to a marked degree. When he started in life his means were extremely limited and he made his money by saving it. The habits of economy and thrift which he formed then, clung to him to the last and although his income of last years was very large, he lived modestly and continued to count his pennies." He was positive in his views, "unbending in will," continued the obituary, and at times appeared to "lack sympathy."

Andrew Borden had been married twice. The first wife, the former Sarah Anthony Morse, died in March 1863 of "eutterine congestion and disease of the spine," leaving two children, Emma Leonora, born March 1, 1851, in Fall River, and Lizzie Andrew, born on June 9, 1860, also in

Fall River. On January 18, 1865, Andrew married Abby Durfee Gray. Six years younger than Andrew, she was short and plump, weighing over two hundred pounds at the time of her murder. No one who knew either bride or groom believed the union was anything but a mutual convenience—the aging spinster got a rich, if stingy, husband and Andrew got a housekeeper and nursemaid.

At the time of the murders the Borden girls were women and living with Andrew and Abby at 92 Second Street. Bought by Andrew Borden in 1872, the home was described in Mr. Moody's opening statement at the trial as "a common type of house in this community and state." Behind it stood a barn. Borden could have easily afforded a finer place in a better neighborhood, but he chose a dwelling, in Moody's words, on "one of the most frequented streets outside of the main business streets in the city." A short distance from City Hall, Second Street was a thoroughfare for carriages and pedestrians.

Separating the house from the sidewalk was a picket fence with two gates. There were three entrances to the house. The front door opened into a foyer flanked by doorways to a parlor and a sitting room. A door on the north side of the house led to a small entryway, which provided access to the kitchen. A third entrance was to the cellar. Upstairs were bedrooms, including a guest room directly above the parlor. Lizzie's room was over the sitting room. A door connected it to Emma's. Mr. and Mrs. Borden slept in a room over the kitchen. A small room on the third floor belonged to the family's live-in maid, Bridget Sullivan. Like all Irish maids, she was referred to as Maggie. She'd been serving the Bordens for three years and had developed a routine for handling all the usual chores of a maid and whatever was requested of her by the four occupants of the house.

Always the first up, she began Wednesday, August 3, at six o'clock by going down a back stairway to the cellar to fetch coal to build a fire in the kitchen stove. That done, she unlocked the side door and opened it and a screen door to bring in that day's delivery of milk. Because her employer did not wish to pay for the installation of gas, another of Sullivan's tasks was to check that the lamps had ample supplies of kerosene. With those lighted as needed, the milk in, and a fire going in the stove, she turned to preparations for breakfasts. But on this day there was one less to be served. Emma Borden was away, visiting her friends the Brownells at their seaside cottage in Fairhaven, about fifteen miles from Fall River.

When Mr. and Mrs. Borden came downstairs, they said they were not feeling well and that they had been so sick all through the night that they had vomited several times. Lizzie also said she had not felt well and after nibbling at her breakfast announced that she was going up to her room. Mrs. Borden was so concerned that she said she was going to see her physician, Dr. Seabury W. Bowen. She arrived at his office at seven o'clock. Moments after she was admitted, she vomited. Allowing that Mrs. Borden did look "sick," Bowen opined that the malady did not appear to be serious. He sent her home. When he crossed the street to Borden's bank to see how he was faring, he was met with a typical Andrew Borden reception. The doctor's attentions were neither welcome nor required, said Borden, and don't dare have the temerity to submit a bill.

What Lizzie Borden actually did in the hours after she said she was going to her room became a matter of heated dispute that would persist in discussions and debates about the Borden case for more than a century. Prosecutor Moody told the jury in his opening at her trial that at noon she appeared in Smith's drugstore "and there asked the clerk for ten-cents worth of prussic acid for the purpose of cleaning a sealskin cape."

At an inquest into the deaths of the Bordens, held between August 9 and 11, 1892, Lizzie had testified she had gone out Wednesday morning, but she later changed her story, saying she hadn't left the house until the evening.

Yet a clerk at Smith's, Eli Bence, stated at the inquest he was "positive" the woman who asked for the poisonous substance was Lizzie Borden.

On cross-examination Bence was unable to describe the color of the dress, hat, purse, and gloves worn by the woman who'd asked for the acid.

The prosecution then called medical student Frank H. Kilroy, who said he'd been in front of the store, "under the fan, and conversing with Mr. Bence, and the lady came in, and Mr. Bence left me, and went behind the counter, and I heard her say 'prussic acid.' Mr. Bence says, 'I cannot sell it without a prescription.' "

This was followed by testimony of another clerk, Frederick B. Harte, who identified the woman as Lizzie Borden. But neither could he describe the woman's clothing. Nor was he able to state the time, other than to say that it happened after ten and before half past eleven.

At some point in this apparently ominous testimony, Lizzie Borden whispered to a friend, Mrs. Brigham, "I was never in that store in my life."

After the proceeding adjourned, Brigham was asked to confirm that Lizzie had made the remark. She replied, "Yes, Lizzie said that she was not out of the house in the morning, when the three witnesses claim they saw her, but she says there is only Maggie now to prove that."

Questioned at the inquest by defense lawyer Melvin Q. Adams, Bridget Sullivan proved to be not as helpful as Lizzie hoped. He asked, "Lizzie stayed in her room all that forenoon, did she not?"

"I suppose so; I did not see her until she came to dinner."

"You knew she was upstairs? They were all sick and ailing that day?"

"Yes, sir."

"She did not go out all that day, did she, so far as you know?"

"I could not say whether she went out or not."

"They ate a little breakfast, and Lizzie went back upstairs to her room?"

"I suppose so. She went out of my sight. I do not know where she went."

It was during this excursion, her prosecutors would allege, that she went shopping for a small quantity of prussic acid. At the trial William Moody expressed no doubt that "the person who made this application for this deadly poison was the prisoner."

The inference was that, having made one attempt to kill her father and stepmother on August 3, but only having made them sick, Lizzie Borden sought a more potent substance, then changed her mind and decided to hack them to death on August 4.

Earlier that day Bridget Sullivan had opened the door to a man who that night would occupy the guest room. His name was John Vinnicum Morse. A brother of Borden's first wife, he'd left Fall River some twenty-five years earlier to explore the possibilities for a young man in the West. Before settling in the town of Hastings, Iowa, in 1880, he had spent a few years in Illinois as a farmer and butcher and managed to save enough money to buy land in Iowa and eventually to acquire two farms on 220 acres. Like his brother-in-law, Morse had a reputation for penny-pinching. Rather than buy a buggy, which he could easily have afforded, he made trips from farm to town in what a neighbor described as "an old rattle-trap lumber wagon." Unmarried, John V. Morse was also like Andrew Borden in having no friends and seeming standoffish with neighbors, who regarded him as a very eccentric and peculiar man.

Unlike Andrew, John paid so little attention to his appearance that to Iowans he looked like a hobo. If he owned more than one suit, no one in Hastings ever saw him in it. Having done nothing to dispel his image as a tall, handsome, mysterious stranger, and wearing the same old outfit, he'd picked up and headed back East, apparently permanently.

Dropping in on the Bordens unexpectedly on Wednesday, August 3, 1892, he arrived without luggage and asked Andrew if he could stay overnight. In sharp contrast to his reputation as a man who didn't care to socialize and despite the strange malady which had gripped him and his wife, Borden welcomed Morse warmly. However, John's niece Lizzie's welcome had been decidedly icy. Rather than greet an uncle she claimed she had never liked, and who evidently knew it, Lizzie remained in her room until at some point she decided to go out, allegedly to buy prussic acid.

The next morning (Thursday, August 4), Sullivan started her daily chores at 6:15. The guest, Morse, was already up. Abby Borden came downstairs at seven, followed by Andrew a few minutes later. They and Morse had breakfast together. Lizzie remained upstairs, evidently preferring not to see her uncle. She came down a few minutes after he had departed to take care of business, around 8:45 A.M. About fifteen minutes later Andrew set out for his office at the Union Savings Bank, of which he was president.

He arrived at approximately 9:30 A.M. but left after only five minutes to call at the National Union Bank, where he was a majority stockholder. Cashier John T. Burrell would later testify that he saw Mr. Borden enter between 9:15 and 9:45. After spending about ten minutes at the bank he had a customary shave at Pierre Leduc's barbershop.

Spruced up, he encountered haberdasher John Clegg, who was soon to be a Borden tenant at a property on South Main Street. Clegg would state that they met at 10:20 A.M. Clegg was sure of the time because he glanced at the City Hall clock. They talked for nine minutes and Mr. Borden proceeded up South Main to look in on the men who were remodeling the property he was to rent to Clegg. When Borden was seen by Caroline Kelly, wife of a doctor and a neighbor, he was returning home at 10:40 A.M. Caroline observed him going along the side of the house toward the front door. Because the door was locked and he did not have his key, Sullivan had to let him in.

At about 10:55 Sullivan went to her room to lie down. Andrew Borden went into the sitting room to do the same on a couch. Fifteen minutes later, Lizzie found him dead and yelled for the maid.

In studying this sequence of events, and assuming as murder investigators always had and still do that the person who "discovers" a murder probably did it, Rufus Hilliard and his sleuths immediately cast suspicious eyes toward Lizzie Borden.

But why on earth would this "woman of good social position, of hitherto unquestioned character, a member of a Christian church and active in its good works, the own daughter of one of the victims," want her father and step-mother dead?

On Thursday, August 11, 1892, six days after she was arrested and charged with murder, her uncle (Andrew Borden's brother-in-law), Hiram Harrington, husband of Lauanna Borden, offered his opinion. "Money," he said to members of the press who were eager for every fresh angle, "unquestionably money."

A blacksmith who saw a bright future in a growing rage for "automobiles," he'd made room on his Fourth Street property, four blocks from the Borden home, for selling Cadillacs. In talking to a reporter from the *Fall River Daily Herald,* Hiram described Andrew Borden as "an exceed-ingly hard man concerning money matters."

Did Harrington personally know of any dissensions among the inhabitants of the house on Second Street?

"Yes, there were, although it had been always kept very quiet. For nearly ten years there have been constant disputes between the daughters and their father and stepmother."

In these disputes, said Harrington, "Lizzie did most of the demonstrative contention, as Emma is very quiet and unassuming, and would feel very deeply any disparaging or angry word from her father. Lizzie, on the contrary, was haughty and domineering with the stubborn will of her father and bound to contest for her rights. There were many animated interviews between father and daughter on this point. Lizzie is of a repellent disposition, and after an unsuccessful passage with her father would become sulky and refuse to speak to him for days at a time. She moved in the best society of Fall River, was a member of the Congregational church, and was a brilliant conversationalist. She thought she ought to entertain as others did, and felt that with her father's wealth she was expected to hold her end up with others of her set. Her father's constant refusal to allow her to entertain lavishly angered her. I have heard many bitter things she has said of her father, and know she was deeply resentful of her father's maintained stand in this matter."

Four days after Harrington's tale appeared, an inquest was convened by Judge Josiah Blaisdell. Notwithstanding the fact that Lizzie was under suspicion and had a constitutional right not to testify, she was quizzed by District Attorney Hosea Knowlton over a period of three days, August 9–11, 1892. Very little of what she said in the following condensation of questions on the key elements of the prosecution's case helped her. [The full transcript of the inquest can be found in the Appendix.]

After a few routine questions Knowlton asked if she had any idea how much her father was worth.

A: No sir.
Q: He never told you that he had made a will, or had not?
A: No sir.
Q: Were your relations with [Abby Borden] cordial?
A: It depends on one's idea of cordiality, perhaps.
Q: Were your relations toward her that of mother and daughter?
A: In some ways it was, in some ways it was not.
Q: In what ways was it?
A: I did not call her mother, [I called her Mrs. Borden].

Q: When did you begin to call her Mrs. Borden?

A: I should think about five or six years ago.

Q: Your usual address was Mrs. Borden?

A: Yes sir.

Q: Why did you leave off calling her mother?

A: Because I wanted to. I had never been to her as a mother in many things. I always went to my sister, because she was older and had the care of me after my mother died.

Q: [On the morning of the murder] had the family breakfasted when you came down?

A: Yes sir.

Q: Where was your father when you came down Thursday morning?

A: Sitting in the sitting room in his large chair, reading the *Providence Journal*.

Q: Where was Mrs. Borden?

A: She was in the dining room with a feather duster dusting.

Q: Where was Maggie?

A: Just come in the back door with the long pole, brush, and put the brush on the handle, and getting her pail of water; she was going to wash windows around the house. She said Mrs. Borden wanted her to.

Q: Tell me again what time you came down stairs.

A: It was a little before nine.

Q: Did your father go down town?

A: He went down later.

Q: What were you doing when he started away?

A: I was in the dining room, I think; yes, I had just commenced, I think, to iron.

Q: How long did you work on the job?

A: I don't know, sir.

Q: How long was your father gone?

A: I don't know that.

Q: Where were you when he returned?

A: I was down in the kitchen.

Q: You were not upstairs when he came home?

A: I was not.

Q: Who let your father in?

A: I think Maggie let him in.

Q: Was Maggie still engaged in washing windows when your father got back?

A: I don't know.

Q: You remember, Miss Borden, I will call to your attention to it so as to see if I have any understanding, not for the purpose of confusing you; you remember, that you told me that you were downstairs and not upstairs when your father came home? You have forgotten, perhaps?

A: I think I was downstairs in the kitchen.

Q: When was the last time you saw your mother?

A: I did not see her after when I went down in the morning and she was dusting in the dining room.

Q: Where did she go then?

A: I don't know where she went. I know where I was.

Q: You never saw her or heard her afterwards?

A: No sir.

Q: What explanation can you suggest as to the whereabouts of your mother from the time you saw her in the dining room until eleven o'clock?

A: I don't know. I think she went back into the spare room, and whether she came back again or not, I don't know; that has always been a mystery.

Q: Had you any knowledge of her going out of the house?

A: She told me she had a note, somebody was sick.

Q: When you found your father dead and you supposed your mother had gone?

A: I did not know. I said to the people who came in "I don't know whether Mrs. Borden is out or in; I wish you would see if she is in her room."

Q: You supposed she was out at the time?

A: I understood so.

Q: Did she tell you who the note was from?

A: No sir.

Q: Did you ever see the note?

A: No sir.

Q: After [your father] went out, and before he came back; a large portion of the time after your father went out, and before he came back, so far as you know, you were the only person in the house?

A: So far as I know, I was.

Q: And during that time, so far as you know, the front door was locked?

A: So far as I know.

Q: Did you see your father after he came in?

A: Not after [Maggie] let him in.

Q: How long was your father in the house before you found him killed?

A: I don't know exactly, because I went out to the barn. I don't know what time he came home. I don't think he had been home more than fifteen or twenty minutes; I am not sure.

Q: When you went out to the barn, where did you leave your father?

A: He had laid down on the sitting room lounge, taken off his shoes, and put on his slippers.

Q: What was the last thing you said to him?

A: I asked him if he wanted the window left that way. Then I went into the kitchen, and from there to the barn.

Q: What doing?

A: Trying to find lead for a sinker [for a fishing outing at Marion, Massachusetts].

Q: Did you bring any sinker back from the barn?

A: I found no sinker.

Q: When you came down from the barn, what did you do then?

A: Came into the kitchen.

Q: What did you do then?

A: I went into the dining room and laid down my hat.

Q: What did you do then?

A: Opened the sitting room door, and went into the sitting room.

Q: What did you do then?

A: I found my father, and rushed to the foot of the stairs.

Q: When you saw your father where was he?

A: On the sofa.

Q: What was his position?

A: Lying down.

Q: Describe anything else you noticed at that time.

A: I did not notice anything else, I was so frightened and horrified. I ran to the foot of the stairs and called Maggie.

Q: Did you make any search for your mother?

A: No sir.

Q: Why not?

A: I thought she was out of the house.

Q: You made no effort to find your mother at all?

A: No sir.

Q: Did you have any occasion to use [an] axe or hatchet?

A: No sir.

Q: Did you know where they were?

A: I knew there was an old axe down cellar; that is all I knew.

Q: Did you know anything about a hatchet down cellar?

A: No sir.

Q: Where was the old axe down cellar?

A: The last time I saw it it was stuck in the old chopping block.

Q: Did you know there was found at the foot of the stairs a hatchet and an axe?

A: No sir, I did not.

Q: Assume they had blood on them, can you give any occasion for there being blood on them?

A: No sir.

Q: Can you tell of any killing of an animal? Or any other operation that would lead to their [the axe and hatchet] being cast there with blood on them?

A: He [Andrew Borden] killed some pigeons in the barn last may or June.

QUESTION BY JUDGE BLAISDELL: Was there any effort made by the witness to notify Mrs. Borden of the fact that Mr. Borden was found?

A: No sir, when I found him I rushed right to the foot of the stairs for Maggie. I supposed Mrs. Borden was out. I did not think anything about her at the time.

Q: You did not suggest that any search be made for her?

A: No sir.

Q: You did not make any yourself?

A: No sir.

Q: Did you go into any drug store and inquire for prussic acid?

A: I did not.

Immediately after Lizzie Borden testified, she was arrested, but she was charged only with the murder of her father. Turned over to a matron, she was confined to a jail cell. When she was arraigned the next morning, she entered court escorted by a clergyman, the Reverend Mr. Buck. One historian of the case saw in the presence of the minister a signal to Lizzie's supporters that she need not fear because she had "this man of God as her shield and buckler." Lizzie Borden was thus safe from the "ravening wolves of the law."

Lizzie Borden's attorney, Andrew J. Jennings, objected to Judge Blaisdell conducting the arraignment on the ground that Blaisdell had presided at the inquest. Jennings was overruled. Lizzie pleaded not guilty. A date was set for a preliminary hearing in district court. Lizzie was taken to the jail in Taunton.

Another clergyman, the Reverend Mr. Jubb, an Englishman who'd been a resident in the United States for a year, denounced Judge Blaisdell's action as "indecent, outrageous, and not to be tolerated in any civilized community."

That same day a transcript of her inquest testimony was run in the New Bedford *Evening Standard* under the title "Lizzie's Story." Five days after its publication, the *Fall River Daily Globe* broke a story promising "developments of a most startling nature" at the forthcoming preliminary hearing into the murders. The August 17, 1892, edition headlined:

VERY IMPORTANT MOTIVE
IN THE UNMADE WILL

The story asserted the paper had been "informed on very good authority" that Andrew Borden "was making preparations" for drawing up a will that "could not possibly affect anyone except Lizzie and Emma Borden and other persons connected to them by blood relationship." Citing "reliable authority," the article said that "the State will prove that Mr. Borden expressed his desire to make a will favorable [to] his second wife and that the daughters did not approve of this method of disposing in the property."

In preparing a case of murder the prosecution looks for three elements to support their murder charge. The two attorneys acting for the *Commonwealth of Massachusetts* v. *Lizzie Borden* believed they'd found them all: motive, means, and opportunity. Having determined that Lizzie had been alone in the house at the time of the murders with access to a hatchet and with greed as motive, the state's attorneys felt confident they could provide ample evidence to prove the charges to a jury. Persuading the public was another matter altogether.

Vast numbers of Fall River residents and like-minded people all across Gay Nineties America didn't think much of the case against Lizzie Borden. In a phenomenon that would mark virtually every "trial of the century" for the next hundred years, they rallied and championed her as a "poor, stricken girl" who was "innocent and blameless." She also became a cause for militant feminists and leaders of the Women's Christian Temperance Union and the Women's Auxiliary of the YMCA. The latter invited prayers throughout the nation for this "unfortunate girl," brushing aside the fact that Lizzie was thirty-two. Exceptionally vocal on Lizzie's behalf was Mrs. Mary A. Livermore, who railed against "persecution" of a hapless woman by "the tyrant Man."

The common thread in all these defenses was an assertion of disbelief that any woman could have committed such a brutal crime.

There was at least one dissenter, albeit also a stalwart Lizzie Borden backer. A member of the extended Borden family sent a letter to another cousin that somehow found its way into print in the *Daily Globe* on August 17, 1892:

> By blood! If she did it, the old Borden nerve, grit and cheek are not degenerated. No woman except a Borden could have done it, and yet it seems impossible that a woman could do it. . . . I have watched her indomitable nerve and bearing with admiration . . . so if this girl done this thing it is the old Borden nerve and grit that has carried her through, and I predict that she will not wilt. No, by blood!

At the end of a pretrial evidentiary hearing held between August 25 and September 1, 1892, before Judge Blaisdell, Lizzie's lawyer, Andrew J. Jennings, assailed the prosecution's evidence. "They haven't proved that this girl had anything to do with the murder. They can't find any blood on her dress, on her hair, on her shoes. They can't find any motive. They can't find any axes." He demanded "the woman's release."

In a kindly and familiar tone, Judge Blaisdell said, "The long examination is now concluded, and there remains for the magistrate to perform what he believes to be his duty. It would be a pleasure for him, and he would doubtless receive much sympathy, if he could say: 'Lizzie, I judge you probably not guilty. You may go home.' But upon the character of the evidence presented through witnesses who have been so closely and thoroughly examined, there is but one thing to be done."

Obviously acutely aware that Lizzie Borden had become a cause celebre among so many women, he continued, "Suppose for a single moment a *man* was standing there. He was found close by that guest chamber, which, to Mrs. Borden was a chamber of death. Suppose a *man* had been found in the vicinity of Mr. Borden, was the first to find the body, and the only account he could give was the unreasonable one that he was out in the barn looking for sinkers; then he was out in the yard; then he was out for something else; would there be any question in the minds of men what should be done with such a man?"

Tears brimmed in the old jurist's eyes as he gazed at Lizzie, looking as composed and impassive as she had been all during the proceeding. He concluded, "So there is only one thing to do, painful as it may be—the judgement of the Court is that you are probably guilty, and you are ordered committed to await the action of the Superior Court."

While Lizzie Borden did her waiting in the jail at Taunton, Fall River was rampant with a rumor that she had written a letter to friends at Fairhaven saying she had a new axe and was having a fine time whetting it. Someone suggested, and uncountable others accepted it as fact, that there'd been no blood found on her and her clothing because she had taken the precaution of killing her father and stepmother in the nude.

However, Marshal Hilliard and his investigators had come up with an explanation of their own, thanks to a story told by one of the Borden's neighbors. Alice Russell had been one of the first outsiders into the house before police arrived and since that terrible day had been solicitous of both Lizzie and Emma, spending a great deal of time with them in the house. On one of those visits she saw Lizzie about to burn a dress. Lizzie said it had been ruined with paint stains. Concerned about the dress-burning, Russell consulted a lawyer. He advised her to relate the incident to the police. The story went a long way in persuading the grand jury to indict Lizzie Borden.

It was while Borden was in a jail, which her supporters took to calling "the Bastille," that nearly everybody seemed to be reciting the anonymous ditty about forty whacks followed by forty-one. Another macabre joke also found its way into circulation. Upon being asked on the fourth of August the time of day, Lizzie replied, "I don't know, but I'll go and *axe* my father."

Black humor aside, as Borden sat in jail there was no sign that sympathy for her was in any way diminishing among the public and in a large segment of the Massachusetts press. Instead, the widespread belief that she was not the murderer had led to criticism of the Fall River police for not pursuing the "real" killer or killers. In a broadside directed to Rufus Hilliard and his force, the *Springfield Republican* declared, "Because someone unknown to them and too smart for them to catch, butchered two people in the daytime, using brute force, far in excess of that possessed by this girl, they conclude that there is probable reason to believe that she is the murderess."

In this atmosphere of ridicule directed against those who would put Lizzie on trial and rampant scoffing at the evidence against her, District Attorney William Moody said in his opening statement to the jury, "The time for idle rumor, for partial, insufficient information, for hasty and inexact reasoning, is past. We are to be guided from this time forth by the law and the evidence only."

But not *all* the evidence.

In two stunning rulings by the court, the prosecution found itself deprived of essential portions of their case. Denied to them was a plan to introduce the testimony Lizzie Borden had given at the inquest. The court ruled that at the time of the inquiry Borden had been "practically under arrest" without having been properly apprised of her Fifth Amendment protection against self-incrimination.

Therefore, declared the court to a stunned prosecution, "the statements so made are not voluntary and are inadmissible at trial."

Also excluded was testimony about the alleged attempt to purchase prussic acid. This was based on the grounds that it had not been proven that the only use for prussic acid was as a poison.

In utter frustration William Moody said the prosecution might as well ask for a directed verdict of not guilty.

Early in the prosecution case jurors heard from Assistant Marshal John Fleet. He had arrived at the Borden house about a quarter of an hour after Lizzie had called up the stairs to Maggie and reportedly said that someone had come into the house and murdered her father. He had interviewed Lizzie in her room.

"I went in there and told her who I was," he testified. "I was then in citizen's clothes, I asked her if she knew anything about the murders. She said that she did not. All she knew was that Mr. Borden, her father, as she put it, came home at half-past ten or quarter to eleven, went into the sitting room, sat down in a large chair, took out some papers and looked at them. She was ironing in the dining room—some handkerchiefs."

Fleet said he'd asked Borden if she had any idea who could have killed her father and mother. Lizzie had answered, "She is not my mother, sir; she is my stepmother; my mother died when I was a child."

Continuing his testimony, Fleet said he'd asked Borden "if there had been anyone around whom she would suspect of having done the killing of these people."

Lizzie replied, Fleet relayed, that about nine o'clock that morning a man came to the door and was talking with her father.

In the room while Fleet questioned Borden on the day of the murders had been a friend of Borden's, Miss Russell, who had interjected, "Tell him all. Tell him what you was telling me."

Lizzie had told Fleet, "About two weeks ago a man came to the house, to the front door, and had some talk with father, and talked as though he was angry."

Fleet then testified concerning the finding of the dust-covered hatchet. He said that the handle was broken and that it appeared to have been done recently.

The most dramatic testimony came on the seventh day, Monday, June 12, 1893. On the witness stand was Dr. William A. Dolan. The subject was the wounds that had killed Andrew Borden as discerned during an autopsy on August 11, 1892, and comparisons he had made of the wounds and two hatchets found at the Borden house.

Using a magnifying glass, he'd found two hairs on one of them and spots "that looked like blood, or rust."

Dolan was presented a plaster cast of a head with the positions of wounds marked in blue.

Q: How many wounds did you find on his head?
A: Ten on the fleshy part.
Q: Which of them crushed the skull?
A: Those last four, and this one, cut into the skull in front.
Q: Did you afterwards remove the skull?
A: Yes sir.
Q: And remove the flesh from the skull?

A: Yes sir.

Q: And have you it in your possession?

A: Yes sir.

Q: In your opinion were the wounds that you found upon the skull of Mr. Borden such as could have been inflicted with a hatchet by a woman of ordinary strength?

A: Yes sir.

This testimony was supported the next day by Dr. Frank W. Draper, who had taken part in the autopsies. On this occasion the skull shown to the jury was not plaster; it was the actual skull of Andrew Borden.

Prosecutor Knowlton showed Draper a hatchet and asked him whether the hatchet head was capable of making those wounds?

After Draper replied that he believed it could, Knowlton had Draper fit the hatchet blade into the cuts in the skull.

Draper then stated, "In my opinion the wounds could have been made by the use of an ordinary hatchet in the hands of a woman of ordinary strength."

After the prosecution completed its presentation, and with much of the state's evidence against Lizzie Borden excluded or undermined, defense attorney Jennings offered an opening address that amounted to a blueprint on how to acquit.

"A reasonable doubt," he said, "is a doubt for which you can give a reason. If you can conceive of any hypothesis that will exclude the guilt of this prisoner and make it possible or probable that someone else might have done this deed, then you have got a reasonable doubt in your mind."

He coupled this with an assault on the evidence heard, then proceeded over two days to bring to the witness-box an array of individuals to testify as to the possibility that the murders had been committed by a stranger or strangers or an unnamed enemy of Andrew Borden who'd been overheard telling Borden, "You have cheated me, and I'll fix you for it."

As to the stained dress Lizzie had burned? John W. Grouard testified that while Lizzie and Emma had been engaged in dressmaking he had been painting the house.

On Friday, June 16, 1893, after eleven days of trial, the defense rested.

When the court reconvened on Monday, counsel George Robinson began his summation for the defense by directing the jurors' attention to Lizzie Borden.

"I noticed one day," he said, "as we were proceeding with this trial, a little scene that struck me forcibly. She stood there waiting, between the court and the jury, in her quietness and calmness, until it was time for her to come properly forward. It flashed through my mind in a minute: There she stands, protected, watched over, kept in charge by the judges of this court and by the jury who have her in charge. If the little sparrow does not fall unnoticed to the ground, indeed, in God's providence, this woman has not been alone in this courtroom, but ever shielded by His providence from above, and by the sympathy and watchful care of those who have her to look after."

His review of the case took a total of five hours, interrupted for a dinner break, and it ended with a plea that Lizzie "may go home and be Lizzie Andrew Borden of Fall River in that bloodstained and wrecked home where she has passed her life so many years."

Following Robinson and taking almost as much time, District Attorney Knowlton apologized for being the one to prosecute Lizzie, calling it "the saddest day of my life," then gave a detailed review of the prosecution's case, stressing that the fatal blows could have been delivered by a woman.

Of the death of Abby Borden, he said, "We find a woman murdered by blows which were struck with a weak and indecisive hand. We find blows which were inspired by hatred, not by lust or lucre."

Having murdered her stepmother, he continued, Lizzie had waited for her father to come home. "We find her then set in her purpose," he said, "turned into a maniac" who "when the old man lay sleeping on the couch was prompted to cover her person in some way [to keep from being covered with blood] and remove him from life; and conceal the evidences so far as she could in the hurried time that was left her."

He painted a picture of Lizzie Borden having all the time she wanted. "She did not call Maggie until she got ready, until she got through. She had fifteen minutes, which is a long time, and then called her down."

He dismissed Lizzie's various stories of having been in the barn and the note that she'd said had been delivered to Abby Borden, causing her to believe Abby was not in the house.

Who else but Lizzie Borden could have done these deeds?

"We find [her] in the house where there is found in the cellar a hatchet which answers every requirement of this case, where no assassin could have concealed it, and where she alone could have put it. We find in the house a dress which was concealed from the officers until it was found that a search was to be resumed and safety was no longer assured. The dress was hidden from public gaze by the most extraordinary act of burning that you ever heard in all your life, by an innocent person."

Borden's motive?

"We get hatred, we get malice."

Borden's actions after the murders?

"We get absurd and impossible alibis. We get contradictory stories that are not attempted to be verified; we get fraud upon the officers."

The prosecution's case?

"It is proven."

After lunch Chief Justice Albert Mason threw aside centuries of Anglo-American law based on the concept of cross-examination by an adversary in a lawsuit by informing Lizzie, "It is your privilege to add any word which you may desire to say in person to the jury."

Lizzie Borden stood and said, "I am innocent. I leave it to my counsel to speak for me."

All that remained before the case went to the jury was the charge.

Given by Judge Justin Dewey, it brimmed with his doubts about the evidence meeting the test of beyond a reasonable doubt, which amounted to a directed acquittal.

Dewey later said, "I was satisfied when I made my charge to the jury that the verdict would be 'not guilty,' although one cannot always tell what a jury will do."

He need not have worried.

After one ballot and no examination of evidence, the jury lingered for seventy minutes to give the impression they had deliberated, then filed into the courtroom and pronounced Lizzie Borden not guilty.

One of the jurors told a reporter for the *New Bedford Mercury,* "We made up our minds when the government finished putting in its evidence."

He also announced, "We are going to form a permanent association and meet from time to time. Tomorrow we are to have our photograph taken, and we shall send one to Lizzie."

Typical of the whoops of joy of sympathetic newspapers, Boston's *Journal* hailed the "vindication" of "a true, modest and upright woman."

In New York City the *Tribune* welcomed Lizzie to "her rightful place in a world of hope and happiness."

The *New York Times* declared there had never been "any serious reason to suppose that she was guilty" and laid blame for "a barbarous wrong to an innocent woman and a gross injury to the community" on Marshal Rufus Hilliard's "inept and stupid and muddle-headed" police department.

Officially exonerated of double-murder, and very

wealthy, Lizzie Borden lived thirty-nine more years, not as Lizzie but "Lizbeth." She bought a fourteen-room house about two miles from 92 Second Street. She named it Maplecroft.

Her sister, Emma, shared it with her until 1905, when she moved out of Fall River and finally settled in New Hampshire. Leaving an estate of almost $500,000, she died on June 10, 1927.

Her death came ten days after her younger sister passed away and into a netherworld of half-truth and legend in which Lizzie Borden will forever be remembered for taking an axe and giving her mother forty whacks, and after she'd seen what she had done, gave her father the same. Plus one.

Nine

Midwest Nightmares

In the twenty years after a horrified but fascinated nation followed events of the Borden case, the voting men of America had gone to the polls five times. In November 1892 as Lizzie Borden sat in a jail cell in Taunton, Massachusetts, they'd taken an unprecedented step in reelecting Democrat Grover Cleveland to the presidency after a four-year lapse in which Republican Benjamin Harrison had occupied the White House. This gave Cleveland the distinction of being the only man to serve two nonconsecutive terms. In 1896 they'd chosen Republican William H. McKinley and then reelected him in 1900. Assassinated in September 1901, McKinley was succeeded by his vice president, Theodore Roosevelt. After winning election to the presidency in his own right in 1904 and declining to seek another term, Roosevelt turned over the reins of government in 1909 to his designated successor, William Howard Taft. Four years later, finding himself disillusioned with Taft's record, Roosevelt decided to run for a third term. "My hat is in the ring," he told a reporter on February 24, 1912. "The fight is on and I am stripped to the buff."

Whether Republicans who would gather in Chicago on June 18, 1912, to nominate their candidate for president would vote to cast aside their incumbent (Taft) in favor of Roosevelt was the number one subject on the lips of politically minded men attending the June 6th Childrens' Day exercises of the Presbyterian Church in Villisca, Iowa.

A small town in Montgomery County, southeast of Council Bluffs, it had been founded by pioneering farmers and was originally named The Forks. Certainly, no man observing the annual Children's Day program was more interested in civic affairs than Frank Fernando Jones.

A resident of the town for thirty-seven years, he had been a member of the city council, was currently serving in the state legislature, and would be on the ballot in November as a candidate for the state senate.

Now fifty-seven years old, Jones had come to Iowa from New York State in 1875 as a twenty-year-old with the intention of teaching school. By the time the farming town's name was changed to Villisca, he had married a local woman, Maude, who bore him two children, Albert and Letha.

In the years since his arrival Frank Jones had observed the nature of American agriculture being revolutionized by machinery for more efficient plowing in the form of the spring tooth harrow, gang plow, reapers, automatic fodder shredders, and equipment for shucking corn. He also noted that a leading maker of these labor-saving and profit-enhancing innovations was the John Deere company, whose steel plow had earned the reputation of "the plow that broke the plains."

Discerning prospects for earning a lot more money by selling farm equipment than he could ever earn as a teacher, Jones obtained an exclusive John Deere franchise, which became the cornerstone of a hardware emporium known to the folks of Villisca as "the Jones store." By 1898 the enterprise proved so profitable that Frank Jones was able to build the biggest house on the town's stylish Fifth Avenue.

Growing fortune allowed Jones to enter a partnership

with several wealthy friends to found the Villisca National Bank. Having become a prominent citizen of the town, he launched the successful political career that in 1912 had him nicely positioned to run for the state senate.

Yet this American success story that would have warmed the heart of Theodore Roosevelt, the country's most famous rugged individualist and advocate of "the strenuous life," rooted in ambition but tempered by personal morality, had not unfolded without a severe disappointment. The cause of this unpleasantness was a young man whom Frank Jones had hired to help run the store.

Fourteen years younger than Jones, Josiah Moore, known to everyone as Joe, had gotten married in 1899 to Sara Montgomery. They had four children: Herman, Katherine, Boyd, and Paul. With a growing family and having worked for Jones for seven years, Moore believe he was entitled to an increase in his pay.

When Jones declined the request, resulting in a bitter argument, Moore quit, borrowed some money, and set up shop as the Moore Implement Company across the street from the Jones store. He also wrangled away Jones's John Deere franchise.

Feeling betrayed, Frank Jones not only never spoke to Joe Moore again, but would invariably cross the street to avoid him. To make matters even more strained between them, Jones discovered in 1911 that Moore was having an affair with the wife of Frank's eldest, Albert.

Consequently, when the Presbyterian church's Childrens' Day program was held on the evening of Sunday, June 9, 1912, Frank Jones steered clear of Joe Moore, whose children were participating in the event. With the Moore family were friends of ten-year-old Katherine Moore, eleven-year-old Lena and eight-year-old Ina Stillinger.

Among the attractions of the church evening, though not on the program, was a well-known traveling preacher and evangelist, the Reverend Lyn George Jacklin Kelly. Thirty-four years old and married, he'd come to the United States from his native England in 1904. He had settled in Macedonia, Iowa, but traveled widely as a preacher.

Confident in the pulpit, well-versed in the Holy Bible, and an articulate advocate of the teachings of the central figure of the New Testament, he spoke so rapidly while sermonizing in a fire-and-brimstone manner that anyone seated close to him was likely to be baptized with saliva. Short in stature (five feet two inches) and slender as a reed (119 pounds), he was known affectionately by those to whom he fervently preached the Gospel of Christ all over the Midwest as "the little minister." He'd been invited to observe the Children's Day exercises as a guest of the Reverend Mr. Ewing and would be staying overnight with the Ewing family.

Welcoming the opportunity to meet the well-known visitor, Josiah Moore proudly introduced Kelly to wife Sara, the four Moore children, and the pretty Stillinger girls. When the evening's program was over, they said goodbye to friends, Mr. and Mrs. Ewing and their guest, and made their way to the Moore house on east Second Street along four blocks whose streetlamps were not lighted because of a dispute between the city and the power company. When the Stillinger girls expressed reluctance to continue on to their grandmother's house in the dark, Moore invited them to spend the night in a downstairs bedroom. With that agreed, the Moores, their four children, Lena and Ina, went into the kitchen for a bedtime snack of milk and cookies. When they finished, the Stillingers retired to the downstairs bedroom, eleven-year-old Herman and ten-year-old Katherine climbed into separate beds in an upstairs room next to one with a single bed shared by seven-year-old Boyd and five-year-old Paul, and Mr. and Mrs. Moore to their room at the front of the house.

In the morning their neighbor, Mary Peckham, looked through a window and thought it odd that the Moore children were not at play in their yard. Concerned that someone might be ill, she went to the Moore house and knocked on the front door.

When the rapping went unanswered, she tried the door and found it locked. After shouting "Is everything all right?" and getting no reply or hearing sounds in the house, her concern became alarm. Returning home, she telephoned a relative of the Moores'.

In the four bedrooms of the house on Second Street as Peckham waited and worried on that warm Monday morning, and the people of Villisca, Iowa, and those on surrounding farms went about their daily routines, the bodies of Josiah and Sara Moore, their four children, and the two Stillinger girls lay murdered in the night with Joe Moore's own axe.

By all appearances they had been bludgeoned while they slept—except, possibly, Lena Stillinger. She had been either awakened during the attacks, or her half-undressed body had been moved by the killer after she was slain.

If that were the case, the police surmised, the motive for the murders of the seven others might well have been to eliminate the likelihood of the killer being discovered in the course of sexually molesting the young girl. However, a far more plausible scenario in the thinking of the police was one in which the intended victim of the attack had been Josiah Moore.

As a businessman he was sure to have made enemies or otherwise provoked someone's wrath—a disgruntled employee, perhaps, or dissatisfied customer of his hardware and farm-machinery business.

As the police investigated, funerals were held for the eight victims on June 12, 1912. A crowd lining the streets of the town was estimated between five and seven thousand. The funeral procession consisted of the town's sole two hearses with some of the bodies placed on wagons, followed by friends, family, and others in fifty carriages.

With no clues or other leads, the police proved unable to solve the worst murder in Iowa history, and one with the largest number of victims in the bloody annals of axe murders. And so the case languished, until the Moore family sought the assistance of the Burns Detective Agency. Sent to Villisca four years after the killings, one of the firm's best operatives, James Newton Wilkerson, pursued both motives.

Digging into Joe Moore's business history, he found himself intrigued by accounts of the townspeople of the "bad blood" between Moore and his former employer, and now state senator, Frank Jones. Quietly probing into Jones's affairs, and that of his son Albert, the detective turned up the name of a man whose wife, daughter, and in-laws had been killed with an axe in 1911 in Blue Island, Illinois.

His name was William "Blackie" Mansfield. Theorizing he'd been hired to kill Moore in revenge for taking over the John Deere franchise, and for Moore's affair with Albert's wife, the detective supposed Mansfield "went crazy" and killed everyone in the Moore house.

Traced to Kansas City, where he was working in a slaughterhouse, Mansfield was taken to Iowa, where a Montgomery County grand jury convened to look into his possible involvement in the murders. After the grand jury refused to return an indictment, he was released. He filed suit against the Burns Agency for false arrest and won a financial settlement.

Furiously denying having had anything to do with the murders, Frank Jones also filed suit against Wilkerson, alleging slander. He lost the case; because many residents of Villisca had become convinced that Jones had, indeed, had a hand in arranging the murders, he also lost his bid in 1916 for reelection to the state senate.

Undaunted by the failure to pin the murders on Jones and Mansfield, Wilkerson switched his investigative skills to an investigation of sex as a possible motive. In following this line of inquiry he discovered that the honored guest of the Reverend Mr. Ewing, the Reverend Lyn George Jacklin Kelly, was not the godly figure he seemed to be. Wilkerson learned that Kelly had been convicted of sending obscene letters to young girls in which he asked them to type for him in the nude. He was also a Peeping Tom.

Checking on Kelly's whereabouts on the night of the murders, Wilkerson learned that Kelly had spent the night in the Ewing home but had left early in the morning in order to take the 5:19 train to his home. During that trip, Wilkerson learned, Kelly had engaged in conversation with an elderly couple and told them about the murders *before* the bodies were discovered.

The detective also found that Kelly had sent a bloody shirt to a laundry in Omaha and that Kelly had been obsessed with the murders. Arrested for the crimes, the preacher confessed, not once, but twice. But before going to trial he recanted. The result was a hung jury. Tried again, he was acquitted. After moving first to Kansas City, then to Connecticut, and finally to New York, he disappeared into the mists of history.

Despite being the site of the worst mass murder in Iowa's history, the house at 508 East Second Street in Villisca, Iowa, had many occupants before being acquired by the Olson Linn Museum in 1994. Restored to how it appeared on the evening of Children's Day, June 9, 1912, it is listed in the National Register of Historic Places.

Although the Moore house offers nothing remarkable architecturally, the modest house does have one thing in common with one of the most famous buildings of the man who is arguably the greatest of American architects. Just two years after Josiah Moore, his wife, their four children, and the Stillinger girls were slaughtered in Villisca, Frank Lloyd Wright's masterpiece of "prairie" architecture, Taliesen, was also the scene of multiple axe-murders.

In American architecture in 1914 no one provoked more admiration and controversy than Wright. Born in Richland Center, Wisconsin, in 1867, he'd studied and apprenticed at the University of Wisconsin with the renowned Louis Sullivan. Setting up practice in Oak Park, Illinois, in 1893, Wright designed a residence for W. H. Winslow in River Forest, Illinois, which expressed his belief that a structure should be human in scale and harmonious with its surroundings. This style of "organic architecture" became known as "prairie house." These houses had low profiles, open floor plans, minimal ornamentation, and blended with the topography of their sites.

In designing and building several such homes, Wright had earned not only a name for himself, but more than enough income to support himself, a wife, Catherine, and six children.

Wright also had no problem affording a custom-made Stoddard Dayton sports roadster. It boasted a cantilevered convertible canvas top, gleaming brass fittings, and brown leather seats. Wright went "automobiling" around the town in a bright yellow car, nicknamed "The Yellow Devil," that was capable of hitting sixty miles per hour. As it raced through Oak Park, the residents could not fail to notice that the driver's companions were married women.

Wright claimed they were either his present or potential clients. Most were his lovers. The woman seen with him in the fall of 1909 was Martha Borthwick Cheney.

Two years younger than Wright and called Mamah (pronounced "May-mah"), she was the wife of Edwin Cheney (pronounced "Chee-ny") and the mother of a six-year-old son and a four-year-old daughter. Described by friends as exceptionally spirited and intelligent, she'd earned a master's degree in teaching and had a working knowledge of German, French, and Italian. Her laugh was called infectious and her nature gregarious, while her husband was so reserved as to be seen as stiff and humorless.

When Edwin Cheney engaged Wright to design and build a house for him and Mamah in Oak Park, wife and architect not only fell in love, they made no attempt to be secret about it. Yet neither Edwin Cheney nor Catherine

Wright asked their spouses for a divorce, not even when
the couple abandoned them and dashed off to Europe.
Wright's biographer, Frank Manson, wrote, "For nearly
two weeks the scandal, while rumored, was kept from the
public; but it broke into print on Sunday, November 7, on
the front pages of every Chicago newspaper. There was
general consternation and speculation, but Chicago heard
nothing from Wright for almost two years. All that was
really known was that he and Mamah Cheney, after a so-
journ in Berlin, were living quietly in a small villa above
Florence, at Fiesole."

They spent a year in Europe.

Shortly after Mamah's return, Edwin Cheney obtained
a divorce on grounds of abandonment and was given custody of the children. They were to be allowed to visit their
mother at "appropriate intervals." Mamah reverted to using her maiden name, Borthwick.

Immediately after his return, the still married Wright
began work on a house at Spring Green, Wisconsin, that
was to be his and Mamah's home. A prime example of
prairie house style, it was named Taliesen (Welsh for "shin-
ing brow"). It also became his headquarters and a magnet
for ambitious young architectural students.

Another Wright biographer, Brendan Gill, wrote that
Wright and Borthwick "were living together in the most
beautiful house he had ever designed, in a setting that was
itself of exceptional beauty. They were on their way to finding a comparatively inconspicuous place for themselves in
the community; they were not, after all, as one must take
care to remember, daring youngsters bent on shocking their
elders. They were in their early forties and therefore entering middle age."

Wright saw their relationship in that special place as a
"spiritual hegira." Hoping to quell the persistent scandal
and denunciations of himself and Mamah for having abandoned their families, he called a press conference for
Christmas Day, 1911. The resulting coverage was the op-

posite of his intention. The reporter for the *Chicago Tribune* wrote of Wright "defying society and leaving Mrs. Wright at her home just west of Chicago . . . and Mamah Borthwick seemed to have forgotten the Christmases of the past which she had spent with her husband and children."

Personal scandal did not keep Wright from designing buildings that only furthered his reputation as the most innovative architect in the country. One of these projects was Midway Gardens in Chicago. Situated on the shore of Lake Michigan, it was a public building described as a "masterpiece of joyous pagan fancy, providing food, drink and entertainment in an Arabian Nights setting." It opened in the summer of 1914, requiring him to be there to supervise an army of artisans still at work on details.

While he was away, Mamah remained at Taliesen, enjoying a visit by her children. The boy, John, was now twelve; daughter Martha was ten.

Also in residence were William Weston, Wright's favorite carpenter/craftsman; Weston's thirteen-year-old son, Ernest; Emil Brodelle and Herbert Fritz, draftsmen; a pair of handymen, Thomas Bunker and David Lindblom; and a recently hired couple to serve as butler and cook, Julian Carleton, a native of Barbados, and his wife, Gertrude.

At noon on August 14, 1914, after a morning's outing as the brilliant sun shone on the snug green valley where Wright had constructed Taliesen as a place from which, he said, he intended to practice "truth against the world," Mamah Borthwick and guests returned, happily looking forward to one of Gertrude's fine lunches. Informed by the butler that everything was ready, they entered the dining room.

As they sat in Wright-designed chairs around a large Wright-designed table, Carleton withdrew, presumably to bring their lunches.

Closing the door behind him, he locked it from the outside and hurried out of the house to stand below the dining room's only window. At his feet was a large can of gasoline. Lying next to it was a hatchet.

Working frantically, he doused the window frame and its surrounding walls with the gasoline and lit a match. As the fumes exploded in an instant inferno, he snatched the hatchet from the ground and raced back into the house.

Standing by the dining room door, hatchet in hand, he listened to terrified cries within. Then came the sound of splintering wood as someone attempted to pry open the door. A moment later when two heads appeared, he swung hard. The first blow split Borthwick's skull. The second sank deeply into Emil Brodell's head. Shoving the bodies aside, Carleton plunged into the dining room swinging the bloody hatchet with deadly force as the others desperately attempted to reach the fire-engulfed window.

Though severely wounded in head and shoulders in a struggle with the butler, William Weston fled from the carnage and ran to the house of a neighbor to tell him to call police and fire departments. He then raced through cornfields back to Taliesen.

Hardly able to stand, he found his son Ernest's savagely hacked corpse lying in a decorative fountain. Locating a garden hose, he attempted vainly to douse the flames. He was still trying when police and firemen arrived.

They counted six dead and four wounded.

The butler was gone.

Reached by phone while lunching with his son John at the bar of Midway Gardens in Chicago, Wright was told only that Taliesen had been destroyed by a fire. That there had been an inexplicable massacre did not become known to him until hours later when he saw a newspaper headline as he traveled by train to Taliesen.

By the time he arrived, a search for Carleton by police with bloodhounds in surrounding woods had failed to locate him.

Two days later, searchers discovered Carleton huddled by a steam boiler in the still-smoking ruins. He'd attempted suicide by swallowing hydrochloric acid. Unable to explain his motive and unable to eat, he died seven weeks later of starvation.

Newspaper coverage of the murder spree included swipes at the character of the man in whose house the murders occurred.

The *New York Times* sniped about the ending of Wright's "spiritual hegira."

The *Chicago Tribune*'s Walter Noble Burns (inspiration for the devious editor in the Ben Hecht-Charles MacArthur play, *The Front Page*) wrote, "The builder of the love bungalow in the hills of Spring Green stood alone at the end of his 'spiritual hegira.' The woman, slain by a frenzied negro axman and incendiary, was laid to rest in the hills where she made herself an exile for an unconventional love."

Wright wrote in his autobiography, "Thirty-six hours earlier I had left Taliesen leaving all living, friendly, and happy. Now the blow had fallen like a lightning stroke. In less time than it takes to write it, a thin-lipped Barbados Negro, who had been well recommended to me as an ideal servant, had turned madman, taken the lives of [six] and set the house in flames. In thirty minutes the house and all in it had burned to the stonework or to the ground. The living half of Taliesen was violently swept down and away in a madman's nightmare of flame and murder."

Ten

Getting the Old Man

From Mexico City on August 22, 1940, the Associated Press flashed:

> Leon Trotsky, world-famous leader of the Russian revolution, died last night, the victim of an assassin whom he accused of being a tool of the Russian secret police.

The news item continued:

> Trotsky's brain was pierced by a pickax wielded by Frank Jackson, who for months posed as a "great admirer" of Trotsky. Jackson was earlier identified as Jacques Vandendreischd.
>
> In his first statement Jackson said he decided to kill Trotsky after being "disillusioned" by the Russian's recently expressed political views. Police added that Jackson was not a Belgian, as he claimed, but an American citizen formerly of New York City.

Except for Trotsky having been killed by blows from a pickax, and Trotsky's assertion that he believed the assassin had acted on orders from someone in the Soviet Union, none of this information was true—not even the name of the victim.

The advocate of a worldwide Communist revolution who called himself Leon Trotsky, and who had written in 1924 that a Communist state could be maintained only "by recourse to every form of violence," had been born Lev Davidovich Bronstein in Ukraine in 1879. He had stolen his revolutionary name from the head jailor in a prison in Odessa from which he'd escaped in 1902. It is what Leon Trotsky did after he bolted to freedom that earned him the reputation as the leading theorist of Russian-style Marxism. That lifetime of violence and revolutionary work in the name of Communism would be as convoluted a plot as found in any novel penned by the Russian authors Leo Tolstoy and Fyodor Dostoyevsky.

When his escape from prison was discovered, the police sent out an alert that placed Lev Davidovich Bronstein, also known as Nikolai Trotsky, on "wanted list 5530." It described him as "twenty-three years old, five foot ten, dark brown hair, goatee beard, wears spectacles."

Traveling on a false passport as Trotsky, he left Russia for Austria. When he moved on to Switzerland, a Zurich editor of a Socialist publication, Pavel Axelrod, gave him the address of another Socialist living in England. In London he called on the man living with his wife in a one-room flat. He was Vladimir Ilyich Ulyanov. The world would soon know him as Lenin.

Many years later Trotsky would write of his relationship with his new comrade, "Lenin and I had several sharp clashes because, when I disagreed with him on serious questions, I always fought an all-out battle. Such cases, naturally, were memorable for everyone, and later on much was said and written about them. But the instances when Lenin and I understood each other at a glance were a hundred times more numerous."

The two men formed personal and revolutionary bonds

that held and strengthened in the following years, culminating in the Bolshevik Party's overthrow of a democratic government in Moscow established after the downfall of the Czar. In the new Soviet government, Leon Trotsky became the commissar of foreign affairs. He negotiated a separate peace with Germany in the First World War, created the Red Army, and led it into victory in the civil war that followed the Bolshevik October Revolution. Although Trotsky found himself second in power to Lenin, after Lenin suffered a debilitating stroke in 1922 he was unable to outmaneuver a competing "troika" consisting of Grigory Zinovyev, Lev Kamenev, and Joseph Stalin.

Upon the death of Lenin in January 1924, Stalin wasted no time in gathering the reins of government into his own hands. Seeking to neutralize Trotsky, he set out to undermine Trotsky's standing in the party and his role in the Revolution. "I have to say that Trotsky played no special role in the October uprising," he asserted. "Trotsky could play no special part either in the party or in the October uprising as a relative newcomer to our party in the October period."

This was a lie and Stalin knew it, as did everyone else; but they were afraid to say so.

From that point on, as Dmitri Volkogonov wrote in his 1999 Trotsky biography, Trotsky "was vilified by Stalin as a spy, scum of the earth, double-dealer, murderer, falsifier and imperialist agent."

Of Stalin's lies about him and Stalin's grabbing of power, Trotsky wrote in 1932, "The revolution itself produces a new ruling stratum which seeks to consolidate its privileged position and is prone to see itself not as a transitional historical instrument, but as the completion and crowning of history."

For Stalin to achieve that goal, he recognized, he had to eliminate Trotsky. Consequently, between 1926 and 1929 Trotsky found himself booted from official positions and expelled from the Communist Party. To deal with a threat that Stalin referred to as "Trotskyism" and its adherents as "Trotskyites," he ordered the Ministry of the Interior "to expose any Trotskyists and other enemies of the state still at large" and put them in concentration camps, where there would be "no reduction of the term of punishment."

The iron-fisted ruler in the Kremlin had much to fear from Trotsky and ordered him expelled from the Soviet Union in 1929. But being kicked out of the country could not stop Trotsky from expressing his views on Stalin's perversion of the goals of the Revolution. He did so in a series of writings, beginning with a periodical, *Bulletin of Opposition,* in 1929. This was followed by an autobiography (1930), *History of the Russian Revolution* (1931), and *The Stalinist School of Falsification* (1932).

Stalin retaliated by stripping Trotsky, his wife, and his son Lev of their Soviet citizenship. But worse fates befell Trotsky relatives still in the USSR. His first wife was exiled to Siberia.

The next year, 1936, as Trotsky published a scathing indictment of Stalin's rule, *The Revolution Betrayed,* two of his nephews were arrested and shot. As a result of pressure from Moscow, that same year, the government of Norway, where Trotsky and his wife had been residing for more than a year, ordered them deported.

Granted political asylum by Mexico, they settled in Mexico in January 1937, only to learn that another son, Sergei, who was still living in the USSR, had been arrested and executed, as had been another nephew. The following year they learned that Lev had been found dead under mysterious circumstances in Paris. Two months later they were informed that Trotsky's elder brother, Alexander Bronstein, had been executed in Moscow.

A fifty-seven-year-old political exile without a passport, Trotsky ensconced himself and his wife in a house on Vienna Street in Coyocan near Mexico City. Bought with help from some American friends, it was immediately fortified and protected by an elaborate security system that included tall fences and a tower with a searchlight. Barricaded against intruders, he hired secretaries, a typist, a house-keeper, and a bodyguard and began work on a biography of his nemesis.

In a letter to the editor of the *Bulletin of Opposition* in March 1938, he wrote, "I am committed to write a book on Stalin."

When this news reached the Kremlin, it was not wel-comed by the heir to Lenin. Seething with anger and trepi-dation about what might be written by a man who knew Stalin better than anyone in the world except himself, Stalin mobilized all the resources of the world's largest and most feared secret police apparatus. The antecedent to the KGB of the cold war era was originally called the Cheka, and later the OGPU and the NKVD.

Stalin ordered Lavrenti Beria, the head of this dreaded worldwide organization, to "get the Old Man."

But there was more from the Old Man in Mexico to irk Joseph Stalin. On May 11, 1940, Trotsky issued "an open letter" to the Soviet people in the hope that somehow it would breach the borders of the USSR and be read by them. Three pages long, it bore the heading, "You are being de-ceived."

After noting that tens of thousands of "revolutionary fighters have perished," he wrote, "Stalin has destroyed the entire Bolshevik old guard, all of Lenin's collaborators and assistants, all the fighters of the October revolution, all the heroes of the civil war. He will go down in history under the despised name of Cain."

The letter called on the people to give "rebirth to the USSR by cleansing it of the parasitic bureaucracy" by way of "an uprising of the workers, peasants, Red Army men and Red sailors against the new caste of oppressors and parasites."

By putting his name to the inflammatory letter, Trotsky in effect put his initials next to the name of Joseph Stalin at the bottom of his own death warrant.

Portrait of victim Helen Jewett, published by H.R. Robinson, was promoted as having been "an original painting taken from life." Copies of the picture were sold as souvenirs. (© *Collection of the New-York Historical Society*)

H.R. Robinson also sold this hand-colored lithograph of Jewett, a prostitute murdered by her lover in a New York City brothel in May 1836. (© *Collection of the New-York Historical Society*)

Richard Robinson's portrait as he appeared on his arraignment for the murder of Helen Jewett. Many of Robinson's friends and scores of other young men copied his attire. (© *Collection of the New-York Historical Society*)

This A. Holly lithograph depicted Robinson fleeing the murder. Because many people refused to believe a young man of Robinson's social status could be a killer, Holly mockingly titled the picture "The Innocent Boy". (© *Collection of the New-York Historical Society*)

Pamphlets like this provided sensational descriptions of the murder of Helen Jewett, who was also known as Ellen.
(*Courtesy New York Public Library*)

Robinson's trial is depicted in this J.T. Bowen lithograph. Despite an overwhelming amount of incriminating evidence, the jury found Robinson not guilty.
(© *Collection of the New-York Historical Society*)

German immigrant Louis Wagner was hanged on June 25, 1875 for killing Karen Christensen and Maren Hontvet and severely wounding Anethe Christensen with an axe.
(*Courtesy Portsmouth Athenaeum*)

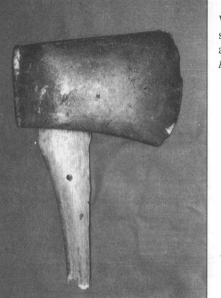

Wagner's attacks were so savage, the handle of the axe broke. (*Courtesy Portsmouth Athenaeum*)

The house on Smutty Nose Island where Wagner murdered the two women in March 1873. (*Courtesy Portsmouth Athenaeum*)

Anethe and Karen Christensen's tombstones bear the epitaph:
"A sudden death, a striking call, A warning voice that speaks
to all, To all to be prepared to die." (*Courtesy* SeaCoast NH)

PORTRAIT OF JOHN C. COLT.

Woodcut sketch of John C.
Colt, convicted for the axe
murder of New York City
printer Samuel Adams in
1841. (*Courtesy New York
Public Library*)

From London's *Police Gazette*, an artist's version of how Kate Webster killed her elderly employer, Julia Thomas, with an axe in March 1879. (*Courtesy New York Public Library*)

Lizzie Borden in 1893. She was accused of killing her father and stepmother. (*Courtesy The Fall River Historical Society*)

Andrew Borden was killed as he napped on a parlor sofa.
(*Courtesy The Fall River Historical Society*)

Abby Borden was slain as she was tidying up a bedroom, an hour
and a half before Andrew Borden was killed.
(*Courtesy The Fall River Historical Society*)

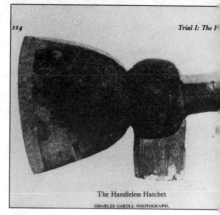

Although broken and bearing no bloodstains, police claimed this hatchet was the weapon Lizzie Borden used. (*Courtesy The Fall River Historical Society*)

The Handleless Hatchet

CHARLES CAROLL PHOTOGRAPH,

Daily Globe.

WEDNESDAY MORNING, JUNE 14, 1893.—TWELVE PAGES.   PRICE TWO CE

NO BLOOD.

AN EXCITING SCENE IN COURT

Experts Yield No Clew to Crime.

Spots on Axes Were from Rust.

Lizzie's Garments Pass the Ordeal.

One Suspicious Blot Found on Her Skirt.

Stains Were Not What They Seemed.

DR DRAPER FITS THE AXE IN THE SKULL OF MR BORDEN.

Local newspaper artist's sketch shows the hatchet being matched to the cuts in Andrew Borden's skull for the jury. (*Courtesy The Fall River Historical Society*)

Artist's view of Lizzie Borden (*left*) and her sister Emma during Lizzie's trial. (*Courtesy The Fall River Historical Society*)

Marshal Rufus Hilliard and his police force were accused of bungling the investigation into the murders of Mr. and Mrs. Borden, resulting in Lizzie's acquittal. (*Courtesy The Fall River Historical Society*)

Karla Faye Tucker was convicted of the 1983 pickax murders of Jerry Lynn Dean and Deborah Thornton. *(Courtesy AP/Wide World Photos)*

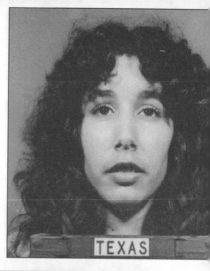

Melchora Vasquez, chief clerk for trial exhibits of the Harris County, Texas court, carries pickax used by Tucker. *(Courtesy AP/Wide World Photos)*

Tucker's accomplice in the double murder, Daniel Garret, in Houston, Texas courtroom waiting for jurors to decide his fate. (*Courtesy AP/Wide World Photos*)

Tucker waits for verdict in court. (*Courtesy AP/Wide World Photos*)

Tucker's conversion in prison led to a worldwide appeal that included Pope John Paul II to spare her from the death penalty. (*Courtesy AP/Wide World Photos*)

Tucker died by lethal injection on February 4, 1998, becoming the first woman executed in Texas since the Civil War. (*Courtesy AP/Wide World Photos*)

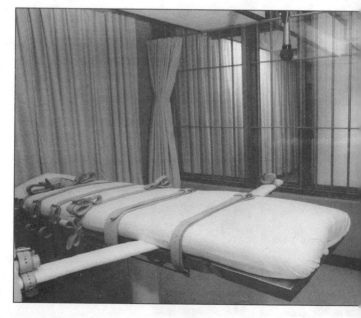

Rita Gluzman was convicted in federal court under a new spouse-abuse law for the 1996 axe murder of her husband Yakov. (*Courtesy AP/Wide World Photos*)

New Jersey police caught Rita Gluzman's cousin Vladimir Zelenin throwing bags containing body parts into the Passaic River. (*Courtesy AP/Wide World Photos*)

Sean Rich, 17, being escorted into Marion County Superior Court in Indianapolis, Indiana to be arraigned for the axe murders of the Reverend and Mrs. Frederick Mathias. (*Courtesy AP/Wide World Photos*)

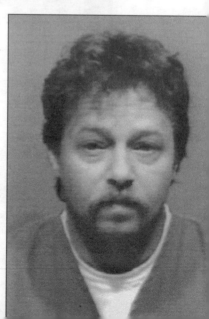

On July 8, 1998, William Lee "Cody" Neal was convicted of first-degree murder, kidnapping and sexual assault in the deaths of three women in Littleton, Colorado. (*Courtesy AP/Wide World Photos*)

Of course, no such document existed. Joseph Stalin ruled his vast empire with whispered decrees, a nod, a wink, a cunning smile, and the twitch of a finger that never passed unnoticed by Beria and those under him in the Dzerzhinsky Square offices and cellar dungeons of the NKVD.

One of the men in the Foreign and Secret Political Sections of the Security Directorate was Naum Eitingon. A veteran NKVD operative, he was acutely aware that after a plan to kill Trotsky in Turkey had failed, the agent in charge, Genrich Yagoda, had been accused of being a Trotskyite, was tried, convicted, and shot for "his vile treacherous activity." Now Stalin was looking for someone who would not botch the job of getting the Old Man.

He told Beria in March 1939, "This Fascist hireling must be liquidated without further ado. Spare no expense. Bring in whoever you want."

After assembling a team of Spanish-speaking agents, Eitingon left Moscow for Mexico with a primary plan of action that would involve many men in an attack on Trotsky's house. It was scheduled for the wee hours of May 24, 1940.

On that morning, after working on the book on Stalin, Trotsky went to bed around 2:30. In the house with him were his wife, Natalya, his grandson, Seva, and two married friends. Several men stood guard inside the house while another, Robert Sheldon Harte, was posted at the gate.

At about four o'clock, according to Natalya's book, *The Life and Death of Leon Trotsky,* the household was jolted awake by gunfire outside. Bullets splintered the walls and sent pieces of concrete flying. The noise was deafening. Rooms became clouded with gunsmoke. In the midst of this din, Natalya shoved Trotsky out of bed and while bullets raked the bedroom's walls they both crouched in a corner. After several terrifying minutes, the attack ended with Trotsky and the others alive and unhurt but badly shaken.

The only casualty was Harte. Kidnapped by the attackers, he was later found dead.

When the police arrived and counted more than 200 bullet holes in the walls of Trotsky's bedroom alone, Trotsky exclaimed, "It was Stalin!"

A message to the Kremlin from Eitingon reported, "Operation carried out. Results known later." When confirmation that Trotsky had survived reached Stalin, the dictator went into a rage that was, in the eyes of his inner circle, unequaled in his sixteen-year history of brutal tirades.

In Mexico, fearing a summons to Moscow to account for his failure and amazed that it did not come, Eitingon resorted to a plan that would rely on a NKVD operative whom Eitingon had met in Spain during the Spanish civil war. His name was Jaime Ramon Mercador del Rio Hernandez, and he was now in Mexico. Using an NKVD-provided name, Frank Jackson, he was living in the Hotel Monteju with a woman named Sylvia Agelof.

An active Trotskyite, Sylvia had a sister, Ruth, who had been Trotsky's secretary. When Ruth gave up the job, she'd recommended Sylvia as her replacement. Working in the fortresslike house, Sylvia did not know that the handsome lover she knew as Frank Jackson and who drove her to the house every day in his Buick automobile was an agent of Stalin's.

Neither did Trotsky and his guards suspect that Sylvia's companion was anything but the polite and sweet-natured young man he appeared to be as he carried packages from his car to the house, helped guests with their luggage, and on one occasion he'd driven Sylvia and Natalya into the center of the city on a shopping trip. The man they knew as Jackson had even offered to take Trotsky for a drive into the mountains, but the Old Man declined.

Guards became so accustomed to seeing him that they paid little attention to his comings and goings. Certainly, they had no reason to suspect that between these visits the amiable youth was meeting with an old friend from the

Spanish civil war who was giving Mercador orders and instructions to carry out "a just sentence" issued in Moscow.

The first of the conversations had taken place two days after the failed attack on Trotsky's house. At the meeting Eitingon promised Mercador that by killing Trotsky he would ensure that his name would be added to the glorious honor roll of heroes of the Soviet Union. Between that day and August 20, 1940, Mercador would visit Trotsky's house at least ten times. On August 17, he'd arrived uninvited and had a brief conversation with Trotsky. That he was wearing a raincoat on a hot day went unremarked upon by either the Old Man or his guards.

The only person to question the raincoat when Mercador appeared at the house on August 20 was Natalya. Mercador explained that he thought it might rain. His reason for visiting the house, he said, was to ask Trotsky to review an article he had written.

Concealed in the coat was a tool used by mountain climbers. Known as an Alpine pick, it was about the size of a hatchet.

Trotsky chatted with Mercador for a few minutes in the small garden behind the house, where Trotsky kept rabbits and chickens. When they moved into Trotsky's office, Mercador would explain at his trial, he "laid the coat on a table in such a way as to be able to remove the ice pick which was in the pocket."

Mercador's statement continued:

> I decided not to miss the wonderful opportunity that presented itself. The moment Trotsky began reading the article gave me the chance. I took out the ice pick from the raincoat, gripped it in my hand and, with my eyes closed, dealt him a terrible blow on the head. Trotsky gave a cry that I shall never forget. It was a long "aaaa," endlessly long, and I think it still echoes in my brain. Trotsky jumped up jerkily, rushed

at me and bit my hand. I pushed him away and he fell to the floor. Then he rose and stumbled out of the room.

He staggered into the adjoining room and, as Natalya wrote in her book, "Leon Davidovich appeared, leaning against the door frame. His face was covered with blood. His arms hung limply by his side."

Trotsky's cry had brought guards running into the room. As they grabbed Mercador, he said, "They made me do it. They've got my mother. They have my mother in prison."

With the guards beating him, Mercador begged, "Kill me now, or stop beating me."

Trotsky managed to say, "No, he must not be killed. He must talk."

A search of Mercador's pockets produced a letter in which Mercador stated he'd acted because he'd become "disillusioned" by Trotsky. The letter had been prepared by the NKVD as part of a cover story to make the attack appear to have been carried out by a Trotskyite.

Trotsky and his badly beaten assailant were rushed to the same hospital. Trotsky clung to life for twenty-six hours. He died at 7:25 P.M. on August 20, 1940.

Natalya said, "This is life."

On the 22nd, the official Soviet news agency, *Tass,* commented, "The person who made the attempt belongs to the followers most closely associated with Trotsky."

Two days later the Soviet newspaper, *Pravda,* repeated the official line by reporting: "Trotsky has died in hospital from a fractured skull, received in an attempt on his life by one of his closest circle."

In New York City, Aleksandr Kerensky, the Russian leader whose revolution overthrew the czar, only to be deposed by the Bolsheviks, said that Leon Trotsky, "most merciless of all Bolshevist terrorists, died by the same means he sponsored. He was the victim of the system of secret police instituted by him, Lenin and Stalin against all opponents."

The survivor of that "troika," Joseph Stalin, outlived Trotsky by thirteen years. It was not until 1964 that Stalin's successor, Nikita Khrushchev, revealed in a then-secret speech to the Communist Party hierarchy the scope of Stalin's crimes and the long arm of the NKVD that in 1940 had reached into Mexico to rid Stalin of the dreaded enemy he'd called "the Old Man."

Tried and convicted of the murder of Leon Trotsky, Jaime Ramon Mercador served twenty years in prison. Released in 1960, he faded into history long before the dreams of Lenin and Trotsky of creating a worldwide Communist society were finally dashed.

Eleven

Something Said Go

Pacing the sidewalk on Monday morning, June 13, 1983, Gregory Travers looked at his watch anxiously. Jerry Dean always showed up in front of the Windtree Apartments on Watonga Street in northeast Houston, Texas, in his blue El Camino pickup truck twenty minutes before they were due at work, but here it was, ten to seven, and still no Jerry. It certainly could not be that he got hung up in traffic. They lived in the same apartment complex.

Wondering if Dean had overslept, Travers walked to Dean's ground-floor apartment, and found that the El Camino wasn't there. Rock and roll boomed from the apartment. Finding the back door unlocked and slightly ajar, he pushed it open a little farther, yelled for Jerry, and heard no reply. This was really odd, he thought as he entered the apartment.

Another yell, and no answer. Moving deeper inside, he looked into the living room where the radio was blasting and where Dean's partially built Harley-Davidson motorcycle ought to have been on a wooden stand. It wasn't there.

Because Jerry Dean did not use the master bedroom, preferring to sleep in a smaller spare room, Travers peered in there. He saw Dean half on the bed and half off, naked.

Tilted back with strands of long blond hair across the face, the head was a bloody mess. The torso appeared covered with black cockroaches, until Travers realized they were blood-caked holes. Then he saw a girl lying on her back on the floor.

A pickax had been driven into the middle of her chest.

Many, many months later an expert on tools would show the pickax to a jury and explain for the benefit of any juror who might not be familiar with such an object that the four-foot tool with half of the head shaped like a long flat tongue with a thick wedge and the other half forming a slightly curved and tapering prong was used for digging holes in the earth. This particular pickax, he informed the jury, had belonged to Jerry Lynn Dean and was kept in the house along with other tools required in Dean's job of installing burglar alarms for Qube Security. The indictment in the case defined the weapon as a "mattock."

From the outset newspaper headline writers who knew what grabbed readers never called it anything but a pickax. So did the police and prosecutors. When a reporter asked a detective if he was investigating a capital murder case, the cop retorted, "No. Capital *pickax* murder case."

In a book on the case published in 1992, author Beverly Lowry explained the difference. "A pickax is a nightmare weapon," she wrote in *Crossed Over, the True Story of the Houston Pickax Murders,* "one of those household and garden tools you know has a useful function, and yet . . . it's the utilitarianism that makes it chilling, the idea that death is all around, that your own hammer, the one we use to hang pictures, can kill us, our sewing scissors, your grandfather's carving knife, this screwdriver I use to open a cranky drawer; that death tools are everywhere, these commonplace domestic items. . . . Lizzie Borden comes to mind. People in Fall River, Massachusetts, knew immediately about the weapon used to kill her parents; when the daughter herself was arrested, so did everybody in the country."

The pickax had been pulled from the body of Jerry Dean's girlfriend, Deborah Thornton, by a member of the medical examiner's staff, S. C. Pilgrim, to facilitate removal of the body to the morgue. The sharp end of the tool, Pilgrim testified, had been driven seven inches into Deborah's chest and through the heart with such force that it had protruded through her back and the point had sunk into the floor.

While the wound to Thornton's body required little description from Aurelio Espinola, the Chief Medical Examiner for Houston, Texas, he did inform the jury that Dean first had been hit on the back of the head with a hammer, and then punctured twenty-eight times. His neck had been hit so ferociously that he'd been almost decapitated.

Since that day in 1836 when James Gordon Bennett entered Rosina Townsend's house of ill repute on Thomas Street in New York City and gazed in horror at Helen Jewett's mangled and partially burned body, no atrocity inflicted upon a human being by another had guaranteed more headlines in America's newspapers, with the possible exceptions of wars and the assassinations of presidents, than murder by axe.

In keeping with that journalistic tradition, the newspapers of Houston and other cities across Texas and the rest of the United States emblazoned front pages with headlines and stories of murders in which the weapon had been a tool that very few citizens of the urbanized and largely white-collar United States in the era of President Ronald Reagan had ever held in their hands, and probably had never even seen. For most, "Texas Pickax Murders" sounded like the plot of a movie made for teenagers or the title of the latest best-selling horror novel.

Headlines and news stories rarely contribute to the solving of crimes. In the opinion of most homicide detectives they fall into the same category as offers of rewards for "information leading to the apprehension and conviction" of killers. More often than not, both news coverage and rewards get in the way of investigations by forcing investigators to waste time in pursuit of "tips" that lead to dead ends. Because homicides do not commonly happen in front of witnesses, they are solved through collection and analysis of physical evidence resulting in the assembling of a sequence of facts that will produce suspects and, hopefully, a confession.

Before anyone can be turned over to a judicial process (in which an individual arrested in the United States of America must, by constitutional rights, be considered innocent until proven guilty, and then only beyond a reasonable doubt), the police are required to demonstrate "probable cause" in making arrests. It was Shakespeare who wrote that "murder will out," but the burden and challenge fall upon the homicide detective and the experts in forensic sciences to assure that it does, starting with the scene of the crime.

Consequently, after Gregory Travers phoned the police on June 13, 1983, to report two murders, there descended upon the Windtree Apartments a swarm of people entrusted by the citizens of the city of Houston and the state of Texas to ferret out the person or persons who in the predawn hours of that morning had come to Watonga Street and entered an apartment with the purpose of killing Jerry Lynn Dean and, evidently by happenstance, a woman named Deborah Ruth Thornton.

When informed by Travers that Dean's El Camino and the frame of a Harley motorcycle were missing, the detectives assumed the motive had been robbery.

Yet the savagery of the slayings hinted at two other possible reasons: a seething hatred for Dean, or because of the theft of the motorcycle frame, involvement of a gang of drug-dealing, leather-jacketed, black-booted, blue-jeans-

wearing, and garishly tattooed inhabitants of a weird sub-
culture of people whose icons were "Harley hogs."

Into the ground-floor apartment along with crime-scene
specialists looking for physical clues—fingerprints and
trace evidence in the form of fibers and other detritus of a
crime—came a team from the medical examiner's office.
Their task was to view the bodies, photograph them, jot
down notes, examine the wounds, ponder, analyze, and
venture educated but nonetheless off-the-cuff opinions as
to which victim was attacked first.

They opined that Dean had been the one, without a doubt
hit with a hammer and then stabbed and slashed. The
woman appeared to have been awakened by the noise and
then killed. This indicated premeditated murder in Dean's
case. Because the pickax had been in the house, its use had
been a simple matter of convenience. But its employment
conveyed more than simple spur-of-the-moment impulse.

Whoever had used it had done so out of pure rage, perhaps drug-induced.

In the history of murder such carnage was generally the
result of a suddenly unleashed anger that had been long
pent-up. In the age of easy-to-get guns, especially in Texas,
killing with a knife, hatchet, or a handy pickax was an
up-close and personal act; the signature of a killer who
vented a deep-seated fury. Else, why so many blows?

In the case of Dean the single assault with the hammer
had been sufficient to kill him. Whoever did it might have
intruded into the apartment with theft as a goal, but the
frenzy of the attacks on Dean pointed to an individual who
also had a score to settle. Probably it was someone who
had always been a real hothead.

In addition to looking for clues, homicide police understand that a way to solve a murder, such as this one, is to
get to know the victim. So what might there have been
about Jerry Lynn Dean that could have set him up for murder?

He'd been married. The wife was Shawn Jackson. She

had been wedded before and had a daughter. After marrying they had lived for a time at Quay Point. The marriage went on the rocks, apparently because Dean learned that Shawn was sometimes a "roadie" with traveling rock bands and that she dabbled in prostitution. Not that Jerry Dean harbored any objections to promiscuous sex. He'd done plenty of sleeping around.

Hardly a saint, he had pretensions of becoming a Harley biker. He hung out with the like-minded and was building a hog in the living room, the very one that had gone missing.

Probing the life of the woman who'd died with a pickax buried in her chest, the police learned that Debbie Thornton was thirty-two, five feet nine inches tall—two inches taller than Jerry Dean—and weighed 111 pounds. Employed as a bookkeeper by the Lawyers Title Company of Houston, she was married and had a son and stepdaughter.

She'd met Jerry Dean at a swimming-pool party at her apartment on Sunday. When Dean invited her to his place, she left the boy and girl in the care of a neighbor, packed the clothes she intended to wear to work the next day, and went to spend the night with Dean in his apartment on what would turn out to be her last day of life.

She had met her brutal death, in the words of the cliche, by being "in the wrong place at the wrong time."

Looking into Deborah Thornton's background, Detectives William Owens and Ted Thomas learned that her father, William List, was a rich homosexual with a penchant for picking up young boys and taking them to his lavish Seabrook home, ostensibly to work. Embarrassed by these activities, Debbie and her brother had changed their last name. Owens and Thomas also discovered that Debbie was to be a witness against her father in an IRS probe of his shady business activities.

Ultimately, it would not be tax troubles that spelled doom for William List. A year after he came to the attention of Owens and Thomas, he would be ambushed and killed in his house by a quartet of young pickups.

While Owens and Thomas worked the Thornton side of the case, the team of James Ladd and Carolyn Newman probed the recent life of Jerry Lynn Dean. This produced chilling stories of a contentious relationship between Dean and a heroin user and a part-time prostitute, Karla Faye Tucker. They heard that Tucker had once punched Dean so hard that she'd shattered his glasses, sending Dean to a hospital to have shards of glass removed from his eye.

Tucker was also said to hate Dean because he'd destroyed a picture of her mother. Believing that she held promise as a suspect, the detectives routinely drove past a house Tucker shared with a group of well-known druggies on McKean Street.

In addition to the "know thy victim" rubric, homicide investigators, such as J. C. Moshier of the Houston Police Department, operated under the maxim that "if you don't close a murder case in the first forty-eight hours you are probably not going to close it." Therefore, when Moshier came to work on July 18, a month and five days after the pickax murders, expectations in the department of a quick solution of the Dean-Thornton murders were not high. Although Moshier was not assigned to the case, he sympathized with his stymied fellow homicide police and kept tabs on the investigation with increasing frustration. That such a widely publicized, brutal, and bizarre double-murder had not been cracked grated on all of them. But he had his own cases to work. Answering his telephone that day, he heard the voice of Douglas Garrett, an ex-husband of one of his high-school friends.

The call was about the pickax murders. Garrett declared that he knew who'd done them. It was his girlfriend Kari's sister, Karla Faye Tucker, he said, and Douglas's own brother Danny Garrett.

Moshier could not believe his ears. "Danny did *what?*"

It was true, Doug Garrett insisted.

Danny Garrett and Karla Tucker had done nothing but brag about it and go on and on about the thrill of killing

Jerry Dean and that woman. Tucker even said that when she was using the pickax she had orgasms. She'd said to him, "Doug, I came with every stroke."

She'd told her sister, Kari Burrell, that every time she "picked" Jerry she'd looked up and grinned and "got a nut" and hit him again. But now Karla and Danny were talking about "offing" two people who knew about the murders, Jimmy Leibrant and Kari's husband, Ronnie Burrell.

What Doug Garrett and Kari Burrell feared was that they might also go onto the hit list, though Garrett did not then explain to J.C. Moshier why he and Kari might have merited such a dubious distinction.

At long last, here was a potential break in the case.

When Doug Garrett refused to talk to anyone but J. C. Moshier, a meeting was arranged. Moshier remarked later that he had never seen two "scareder" people in his life. During the two-hour conference, Moshier told Garrett and Burrell that what Karla Faye Tucker said to her sister and Danny Garrett's brother was, in the parlance of criminal courts, "hearsay." It was not admissible as evidence. It was not even definable as reasonable cause for J. C. to make arrests.

What was needed was an admission from either Karla or Danny.

Would Doug be willing to try to get them to talk some more about the murders while wearing a concealed microphone, tape recorder, and transmitter?

Doug agreed.

On the afternoon of July 20 Lieutenant Kenneth Rodgers of the Special Crimes Bureau of the Houston Police Department wired Garrett by strapping a mike and transmitter to his chest. A miniature tape recorder was concealed in his boot. To conceal the equipment, he wore a long-sleeve green shirt.

"Let them talk," Moshier said to Garrett. "We want to

hear them talk. You must be quiet. I want to hear what they have to say."

What they needed on the tape was an admission that they'd gone to Dean's apartment with the intent to kill him.

They also wanted a tape of Karla Faye Tucker saying that she'd gotten sexual pleasure in killing Dean with the pickax. Should Garrett get the feeling that he was in danger, he was to say "Jesus Christ."

Wired and briefed, Doug Garrett walked into the McKean Street house just before five in the morning and found the residents awake and drinking.

Greeting him from a couch were Jimmy Leibrant's sister Marla, Ronnie Burrell, and Mary Lou Moore, whom Garrett knew only as "Cookie." One of them asked Garrett why he was wearing a long-sleeve shirt on such a hot day. He replied that it was his only clean one. When Doug inquired as to the whereabouts of Tucker and his brother, he was directed to a bedroom.

Casual and calm as could be, Garrett went in. After a few minutes of small talk, he said to his brother, "I been wondering. Did y'all go over there with it in mind to kill them people?"

Having already told Doug and others how they'd killed Dean and Thornton, Danny Garrett replied. "It was a freak thing. It happened. We freaked out."

"They say you're the center of the wheel," said Doug to his brother. "Everybody else is spokes. They say you're number one."

"They got nothing, Doug. No fingerprints, nothing."

How and why did it happen?

"We were very wired and we was looking for something to do," Tucker said. "We went there to case the place, and something said go."

What about the pickax?

"It was there," said Tucker, between popping pills. "It was there."

"Tell me something, Karla, is it true you got sexual gratification?"

As the detectives listened, they knew they had everyone involved in the murders but one. Jimmy Leibrant was not in the house. Then—miracle of miracles—he appeared. Now all they had to do was wait for Doug Garrett to leave the house. He did so after six o'clock, roaring away astride his Harley.

Some minutes later, Ronnie Burrell wandered to a window, looked out, and announced, "It's the fuckin' law."

By midnight the police had finished questioning everyone without getting confessions, the suspects were locked up in the Harris County jail, and newspapers everywhere were readying stories for morning editions to inform the nation and world that the murders of Jerry Lynn Dean and Deborah Thornton appeared to be solved.

After his first meeting with Karla Faye Tucker on July 18, 1983, Joseph Magliolo, a veteran of the Harris County district attorney's office, and no stranger to homicides and those accused of committing them, decided she was someone he'd never choose to turn his back on.

"Her attitude and the way she looked and everything about her," he said grimly, "was the personification of evil."

Had not years of shooting heroin and doing every other kind of illicit substance ravaged her face and body she would have been a very pretty woman—high cheekbones, curly black hair, brown eyes. But the drugs and all that went with it—the wild days and sleepless nights on end, erratic eating, constant boozing, indiscriminate sex—had given her the sallow, drawn, almost emaciated appearance of a walking dead woman.

The cops and prosecutors and jailors who saw her that first night in jail, and in the weeks and months ahead, thought they saw beneath all that a young woman who with a few good breaks in her life could have turned out differently.

Who was Karla Faye Tucker?

How did she end up in the Harris County jail on a double-murder rap?

When someone snuffs out someone else's life and the laws define the act as murder, there can be no secrets. Shakespeare was right. Murder *will* out. It will force out everything about the lives of both victim and accused. For Karla Faye Tucker the story that detectives put together was typical of far too many members of a generation born, weaned, and having grown up in the age of sex, drugs, and rock and roll.

She was twenty-three, born in 1960 to a mother, Carolyn, who smoked marijuana, and when her two girls, Kali and Karla, were old enough, she shared the joints with them.

Heroin entered Karla's life when she was ten. It was given to her by a biker who thought it would be fun to have sex with a ten-year-old. That plan went awry when Karla got sick from the dope. In retrospect, she realized she'd liked how she felt doing heroin. From that point on, she could not get her fill of anything that gave her a high.

When the marriage between Carolyn and Larry Tucker broke up, he was awarded custody of the girls. When they were old enough to decide with whom they wanted to live, they chose their mother. By now Karla was a girl out of control. According to Beverly Lowry in her book about Tucker, *Crossed Over,* she was "strung out, shooting up, getting into fistfights, getting kicked out of school. How much worse could it get?"

Married in her teens to a carpenter named Stephen Griffith, she divorced in May 1983, shortly after Carolyn suffered a stroke. When Carolyn died, Karla was a young woman out of control, mad about having sex, and exhibiting no qualms about financing her drug habit by turning tricks.

When Tucker moved in with her sister and Danny Gar-

rett, he was madly in love with Kari. They were soon joined by Jimmy Leibrant and Ronnie Burrell. The common denominator of their lives on McKean Street was drugs, sex, and everything about the biker life.

She'd met Jerry Lynn Dean in 1981 and despised him from the start. He owned a Harley, but in Tucker's opinion, he fell miserably short of being a true biker. Among his many failings was his appearance: five feet seven inches, a scrawny 142 pounds, long blond hair, measly mustache, and not a shred of the flair of true bikers. A genuine Harley man wore skintight T-shirts and jeans and knew how to drink and to handle his drugs. Jerry Dean possessed none of these qualities. He was a "pussy of a man," a disgusting pretentious pussy. He'd also committed unforgivable sins. He'd mistreated his wife, Shawn, Karla's dearest friend. And he'd destroyed a photograph album containing a cherished picture of Karla's beloved Mama Carolyn.

Along with this history the investigators working the Dean-Thornton murders found in Karla Faye Tucker's past all the signs of a girl heading for trouble: Hotheaded. Willful. Tough. Unforgiving of slights. Capable of cold and unrelenting hatred. Not a person to cross or double-cross. A young woman who knew how to settle a score.

Now, here she was, locked up for taking part in one of the worst murders in Houston's history, or at least the worst in recent memory. There was no getting around it. Doug Garrett had gotten her and his brother to talk, with every word that they'd said about killing Jerry Dean and Deborah Thornton on tape. Open-and-shut case.

However, it would be a much tighter case if there could be a formal, written-down, and then neatly typed-up and signed confession. Whichever mouth it came from didn't matter.

Karla Faye Tucker was the one who talked.

"I wanted to tell the truth," she said in 1984 about why she confessed. "I wanted the real story to be told. I had to do something about how sick-minded we must have been to think about something like this."

Part of the motivation was a story that Jerry Dean had put out a $300 contract to have someone hurt Tucker by burning her face. For Tucker, that was it; the straw that broke the camel's back concerning Jerry Dean. The thing to do about Dean, they agreed—Karla, Danny, and Jimmy—as they talked in the McKean Street house, shooting crystal methaline and drinking tequila, was to steal Dean's Harley stuff and sell it. At some point Jerry Dean had left keys to his house and car at McKean Street. Now Karla had them.

"We were very wired," Tucker said in the confession. "We was looking for something to do. Something said go."

Theft was the ultimate goal. The plan on Sunday night, June 12, 1983, was to simply case Dean's house, five and a half miles away. They would use Danny's Ranchero. Danny Garrett had a shotgun and brought it along.

When they arrived at the Windtree Apartments around three in the morning (Monday), they got out of the Ranchero. Garrett grabbed a hammer from the bed of the Ranchero. Tucker and he walked into the apartment. She unlocked the door and they darted inside.

From the spare room Dean shouted, "What's going on?" Danny Garrett moved into the doorway.

"I was right behind him," Tucker confessed. "The light was out and the window was on the far wall and there was a little crack in the curtains and a little bit of light coming in. And I could see the silhouette of a body that sat up. I couldn't see detail, faces or Jerry's clothes, anything like that, but I could see the outline of everything, like a shadow on the wall. And I walked past Danny and went and sat down on top of him [Jerry]."

"Karla," exclaimed Jerry, pleadingly. "We can work it out."

"Move and you're dead, motherfucker," said Karla.

Dean struggled up and shoved Tucker off the bed.

Getting to her feet, she saw Danny Garrett's silhouette as he struck Dean's head with the hammer. Dean tumbled onto a mattress on the floor, facedown, and Garrett turned and left the room. Tucker heard a revolting gurgling noise.

"I kept hearing that sound and all I wanted to do was stop it," Tucker related. "I wanted to stop him from making that noise."

But it didn't stop.

"So I looked," Tucker continued, "[and] I seen a pickax against the wall. I reached over and grabbed it and I swung it and hit him in the back with it . . . four or five times."

Jimmy Leibrant walked into the room and saw Karla Faye Tucker with one foot on Dean, both hands on the handle of the pickax, struggling to pull it from Dean's back. "Wriggling it," Leibrant would tell the police. When she'd wrenched it free, she lifted the axe over her head, turned, looked at Leibrant, and with a smile hit Dean again.

It was while she was battering Dean, Tucker had told Douglas Garrett and others, that she experienced orgasms.

Leibrant turned and left the room and the house to find a telephone to call Ronnie Burrell and tell him to come and pick him up. Jimmy would tell anyone who would listen, "I burned off because I didn't buy in for that. That's not what it's supposed to be. I hadn't gone for that. That's not my way."

While Leibrant fled and Tucker continued to hear the gurgling sounds, Danny Garrett was loading Harley parts into the bed of the Ranchero. At some point he returned to the spare room, took the pickax from Tucker's hands, and drove it into Dean's chest. He then returned to his looting.

Tucker noticed someone under covers against the wall by the door.

"The head was under a pillow," she explained, "and the body was shaking under the covers. At that point my mind was, I don't know where it was at. I picked up the pickax again. I swung it and hit the person in the upper part of their shoulder. I tried again the second time, and the person came up from under the covers. It was a woman. She grabbed at the pickax."

With the tool embedded in her shoulder, Deborah Thornton managed to struggle with Tucker until Garrett burst into the room and pulled them apart. Tucker left the room briefly and returned to find Thornton trying to remove the pickax. "It hurts," she cried. "If you are going to kill me, hurry up."

"And Danny kicked her in the head and pulled the pickax out at the same time," Karla testified, "and when he kicked her, it knocked her flat on her back and he hit her and put the pickax right there in her chest. When I seen that—it happened that quick—I turned around and walked out of the bedroom and Danny was behind me, and we got the motorcycle frame, carried it out, and put it in Jerry's vehicle."

Danny Garrett left in the Ranchero. Karla Faye Tucker drove Jerry Dean's El Camino. When they returned to McKean Street, it was 6:30 A.M., a half hour before Jerry Dean customarily picked up Gregory Travers to go to work.

More than a half-century before Karla Faye Tucker confessed to grabbing a pickax to kill Jerry Lynn Dean, and less than a half-century after Lizzie Borden had been accused of killing with a hatchet, historian Edmund Pearson published *The Borden Case.* In the 1924 book he propounded one of history's verities: "It is one of the great sensational moments in our civilization, the trial of a woman for her life."

It had always been so. In a preface to a compendium of female criminality, *Look for the Woman,* crime historian Jay Robert Nash wrote, "Interestingly, it is the off-beat and the inexplicable that dominate among the crimes of female offenders. In all recorded history, the female criminal has many times overexcelled her male counterpart in daring robberies, labyrinthine confidence schemes, and heinous

murders. In fact, the female murderer had proved herself easily as deadly as any male and certainly more insidious. Her motives, as a general rule, lack the clearheaded and darkly reasoned purposes of the male. Whim and fancy often rule her. Long-smoldering emotions often burn themselves out only after the victim of the female killer, whether male or female, has been subjected to excruciating agony. Seldom is there the quick, clean stroke of death as with the male."

This was certainly what happened to Jerry Dean. With a pickax that was so heavy that it made her arms tired, Karla Faye Tucker pounded Dean's body more than two dozen times.

"It was the murder weapon and the boasts of the pretty woman who wielded it," wrote reporter Lee Hancock in the *Dallas Morning News,* "that stunned even crime-numbed Houston." But not only Houston.

In the ninety-one years since Lizzie Borden called up the stairs to a maid, "Someone killed father," news reports of sensational murders, which had been mostly limited to the front pages of local and regional newspapers, had gone nationwide—first in newsreels in movie houses, then on radio, and finally into living rooms via television. In a medium of mass communication, in which a rule of newscast selection was "If it bleeds, it leads," Houston's pickax murder case not only got space in newspapers but precious newscast airtime across the country.

The pickax did it.

Without the pickax the killings of Jerry Lynn Dean and his unlucky one-night-stand girlfriend would have gotten into print and on the six and eleven o'clock news as an apparently drug-related homicide and been greeted with a shrug of shoulders by a city and a country in which drugs and violent death were commonplace.

"[It was] the weapon," said Joseph Magliolo, Harris County assistant district attorney, for whom this would be the first capital case since he was named Harris County's chief prosecutor. "The morning they found the bodies it was all over the courthouse. I heard it everywhere I went. I knew about it the first day, because of the weapon."

If *murder by pickax* was an attention-getter even among prosecutors, a murder with the pickax in the hands of *a woman* made it unique.

Detective Moshier told voracious reporters, "It was one of the most gruesome, heinous murders that anyone could remember. It was just such an awful, awful crime."

So awful, in fact, that as Karla Faye Tucker emerged from her drug stupor she had felt so repulsed by the viciousness of what she had done that she needed to purge herself of it by talking about it for hours to detectives and prosecutors.

Because Tucker had confessed and had agreed to testify against herself and Danny Garrett, there would be separate trials. Believing they had more evidence against Tucker for the murder of Jerry Dean, prosecutors would try her for that crime only.

Garrett would be tried for the murder of Deborah Thornton in Harris County District Court 232, presided over by Judge A. D. Azios.

There would not be a murder trial for Jimmy Leibrant because prosecutors had concluded that he hadn't actually murdered anyone. He had also agreed to be a witness for the prosecution.

Assigned by the court to act in Tucker's defense were two former murder prosecutors, Henry Oncken and Mack Arnold. Oncken had been in the D.A.'s office before being appointed to fill a vacancy caused by the death of a judge. When he'd sought the elective post permanently in 1982, he'd lost and gone into private practice. He agreed to take on Tucker's defense because he needed the money. After his first meeting with her in October 1983, he said, "I couldn't stand her. The drugs were still in her. She didn't care about anything."

Oncken was a fatherly figure, quiet and contained. Ar-

nold had a reputation for courtroom theatrics. They agreed on a trial strategy in which Arnold handled the day-to-day proceedings while Oncken acted as his second and looked after their client.

Put on the docket of the 180th District Court of Harris County, the trial was scheduled to open on April 11, 1984, with Judge Patricia Lykos on the bench.

Among defense lawyers and prosecutors alike, the Republican jurist (judges in Texas are elected to their posts) had a reputation described in such unlawyerly adjectives as Greek tyrant, unpredictable, grandstander, publicity hound, political animal, and bitch. Beverly Lowry in her book about Karla Faye Tucker saw in Judge Lykos "an extremely attractive woman, late fortyish, olive skinned, with lush Mediterranean features, dark-haired with some gray" worn "in a great comb-back" style. Rather than the traditional judge's robe, she usually wore bright suits. During a trial she often drank coffee from a wide-bottomed, non-spillable ceramic cup. She also smoked cigarettes, a privilege she afforded jurors, so long as they sat in the last row of the box.

Among the rules she imposed on a trial—which was seen as good or bad in the eyes of lawyers on both sides of a case, depending on who was being addressed—was "no theatrics." In her court lawyers were not permitted to "waltz around," a la the famed defense attorney of an earlier era, Clarence Darrow, or TV's fictional Perry Mason, tossing off questions to a witness over a shoulder. Prosecutors and defenders were to stay put at their respective tables. A witness may not be approached without her permission. No attorney was to leave the court, even to use the men's room, without seeking her approval.

Karla Faye Tucker sat beside her attorney Henry Oncken, facing the jurors. From a necklace hung a small white plastic cross.

She wore it because between arrest and trial she had become a born-again Christian.

* * *

The indictment charged "that Karla Faye Tucker, hereafter styled the defendant, heretofore on or about June 13,
1983, did then and there unlawfully while in the course of
committing and attempting to commit the burglary and robbery of Jerry Lynn Dean, hereafter styled the complainant,
intentionally cause the death of the complainant by striking
and stabbing the complainant with a mattock."

Representing the dead complainant and in the interests
of the "peace and dignity of the state" and on behalf of
the people of Harris County and the state of Texas, D.A.
Joseph Magliolo followed his opening statement's review
of the basic facts of the case as seen by the prosecution by
calling Gregory Travers. His testimony about the discovery
of the bodies was augmented by a series of police photo-
graphs of the murder scene and the murdered.

Through testimony of policemen, homicide detectives,
and Aurelio Espinola, the chief medical examiner, the state
proved murders had been committed. S. C. Pilgrim, the
M.E.'s assistant, described how he pulled the pickax from
Deborah Thornton's chest, therein establishing that it was
the murder weapon. The pickax was produced by Melchora
Vasquez, chief clerk for Harris County's trial exhibits, and
shown to the jury.

The issue for the defense was whether Jerry Dean died
as a result of being struck with the pickax, or was Dean
already dead as a result of Danny Garrett hitting him with
a hammer?

Next came the clandestine taping by Doug Garrett, with
Doug on the stand to verify the tape and what his brother
and Tucker had told him about the killings. It was compelling testimony.

When Jimmy Leibrant took the stand, jurors heard about
the gurgling noises. Leibrant had heard them, too: "Like,
and we have all heard the low hum of an aquarium pump

and then we hear it broken, gasping, the air sucked, released, sucked, released."

He also spoke of seeing Tucker, pickax in hand, smiling with pleasure.

Next up was Tucker's sister, Kari, now married to Doug Garrett. Sisterhood notwithstanding, she testified that Karla had "picked" Jerry, and while she was doing so, she had orgasms, or in Kari's words, quoting Tucker, "got a nut." After the murders, Kari went on, her sister's face "had a flush." On the fate of Deborah Thornton, Kari again quoted Karla: "The girl was a tough motherfucker to kill."

The press had another sensational angle: "Sister testifies against sister."

To rebut the defense's position that Dean was killed by the hammer, not by the pickax, the prosecution recalled Aurelio Espinola to emphatically reassert that Dean died as the result of any one of thirteen pickax punctures.

With that, the state rested. Calling no witnesses, so did the defense. Then came the two closing arguments. At issue was not that Karla Faye Tucker was a murderer—she had admitted that. The issue was whether she was culpable to the extent that she deserved to die for her crime. Whether she would be condemned to execution by lethal injection would be up to the judge and the jurors, who now were asked to render a verdict of guilty or not guilty.

They took seventy minutes to choose the former.

Now the case would move to the penalty trial. The prosecution would press for the death penalty. The defense would attempt to show mitigating circumstances. They hoped to lay a solid foundation for mercy.

Jurors would answer two questions. Did Tucker's conduct cause the death of Jerry Lynn Dean deliberately and with reasonable expectation that death would result? Was there reasonable probability that she would commit an act of violence that would constitute a continuing threat to society as a whole?

Judge Lykos would decide between life in prison and

death. But not until Monday, April 23, after a recess for Easter.

To counter the prosecution's attempts to show with testimony from Kari and Douglas Garrett that Karla Faye Tucker was an inherently violent individual, defense counsel Arnold used members of Karla's family, a psychiatrist, and Karla herself to show that the Karla in the courtroom was not the same Karla Faye Tucker described from the witness chair as the drugged, hateful, smiling, orgasmic woman with a pickax in her hands.

The thrust of all this was that she had changed, that she had been rehabilitated to a point that justice demanded life imprisonment, not execution.

In her instructions to the jurors Judge Lykos advised that they could not consider Tucker's drug abuse as a mitigating circumstance in assessing penalty unless they felt that she had been so intoxicated, she did not know right from wrong.

While her attorney was fighting for her life, Tucker sat as she had all through phase one of the case. She sat as demurely as possible, often jotting notes, and frequently raising a hand to finger the little white crucifix.

Wearing it on Wednesday, April 25, 1984, with a striped blouse open at the neck, and a harlequin-plaid sweater, her face bracketed by long tumbles of curly black hair, she sat in somber silence as the jurors replied in the affirmative to both questions—and Judge Lykos sentenced her to death.

Men and women condemned to death in the United States of America do not meet that fate speedily. They have rights to appeal both convictions and sentences. For Karla Faye Tucker there was yet another trial at which she would be the center of attention, not as the accused, but as the star witness against Danny Garrett.

It would be a lengthier trial because Danny Garrett had not confessed.

When the proceeding ended in December 1984, Garrett was convicted and sent to death row at the Texas state prison in Huntsville.

Tucker was conveyed to the death row of the prison at Gatesville to wait out the process of appeals to higher courts. When the death sentence was upheld by the Texas Court of Criminal Appeals in December 1988, her lawyers carried the issue to the United States Supreme Court. It declined to overturn the decision in June 1989.

With all appeals exhausted, Karla ultimately returned to the courtroom of Judge Patricia Lykos on April 19, 1992, to learn the date for her execution. Judge Lykos set it for dawn, June 30.

Texas Department of Criminal Justice spokesman Charles Brown announced that if the execution were indeed carried out, Karla Faye Tucker would become the first woman to be put to death in Texas since Chipita Rodriguez was hanged in 1863 for murdering a horse trader. With the U.S. Supreme Court having ruled in 1976 that the death penalty was within constitutional bounds, Texas prisons had administered lethal injections to fifty men, starting in 1982—by far the highest total among states with capital punishment. They included men who were teenagers at the time of their crimes, men who claimed innocence, and men who claimed mental problems.

In going to a cell on death row, Tucker joined three other women under a death sentence in Texas (there were 353 men awaiting execution).

She was one of only forty-one women among nearly 2,600 condemned inmates nationally.

Immediately after the imposition of sentence by Judge Lykos, Tucker's attorney, George Secrest, announced that an application for a stay of execution was pending in the Texas Court of Criminal Appeals.

He told reporters, "We have raised substantial constitutional issues. I hope Karla Faye Tucker lives and doesn't die. That's what we all want."

Tucker said, "I think whatever happens will be okay."

Deborah Thornton's brother, Don Carlson, himself a born-again Christian and a death penalty opponent, declared his opposition to Karla's execution. "What I saw when I spoke with her was something totally different from what I saw eight or nine years ago when the trial was going on," he said. "If there is somebody who's totally rehabilitated and has changed, should you go ahead and kill them anyway? She was blasted out of her brain on the night of the killings, and jurors were not allowed to consider that in deciding punishment."

Prosecutor Joe Magliolo retorted, "She took and pickaxed two people to death. I think since the jury said—twelve individual citizens said—she deserved to die for what she did, then that's the verdict."

What worried Magliolo was the fact there had arisen across Texas, the nation, and the world a groundswell of opinion that Karla Faye Tucker had rehabilitated herself to such an extent that she was, as Don Carlson claimed, "not the same woman who'd used a pickax to murder."

Was she *not* the same person? Had Karla Faye Tucker *really* changed? If so, in what way?

By all accounts of prison officials and others who came in contact with her as she sat on death row, she began turning herself around in December 1983. At a meeting of Alcoholics Anonymous she met prison chaplain Rebecca Lewis. This encounter led to Bible classes and religious conversion. She would eventually meet and marry a minister, Dana Brown.

Among those attesting to Tucker's rehabilitation was novelist Beverly Lowry, whose teenage son had been a murder victim. After reading an article about the failure of Tucker's appeal in the *Houston Chronicle* in 1988, Lowry traveled to Gatesville to meet Tucker and, perhaps, write a book that would deal with both the murder of Lowry's son and Tucker's crimes. The Karla Faye Tucker she met was clean of drugs for the first time since she was a child: no

heroin, no acid, no pills, no speed, no crystal meth. She had found God, taken up aerobics, and crocheting. She'd earned a high-school diploma and was taking college courses. She and Lowry became friends. Lowry's book championed the cause of winning a commutation of Tucker's death sentence.

In a column devoted to Lowry's book, *Crossed Over,* published in 1992, Anna Quindlen wrote, "It is about redemption, about how one superlatively messed-up little girl—a doper at eight, a needle freak behind heroin by the time she was eleven—went straight. Just in time to die."

Lowry's dedication of the book read: "For Karla: long life."

Hopes for that eventuality were lifted in 1993 when the Texas Court of Criminal Appeals vacated the execution date and ordered Judge Lykos to conduct an evidentiary hearing to look into allegations that Jimmy Leibrant perjured himself when he said at the trial that he had made no deal with Tucker's prosecutors for his testimony. This and other legal maneuvers resulted in further postponements of the execution date for four years.

On December 8, 1997, the U.S. Supreme Court rejected for the last time attempts to spare Tucker from the death penalty.

Eleven days later, Texas District Judge Debbie Strickland fixed the date of execution at February 3, 1998. This left Karla Faye Tucker with one recourse—a review of her case by the Texas Board of Pardons and Paroles.

Should the board recommend commutation of the sentence to life in prison, the final decision rested with Governor George W. Bush. As of that date, the son of former President George Bush, and a potential candidate for the presidency in 2000, had not reduced a death sentence to life.

While the board members consulted by telephone, supporters of Tucker's cause launched a worldwide campaign on her behalf. An amazing coalition included such disparate peronalities as the Reverend Pat Robertson and Bianca Jagger, the former wife of Rolling Stones singer Mick Jagger and an executive board member of Amnesty International.

After meeting with Karla Faye Tucker at Gatesville, Bianca Jagger said, "All those who meet her agree on one thing: She is fully rehabilitated."

Deborah Thornton's brother, Don Carlson, came forward again to say of Tucker's work as a religious adviser to other inmates, "She has done more for Jesus in that six-by-nine cell than anyone I've ever met in my life."

Based on opposition to the death penalty, a plea for mercy was voiced by the pope.

Tucker's attorney, David Botsford, asserted, "We see mercy and rehabilitation forming the basis for commutation in Virginia, Montana, Illinois, and Georgia. Why not Texas?"

As the chorus for commutation expanded and grew louder, a Christmastime editorial of the *Dallas Evening News* noted, "Karla Faye Tucker has more friends than you'd expect for a pickax murderer." It continued, "Ms. Tucker says she has changed. She kicked the drug habit that fueled her violence and underwent a religious conversion in prison. Her guards confirm her rehabilitation. Should the system respond to her reform? Could anyone prove a rehabilitation is sincere? These questions should trouble thoughtful supporters of the death penalty. Certainly, Ms. Tucker's gender, race and religious faith have helped her win more sympathy than most condemned prisoners. . . . What if a convict is truly rehabilitated, and the victims' families feel no need to pursue the death sentence? Death row is crowded. This is the time to decide whether an occasional act of mercy would make our criminal justice system more or less just."

Harris County prosecutor Rusty Hardin joined those favoring commutation. "It was a brutal crime," he said. "On

the other hand, if you're going to have that process [commutation], she's the most appropriate candidate I've seen."

On the other side of the issue, J. C. Moshier, now a chief deputy Harris County constable, said, "It's wonderful that Karla Faye's become a better person. I just don't know in my mind if it should make any difference."

Dianne Clements, president of the victims' rights group Justice for All, asked, "Is Karla Faye Tucker a future danger? The answer has to be yes based on her behavior in the free world."

As to public opinion, a poll by the *Dallas Evening News* found that a clear majority of Texans favored the death penalty on principle, but less than half favored executing Tucker. Over a two-month period the governor's office in Austin received almost 25,000 letters, fax messages, and phone calls that ran about five to one in Tucker's favor. On the day of her scheduled execution there were four thousand such calls.

After another appeal to the U.S. Supreme Court for a stay was rebuffed, the only opinion that mattered was Governor George W. Bush's.

Stepping before television cameras at 6:10 P.M. in the state capital in Austin on February 3, 1998, Bush announced he had denied a thirty-day reprieve to allow further review of the case, that he had "sought guidance through prayer," and that he had "concluded that judgments about the heart and soul of an individual on death row are best left to a higher authority." He finished with, "May God bless Karla Faye Tucker, and God bless her victims and their families."

Moments later Karla Faye Tucker was on a hospital gurney in the prison death chamber awaiting the fatal injection. She asked forgiveness from the Thornton and Dean families and said she was sorry.

"I hope God will give you peace with this," she said. "Everybody has been so good to me. I love all of you all very much. I'm going to be face to face with Jesus now. I will see you all when you get there. I'll wait for you."

She closed her eyes, licked her lips, and appeared to say a silent prayer. She coughed twice, groaned softly as the drugs took effect, and went silent. Karla Faye Tucker was declared dead at 6:45 P.M.

Douglas Garrett, convicted of the murder of Deborah Thornton, did not have to face the ending that came to Tucker. He had died in prison in 1993 of liver disease.

When word of Karla Faye Tucker's death reached a group of people who had not bought into the story of her rehabilitation and religious conversion, a cheer went up.

On February 10, 1998, seven days after Karla Faye Tucker's execution, a newspaper in Hannibal, Missouri, the *Courier Post,* editorialized, "We have to wonder that if Ms. Tucker had been a Karl instead of a Karla, would there have been so much attention to this case? If a man were to be executed today after professing a Christian conversion, would anyone care to the degree that brought Ms. Tucker so much attention? The focus was on the conversion. The reason for the focus was gender."

Borden case historian Edmund Pearson was right. One of the great sensational moments in our civilization is the trial of a woman for her life.

Twelve

That Evil Man

In late May 1996, elementary-school teacher Marian Whitehurst looked at the deplorable condition of the lawn around the unoccupied house she owned and hoped to sell in the Walden Lakes subdivision near Plant City, a suburb of Tampa, Florida. She decided to hire somebody to mow the grass and do some overall tidying up.

The ideal person for the job, she figured, would be the teenage son of Sharon and Sam Smithers. She knew Sharon as an elementary-school aide. Sam was a former deacon and the head custodian of the First Baptist Church. A well-liked forty-five-year-old gentleman whom no one ever heard using rough language, he took an interest in activities of the PTA and drove a church van. Employed as an electrician's helper, he went to and from work in a pickup truck adorned with a decal that seemed to have nothing to do with his genial character. It read "Bad Boys."

The Smithers' son, Jonathan, was planning to go to college and hoped to play shortstop on the school's baseball team. Consequently, when Marian Whitehurst talked to Sam Smithers about hiring Jonathan, Smithers said the youth was too busy honing his baseball skills to take on the task. Smithers volunteered to handle the yard work himself. Satisfied with the arrangement, Whitehurst gave him the address and instructions as to what needed to be done.

Although confident that she'd hired the right man for the chores, Whitehurst found herself in the vicinity of the property on May 28, 1996, and drove to the house to check how the work was going. Parking her car, she saw Smithers's truck in the driveway. Locating him in the backyard, she saw that he was hosing down a long-handled axe. While there were trees on the property, she had not asked him to cut down or trim any of them. Setting aside curiosity, she complimented him on the quality of his work. But as they passed the open door of the garage, she noticed what seemed to be a puddle of blood about the size of a dinner plate on the concrete floor. Scattered around it were bits of potato chips.

Sam Smithers speculated that an animal must have killed a squirrel there. He promised to clean up the blood.

Dubious of this explanation because there seemed to be too much blood to have come from a squirrel, Whitehurst noticed that something appeared to have been dragged across the ground in the direction of a small pond at the rear of the property.

Although she felt uneasy, she said to Smithers, nonchalantly, "Well, if it's not one thing, it's another."

Keeping her concern to herself, she left.

At home and growing increasingly troubled, she called the Hillsborough Sheriff's Office and reported the blood, Sam Smithers's explanation, and the drag marks on the ground.

Told to meet deputies at the house, she arrived to find Smithers's truck was gone and the blood and bits of chips had been washed away. Still visible, however, were the drag marks.

Following them to the pond, the deputies saw the floating bodies of two women.

When the corpses were removed from the water, the medical examiner estimated that one had been in the pond

for at least ten days. The other appeared to have had been placed there only a few hours earlier. Both women had been strangled. The most recent victim had suffered chop-type wounds to her head, a fractured skull, and a broken jaw.

Investigators immediately turned their attention to the vacant house. In the garage they found an almost empty Minute Maid orange juice bottle and a faint spot of blood. On the stairs of the house leading to the second floor, they discovered a piece of potato chip. In one of the bedrooms were found a slightly rumpled bed and a Trojan condom wrapper.

A deputy asked Whitehurst if Sam Smithers had been given a key to the house.

She replied, "No."

Convinced by the circumstances that Sam Smithers was the most likely murderer of the women, deputies arrested him. He denied any knowledge of what had happened. He asked if he seemed to be the type of man who could do such a thing? Was he not a respectable family man? Gainfully employed? A churchgoer? Ask his coworkers and friends about him and they will all attest to his exemplary character.

Indeed, those who knew Sam Smithers told investigators of a "very religious" man and a "likeable guy." Employees where Smithers had been working for six months as an electrician's helper at a Nebraska Avenue business said he was always eager to please, and they described him as a "country bumpkin."

Yet sheriff's investigators soon learned of another side of Sam Smithers. In 1980 he'd been charged with arson of his hometown church in Chattanooga, Tennessee. He'd been put on probation. In 1994 he'd been turned down when he applied for a handyman position with the Hillsborough Sheriff's Office. And he had been forced to resign as head custodian at the First Baptist Church in Plant City after allegations that he'd offered to falsify the hours of a woman doing community service at the church in exchange for sexual favors.

As this revelation lent credence to suspicions that sex had been Smithers's motive for murder, other investigators had been working to identify the two women. Their purpose and their hope was to link them to Smithers.

The first to be identified was the more recent victim. Reported missing by a friend, she was thirty-one-year-old Christy Elizabeth Cowan. A native of Connecticut, she had graduated at the top of her high-school class and once dreamed of becoming a nurse. Falling into a life of drug use and prostitution, she had two children and a lengthy record of arrests.

Identification of the woman who had been in the water for ten days was made through fingerprints. A drug addict since age thirteen and a prostitute, twenty-four-year-old Denise Elaine Roach had been born in Jamaica. Her two daughters were living with relatives. Detectives learned that her brother had been looking for her to get her to sign adoption papers. An autopsy showed she had suffered skull fractures and broken facial bones before being strangled.

In order to connect the dead women to Smithers, detectives descended upon a stretch of Hillsborough Avenue that was the working turf of Tampa's street prostitutes. Many of them knew both Cowan and Roach, but none better than thirty-four-year-old Bonnie Kruse.

Working out of the Luxury Motel, she sold her favors for enough money to buy crack cocaine. "Unless we were sleeping," she told detectives, "all us girls on Hillsborough Avenue were smoking crack."

They did so without using pimps, she explained, adding proudly, "We were what were called renegades."

She and Roach had been "best friends," she said. Roach's street name was "New York." The two of them usually checked on one another every day, but she hadn't seen Roach around for about two weeks.

Did Kruse know Sam Smithers?

Indeed she did. He drove a pickup truck with a "Bad Boys" decal and once had tried to coax her away from the motel room and go somewhere else with him.

She refused, she said, because, "the look in his eyes scared me."

Another prostitute, Sharon Shepherd, related seeing Christy Cowan on the day she died. She said she had given Cowan $10 and a wrapped Trojan condom. She had taken the condom from an economy-size box.

The condom found in the bedroom of the house, detectives noted, bore the same batch number as those in Shepherd's supply.

Satisfied that Smithers could be shown to have known one of the women, detectives still did not have any physical evidence to connect him to the murders. The only tangible things were a potato chip, a condom wrapper, and a Minute Maid bottle.

To pursue these clues investigators canvassed all the stores in the vicinity of the murder scene that sold both Minute Maid products and potato chips. Their hope was that an employee of one of the stores might remember Smithers buying chips and juice on the day Cowan was killed.

One of the convenience stores visited, Presto, was close to the murder house. While no one could remember seeing either Smithers or Cowan, the store had a security system with a TV camera connected to a recorder. The videotape for the day of Cowan's murder showed her and Smithers entering the store, buying a bag of chips and an orange drink, and leaving togther, with Smithers holding the door open for Cowan.

Confronted with the tape, Smithers confessed.

He had killed Roach, he told Detective Dorothy Martinez, by battering her with his fists and slamming her head against a wall. A large piece of wood fell onto her face, knocking her unconscious. He thought of giving her

CPR, but decided she didn't deserve it. He dragged her to the pond and pushed her in.

"I didn't know if she was dead that day," he told Martinez, "but she was definitely dead the next day when I came back."

Cowan had been killed in a dispute over money. He hit her with a hoe and the axe on the day that Marian Whitehurst had seen him washing blood from the axe. He'd dragged Cowan to the pond by her feet and threw her in, still breathing.

He was charged with two counts of first-degree murder, indicted, and held for trial.

But between the end of May 1996 and December 1998, his account of what happened to Cowan and Roach would change dramatically and shockingly.

On Tuesday, December 15, 1998, prosecutor Ed Schmoll stood before a jury in the courtroom of Hillsborough Circuit Court judge William Fuente and spoke of Christy Cowan's hard life on the streets of Tampa, making dates with strangers to get money to buy crack, and on a spring day in 1996 climbing into a man's pickup truck.

"She didn't realize that this was going to be her last date," he said, as Sam Smithers sat listening a few feet away in a navy-blue suit. "She didn't realize that Denise Roach, another girl that worked the streets, had been missing for at least fourteen days."

Schmoll sketched the case against Smithers—the convenience store videotape, the juice bottle, the potato chip, the pool of blood seen by Marian Whitehurst, the drag marks, the floating bodies, bloodstains in the garage and house and on one of Sam's shoes, and other evidence.

Then it was the turn of Sam's defense attorney, Danny Hernandez.

Smithers had exercised "terrible judgment" by associating with "some bad people," he said in his opening.

Sam did have contact with the two women.

"He knows how they died."

But "he did not murder them."

Covering the trial for the *Saint Petersburg Times,* reporter Sue Carlton wrote for the next day's paper, "It was unclear on Tuesday whether the gray-haired Smithers will ultimately take the stand to explain that account."

Testimony began with Marian Whitehurst's account of stopping by her property on May 28, 1996. She was surprised to find Smithers there that day, she said. He was calmly washing an axe. He pointed out a pool of blood in the garage and said an animal must have killed a squirrel, but not to worry, he would clean it up. Smithers, she said, was "very normal-acting and casual."

When she came back to the house and met sheriff's deputies, she said, the garage floor was wet and clean. She saw only one sodden potato chip.

Moments later, the bodies were found in the pond.

To the witness stand the next day, Wednesday, December 16, came Bonnie Kruse. She was wearing an outfit that Sue Carlton described as "jail blues" because of a recent arrest. Her testimony dealt with the life of Tampa prostitutes and how she and the murdered women were known as "renegades" because they did not work for pimps. Under questioning by Schmoll, she related her scary encounter with the man who drove a pickup truck with a "Bad Boys" decal, and she identified him as Sam Smithers.

In cross-examination, Danny Hernandez asked her about drug dealers, pimps, and people named "Bobo" and "Flavor."

Kruse said she'd never heard of them.

The prosecution brought on an expert to tell about finding blood on Smithers's shoe, on a garage wall, and a mop.

Detective Martinez told the jurors of Smithers's confession.

When the day's proceedings concluded, reporters interviewed Sharon Smithers. Now divorced from Sam, she said, "The man I married never could have done this."

With the prosecution's case completed, the question of

whether Sam Smithers would be called to testify was answered on Thursday, December 17, 1998. Defense attorney Hernandez put his client on the stand.

At the end of the day Sue Carlton would write for readers of her newspaper, "A man who once told detectives he beat two prostitutes and then dumped their bodies in a pond told a jury the murders actually were part of an elaborate drug and blackmail scheme. He killed no one."

Smithers asserted that he had been alternately hired and blackmailed into cooperating with shady figures who used Marian Whitehurst's vacant house to store and deal drugs.

Observers of criminal trials and students of some of America's most sensational murder cases could not help but be reminded of Lizzie Borden claiming that "someone" had come into the house and murdered her father. Fifty years later a "bushy-haired man" was named by Dr. Sam Sheppard as the murderer of his wife, spawning the TV series and a movie, *The Fugitive*. In the 1970s, army doctor Jeffrey MacDonald blamed the slaughter of his wife and two children at Fort Bragg, North Carolina, on intruding hippies. Lyle and Eric Menendez had suggested to police their parents had been shotgunned to death by members of organized crime. O. J. Simpson had attributed the murders of his ex-wife, Nicole, and Ronald Goldman to vengeful drug dealers.

Now, here was Sam Smithers telling a Florida jury that he had lied in his confession to the police in order to protect his wife and son, whose lives, he said, had been threatened by one of the mysterious individuals who were blackmailing him.

Blackmailing him about *what*?

He had been working in the yard of his Walden Lake home one day, he testified, when a bearded man who knew him from a previous job showed him an incriminating photograph of him and a woman who was not his wife. The man threatened to tell Mrs. Smithers and officials of Smithers's church. To avoid this, Smithers was to arrange for the bearded man to use the house at which Smithers had been hired to tend the lawn. He would be paid for this service.

"He needed a place," Smithers said, "and I needed the money."

For $200, he continued, he unlocked the gate for "drop offs" that sometimes involved women and probably were drug-related.

One night at the house, a woman Smithers later identified as Denise Roach got into an argument with the bearded man. He hit her on the head with a hatchet.

"He killed her right in front of me," Smithers told the jurors, "and then he beat me and ordered me to put the body in the pond."

A week and a half later, another fight resulted in the death of Cowan. For helping to cover up this "accident," he said, he was paid $400.

"I had never done anything like this before," he said, "but it was easy money."

On Friday, December 18, 1998, prosecutor Ed Schmoll looked into the faces of the jury of seven women and five men, and thundered, "There is no mystery man." Pointing at Smithers, he said, *"He* is that evil man."

Seated in the audience, Sharon Smithers sobbed. Smithers sat quietly, staring at her as the jury left the courtroom to begin deliberations.

An hour and thirty-five minutes later, they returned with a verdict of guilty on two counts of first-degree murder. The maximum penalty, to be determined in the sentencing phase of the trial, slated for January 22, 1999, was death in Florida's electric chair.

After the trial, prosecutor Hernandez said of Smithers, "I think he had expectations that he was going to be acquitted." Looking forward to the penalty phase at which the state would argue that the murders were especially heinous, atrocious, and cruel—and therefore deserving of the death penalty—he added, "A lot of his character would indicate that this is not your typical criminal defendant."

Also looking ahead, reporter Sue Carlton wrote in the *Saint Petersburg Times*, "They (Smithers's attorneys) are expected to argue that Smithers suffered brain damage, and that he was a good suburban husband, father, churchgoer and working man."

There was much to support this portrait of Sam Smithers. Called as a character witness in the penalty phase, one of his four brothers testified that in the intensely religious Tennessee home of Sam's childhood, he had regularly "felt the sting of a leather belt" swung by their mother during nightly "devotions" of singing and reading. The lashes were intended to "beat the devil" out of him. Robert Smithers told jurors how the brothers listened as their father beat their mother.

Sam had first gotten into trouble, Robert continued, after he put out a fire at church and became a local hero. Sam had been so thrilled at all the attention, he set other small fires, always making sure he was on hand to put them out.

As a baby, Sam had fallen on his head and had once been hit over the head with a shotgun by a robber at a gas station.

A defense psychiatrist said Smithers suffered from extreme mental and emotional disturbance when he murdered the women.

Sam's son, Jonathan, testified that Sam had been "the best kind of dad."

During a rare Saturday session of court, Sharon Smithers (now remarried) testified that nothing in her 23-year marriage could have prepared her for the day her mild-mannered husband was charged with murdering two prostitutes. "Not Sam," she said, shaking her head. "No way."

When she asked him how he could have done such a thing, she told jurors, Sam replied, "Sharon, it was like I was just standing back and watching somebody else do it."

As expected, the prosecution countered by arguing that Smithers had been deliberate in carrying out the murders

and in trying to conceal them. On an even rarer Sunday session of the court, Ed Schmoll asked for the death penalty for two murders carried out with "cold, calculated, and premeditated design."

After ninety minutes of deliberation, the jury recommended to Judge Fuente that Smithers be sentenced to death.

Before a presentence hearing convened on April 15, 1999, John Cowan, the father of one of the victims, sent a letter to Judge Fuente to plead for Smithers's life. He wrote, "My hope for Mr. Smithers is that he will live long enough for the hate and rage to die out, and that sometime in his life he might do something that will change the life of a fellow prisoner for the better. If sometime in the future, Mr. Smithers comes to fully understand the horror of what he has done, and if he is truly and deeply sorry for it, and if he tries to make his remaining time on Earth count for something—inside the prison walls—then I will feel some easing of this awful pain that seems to have no end."

Judge Fuente rendered his decision on June 25, 1999. He termed Cowan's letter "very genuine" and said he gave it great weight in making his decision. But he found that those considerations were outweighed by the cold and calculated nature of the murders. In accepting the recommendation of the jury that Smithers be sentenced to death, he stated, "Each homicide was extremely torturous to each victim."

Said prosecutor Ed Schmoll, "Frankly, I think what the judge did was the only thing he could do."

Thirteen

From Russia With Malice

In 1971 there were better places for a young woman with an appetite for luxuries to be than the Ukraine in the Union of Soviet Socialist Republics. That Rita Gluzman was Jewish in a region that had never been hospitable to Jews didn't make living any easier. Going to Israel with her husband, Yakov, she decided, was the answer to her problem. Her parents had moved there in 1970 and seemed very happy.

Born in 1948, Rita Shapiro had met Yakov Gluzman and fallen in love with him when they were teenagers. The brilliant young man she called "Yasha" planned to become a biologist. Because this goal required years of study, marriage had to be delayed until he'd earned a degree from Moscow State University. With that accomplished, the Gluzmans applied for permission to emigrate to Israel. Rita was granted an exit visa, but the answer from the bureaucrats in Moscow regarding Yakov leaving the country was *"nyet."* The Soviet Union was engaged in a prolonged life-and-death struggle with the United States in which science was more and more vital to victory. In such a state of crisis, Yakov Gluzman was "too valuable" to lose.

Infuriated by the denial of a visa, he retaliated against the red tape by giving up being a biologist and taking up carpentry. But Moscow was unrelenting. No matter what Yakov called himself, he was still a scientist and people in that category were not given exit visas. Rita was free to go, the bureaucrats said, but Yakov must stay.

After a year of continuous pleading, the Gluzmans decided that they might have more luck in winning his freedom if she carried on the fight from Israel. The government of the Jewish state was achieving some success in wrenching permissions from Moscow for emigration of what sympathetic Western governments and a worldwide press termed "Soviet Jewry." Reasoning that diplomatic pressure from Tel Aviv might attain what a mere husband and wife had been unable to achieve, the Gluzmans agreed that she would accept her departure visa, go to Israel, and then carry on the struggle.

She left in the spring of 1970 and soon after arriving in Israel learned that she was pregnant. Born in December, the boy was named Ilan. Pleading with Moscow on behalf of a child in need of a father, Rita Gluzman was again rebuffed. So were Israeli diplomats. Undaunted, feisty, and smart, Rita set her sights on a bigger world power. Traveling to the United States, she gained a meeting with Congressman Benjamin Rosenthal. A member of the Foreign Relations Committee of the House of Representatives and chairman of its subcommittee on Europe, the New York Democrat was a vociferous fighter for free emigration of Soviet Jewry and was constanly pressuring Secretary of State William Rogers to in turn put the squeeze on Anatoly Dobrynin, the Soviet ambassador in Washington, D.C. Unfortunately for the Gluzmans, the Nixon administration had other fish to fry in its delicate relations with the Soviets.

If Rita Gluzman understood anything about how to get things done in the United States, it was the truth of the old American saying, "The squeaking wheel gets the grease," and the most effective way for squeaking to be heard was through the American news media, especially television. In a daring attempt to attract the ears and eyes of the men who decided what was a newsworthy story, she arrived one day on New York City's First Avenue. Directly opposite the headquarters of the United Nations, she announced that until the Soviet Union let her husband go she would stay on First Avenue and conduct a hunger strike. Reporters and camera crews flocked to her.

"My child will soon be old enough to speak," Gluzman said to a reporter from the *New York Daily News,* "and I'm afraid he will be asking, 'Where is Papa?' "

Day after day when the United Nations' Secretary General U. Thant looked down on First Avenue from his thirty-eighth floor office, he saw Rita Gluzman holding a placard demanding the release of her husband from "Soviet captivity," surrounded by crowds of New Yorkers, tourists, and journalists. The daily circuslike scene also confronted members of the USSR's mission to the U.N. Located in the middle of a block of East Sixty-ninth Street, the converted apartment house had to be shielded by police department barricades at each end of the street to keep away growing throngs of protesters sympathetic to Rita's plight. At a moment when Moscow and the Nixon administration were engaged in sensitive negotiations on contentious cold war issues, such as the war in Vietnam and the powder keg that was the Middle East, the hunger strike of a nettlesome woman on behalf of a scientist-husband masquerading as a carpenter was not only an insult to the dignity of a superpower, but an embarrassment to communism in the heart of the capitalist world.

Finding similar protesters outside the Soviet embassy in Washington, D.C., and under constant pressure from the USSR's diplomats in New York, as well as fielding almost daily inquiries from the U.S. Department of State, Ambassador Dobrynin finally had quite enough of the Gluzmans. He cabled Moscow that in his opinion the only recourse for ending the woman's hunger strike was to send Yakov Gluzman merrily on his way.

Yakov arrived to Rita's warm embrace in December 1971. Settled with husband and son, the wife whom Yakov described as "very single-minded and uncompromising" made up her mind to improve her status by earning a master's degree in chemistry. This did not sit well with Yakov. Nor was Rita happy to discover that her husband was required to serve a tour of duty in the Israeli Army before proceeding to earn a doctorate in molecular biology.

A further irritation to Yakov Gluzman upon his return from army service was learning that Rita had incurred large debts while he was away. By 1977 the marriage was shaky. However, each hoped that it could be saved—and their fortunes improved—if they left Israel for the United States. If Yakov accepted, he could have a position with the prestigious Cold Spring Harbor Laboratories on Long Island. A further enticement to go to New York was an opportunity for him to work with Nobel Prize–winning scientist James Watson.

Yakov Gluzman would stay with the organization ten years and distinguish himself by making a scientific breakthrough in cellular biology that would be used in cancer research worldwide.

America also proved a boon to Rita. She developed a promising career in a company that manufactured sophisticated electronic test-and-control equipment. It seemed that the girl from the Ukraine had achieved the American dream. She enjoyed vacations, dined in the best restaurants, shopped in the most upscale stores, and looked forward to sending Ilan to one of the finest universities in the country. So never mind that from time to time her husband complained about her extravagances and griped to her and their friends that she was a spendthrift.

These grousings notwithstanding, when she informed Yakov she intended to start an electronics business, he lent a generous hand in financing a firm she named ECI Technologies. But when he came home one day with the news that he had accepted a better-paying job with the Lederle pharmaceutical firm in New Jersey, Rita was shocked. She complained that the move would ruin her fledgling business. Yakov replied that they were moving, and that was that.

Very well, said Rita, if they had to go to New Jersey the only acceptable place to live was exclusive Saddle River.

She also insisted that they would be joined there by her sister and her three children, who were on their way to the United States from Russia. There would be plenty of room, she pointed out, because Ilan was soon to leave home to enroll at Berkeley University in California.

The Saddle River home cost $530,000. But it soon turned into a disaster. It had severe flooding and septic problems. Rita started calling it "the shack." Yakov bridled at what he said was her constant complaining and condescending attitude.

In part to get away from the domestic unpleasantness, partly for business reasons, and to see his parents who had settled in Israel from Russia, Yakov Gluzman began making trips to Israel without his wife. Each time he returned from these excursions he spoke about returning to Israel permanently and starting a business there. Rita was not amused.

Increasingly distraught over Yakov's frequent trips, and not at all pleased that her electronics firm was not as thriving an enterprise as she'd hoped, Rita discovered letters between Yakov and the office of Senator Bill Bradley of New Jersey seeking the U.S. Senate Democrat's influence in obtaining a visa for an Israeli woman to come to America. She suspected the woman was a girlfriend of Yakov's. She was right.

He'd met Raisa Korenblit at a shopping mall in Hadera, Israel, in August 1974. She was a twenty-nine-year-old immigrant from the USSR, having arrived in 1990, who worked as a bacteriologist in a laboratory near Hadera. After Gluzman returned to the United States they kept in touch by exchanging letters. When he was in Israel again on business, friendship blossomed into romance—Raisa's first. In September 1995 Gluzman ended her virginity.

Confronted with his wife's suspicions, Gluzman denied engaging in an affair. He said he was merely helping the young woman. Rita declared the denial "incredible" and went on to accuse him of secretly sending thousands of dollars of "our money" to his parents. Yakov said he was returning, a little at a time, some $100,000 his father had asked him to hold for him. Rita believed not a word.

After twenty-seven years of marriage, forty-seven-year-old Rita and forty-nine-year-old Yakov separated. He left the Saddle River house and took up residence in an apartment in the town of Pearl River in nearby Rockland County, New York. Then came a series of meetings with lawyers to hammer out details of the dissolution of the marriage. But, inexplicably, on April 5, 1996, Rita did not show up for what was to have been a crucial discussion of unsettled issues.

Rather than meet with her husband, Rita sought out a cousin she had assisted in leaving Russia, Vladimir Zelenin. A forty-year-old employee in Rita's company, he lived in Fair Lawn, New Jersey, and depended entirely on Rita for his livelihood. He also appreciated that there were no guarantees that Rita would come out of the divorce with sufficient resources to keep her business and to maintain the lifestyle to which she'd become accustomed.

Sitting in Zelenin's modest home, they talked and talked about their possibly grim prospects and what they might do to secure both their futures. On that topic, Vladimir soon learned, Rita had a plan.

The goal was to murder Yakov. And she had a date in mind.

"It must be before April seventh," she explained, because on that Sunday—the Christian holiday of Easter—Yakov would be coming to the Saddle River house to collect his things. For that reason they had to kill him the night *before* at his Pearl River apartment.

Zelenin asked how this could be done.

They would need axes. They would wear rubber gloves. And they would need lots of large plastic garbage bags. The body would be cut up and placed in them, and Zelenin would take them in his car for dumping in the Passaic River, near his home.

At 10:40 on Easter Sunday morning Officer Richard Freeman of the East Rutherford, New Jersey, police department, on a routine patrol of an industrial area along the Passaic River waterfront, drove past a deserted parking lot and spotted a blue Ford Taurus with its trunk wide open. Suspecting the car might have been stolen and abandoned, he stopped next to it and started to run a routine check of the license plate number. At that moment he saw a man running toward the car from the riverbank. Confronting him, Freeman demanded to see his driver's license and auto registration. As they were produced, Freeman noticed that one of the very nervous-looking man's hands was bandaged and both hands were bloody. The name on the driver's license was Vladimir Zelenin. The registration was in the name of nearby ECI Technologies.

Looking into the front of the car, Freeman saw several bulky plastic bags. Some of them also had blood on them. While his immediate thought was that Zelenin was dumping trash in the river, a criminal offense, the blood suggested something more sinister was afoot. This suspicion provided him, under police procedure, with probable cause to search the bags. In the first he found a rubber glove, shower curtain, scrub brush, kitchen knives, hacksaw, hatchet, and an axe.

Advising Zelenin that he was under arrest, Freeman handcuffed him and informed him of his right to remain silent and to have the services of a lawyer. Asked if he understood, Zelenin gave a nod and muttered something in broken English that sounded to Freeman like Polish. He used his radio to summon help. Three minutes later, Police Officer Todd McQuade arrived. Briefed by Freeman, he watched Zelenin while Freeman opened other bags.

In the first he found what appeared to be a human liver and gallbladder. Turning to McQuade, he said, "Todd, this isn't animal guts."

A second bag held a skinned human skull.

At this point Freeman realized he had evidently stumbled onto a homicide, and that if the man in custody was to be questioned, a translator would be required. He radioed police headquarters a report of the find and requested someone who spoke Polish.

"No, Russian," blurted Zelenin. "I speak Russian."

"Vladimir," said Officer Freeman, hoping he'd be understood, "are these parts from a human body?"

"Yes."

"Male or female?"

"Male."

"Whose are they?"

Zelenin exclaimed, "More, more."

"More what?"

Zelenin pointed to a Maxima automobile, at the rear of the lot. "More parts."

The Maxima was stuffed with bags of body parts, too.

Presently, the parking lot swarmed with police, including Sergeant Tom Goldrick, the senior investigator for the Bergen County D.A.'s office. While they established a crime scene and launched the painstaking work of collecting and preserving evidence and cataloging which body part came out of which bag, Freeman and McQuade took Zelenin to police headquarters.

At three in the afternoon Goldrick arrived in the detectives' squad room to question the prisoner as best he could, pending arrival of a Russian interpreter from the FBI. Goldrick's first aim was to identify the victim. He asked, "Whose body is it we found in the car, Mr. Zelenin?"

"Body is Yakov Gluzman. He is scientist. We killed him in Pearl River."

"We?"

"We, me and Rita, his wife."

"Rita? The deceased's wife is named Rita Gluzman?"

"Yes."

Because the murder had occurred in Pearl River, New York, Goldrick recognized the likelihood that the case would be transferred there for prosecution. But its success would depend in large measure on the quality of the investigation being conducted in East Rutherford, New Jersey. With luck, by the time the case was handed over, it would be iron-clad. It might even be closed in short order if Vladimir Zelenin could be persuaded that it was in his best interest to continue talking.

No persuasion was needed. Over several hours, assisted by the FBI interpreter, Zelenin related a tale of cold-blooded planning and execution of a grisly axe murder that fascinated and horrified veteran detectives accustomed to investigating shootings, strangulations, knifings, and even bludgeonings. This was murder by axe and hatchet in which the corpse had been cut up with a hacksaw by a man who'd been bullied into helping a coldhearted woman by the name of Rita Gluzman. Why? Because she feared that if her husband divorced her, she wouldn't be able to continue enjoying a life of luxury.

Zelenin proved to be a storyteller as riveting as anyone who'd ever spun a horror yarn. In halting English and through the smooth translation of the interpreter, he related how Yakov Gluzman had walked into a murderous trap designed and laid by the very woman who had gone to such extraordinary lengths—they could only be described as heroic—in order to pluck him from behind the Iron Curtain.

The woman who'd told a newspaper reporter, "My child will soon be old enough to speak and I'm afraid he will be asking, 'Where is Papa?'" had on the previous night, if Zelenin were to be believed, lurked in the dark in her husband's house in Pearl River, waiting for him to come home while she gripped an axe with one hand and held a hatchet in the other.

Gluzman had entered the apartment around 11:30 Saturday night. Zelenin was sure of the time because two o'clock Sunday morning was the change-over hour from standard to daylight savings time, and Rita was worried that with clocks being moved forward they would have one less hour to carry out her plan before the sun came up. They'd bought what they needed—the hatchet and hacksaw and large plastic bags—at a home-supply store. The axe belonged to Yakov.

The moment Yakov opened the door, Rita swung the hatchet, then the axe. In two swift strokes that split and crushed his head, she aborted a divorce.

Goldrick asked Zelenin, "Why not dump the body in the woods?"

"Yakov was too big to carry out in one piece."

Later, Zelenin would be asked by a prosecutor how he knew how to dismember a body.

"I didn't have any experience ever about how to cut a body," he replied. "But I did—I used to take animals apart where I lived. It was natural. Everybody knew how to cut up an animal. Also, I did hunting, so I knew how to cut up an animal. I broke the knife. It got stuck in Yakov's body and it broke, the blade."

How had Zelenin cut his hand?

It got in the way when Rita Gluzman swung the axe. On the way back to New Jersey after they had killed Yakov, they'd stopped at a drugstore to buy bandages. The plan had been to murder Gluzman, dismember the body in the bathtub, clean up the mess in the apartment, and dispose of the bagged body parts in the river. They needed two cars. Zelenin would then drive Rita Gluzman home to Saddle River so she would have an alibi. He would then return to the river to get rid of the bags. Rita had selected the spot to dump the bodies because it was near her company's offices, where cars that belonged to the firm would not seem out of place.

While Zelenin was telling his story, detectives headed to Rita's house in Saddle River. It was possible that Zelenin's story implicating Rita Gluzman was a tissue of lies. But if it was true, she ranked in history's roster of axe-murdering women right up there with Kate Webster, Miss Lizzie Borden, and Karla Faye Tucker. When the police discovered Rita was not at home, Detective Goldrick asked Zelenin if he had any idea where she might be.

"Nyet."

Until she could be found and questioned, there was no knowing if she were the stone-cold killer Vladimir Zelenin had described. She might be innocent. She might be a material witness. She might be dead, killed along with her husband. But the fact that she couldn't be located dead or alive tipped the scales toward suspicion that everything Zelenin had said was the awful truth. In addition to law enforcement agencies and security personnel in the New York metropolitan region's airports, train stations, and bus depots to be on the lookout for her, the news media were provided photos of Rita Gluzman and told that she was wanted for questioning.

With the top stories of Easter Sunday night and Monday's wake-up TV news shows, drive-time radio newscasts, and morning newspapers—not only in New Jersey and New York, but across the country—all focused similarly, Americans again proved the truth of Edmund Pearson's maxim that one of the great sensational moments in our civilization is a woman on trial for her life. While Rita Gluzman was yet to be found, *hardly* anyone who heard or read that she was the object of a vast police dragnet voiced that other maxim of the American way: Anyone accused or even only suspected of a crime must be considered innocent until proven guilty at the bar of justice.

Another popular saying holds that the wheels of justice turn exceedingly slowly, and in many instances this cliche, like all cliches, is based on experience. But in the murder of Yakov Gluzman the wheels were turning rapidly as the case moved out of the hands of the East Rutherford police and the Bergen County D.A. into those of the District Attorney of Rockland County, New York, Michael Bongiorno. Along with the case went the admitted participant and the key witness against Rita Gluzman. Transported from a jail in Hackensack, New Jersey, Zelenin took up residence in the Rockland County jail, a foreboding old structure adjacent to the relatively new Rockland County administration building whose top-floor offices housed Bongiorno and his staff.

Appointed district attorney by Governor George Pataki in May 1995 after the resignation of Kenneth Gribetz, Bongiorno was a Rockland County native, Republican, magna cum laude graduate of Washington and Lee Law School, and for fourteen years had served as an assistant D.A. in New York City. He'd been elected to a four-year term as Rockland D.A. in November 1995. Now, ten months after taking over as D.A., he'd received a murder that qualified under a new state law as a death penalty case. But there were two problems, one legal and one practical. First, under New York law no one could be convicted of murder solely on the testimony of an accomplice. Second, the primary suspect in the murder of Yakov Gluzman was not in custody.

By all appearances she had driven away from Saddle River in her blue 1995 Taurus and then vanished, but evidently not by way of the region's airports, assuming she did not possess a passport bearing her picture but someone else's name. A check of credit card companies showed that her credit cards had not been used since the day before the murder. Neither her family nor friends knew where she might be, or if they did, they weren't saying. All that could be done was wait for a break of some kind, perhaps a sighting of the car. By Thursday evening, no such break had come along.

All that changed the next morning when Bongiorno's assistant, Lou Valvo, took a call from the police in Laurel Hollow, a village in Nassau County, Long Island, informing him that Rita Gluzman was in their custody. She had been discovered on the campus of Cold Spring Harbor Laboratories, Yakov Gluzman's former employer, and was being held for trespassing. In her possession, the caller reported, were several maps, travel guides for Switzerland, hair coloring, several passports, and a set of Henckel knives. When her car was found in a parking lot, it bore a set of stolen New York state license plates. In due course, Nassau County police would charge her with trespassing and the added offense of possessing stolen property.

On the basis of the possibility that murder might be added to the charges, and deeming her a flight risk, Nassau County judge Claire Weinberg ordered Rita Gluzman held without bail. Under New York law the Rockland D.A. had six days to file a murder charge. But there was the serious problem of the New York law excluding conviction on the basis of the uncorroborated testimony of an accomplice.

This provision had vexed Bongiorno's predecessor, Kenneth Gribetz, in a case that the press labeled the "Death Mask" murder. A man who confessed to killing a male model, Eigil Dag Vesti, whose naked body had been found wearing a black hood used in sadomasochistic rituals, claimed that the murder had been carried out on the orders of a wealthy and influential art dealer, Andrew Crispo. Without corroborating evidence, he could not be charged and went free.

Possessing no solid evidence to corroborate Vladimir Zelenin's story, D.A. Bongiorno faced a similar unhappy prospect with Rita Gluzman, with time running out on the statutory requirement that unless Gluzman was charged, she must be released. Were that to happen, Bongiorno knew that Gluzman would make a hasty departure, probably to the safe haven of Switzerland, where the law did not permit extradition of anyone who might face a death penalty.

Enter, the U.S. government in the person of an assistant to the United States Attorney for the Southern District of New York, Cathy Seibel. Her assistant, Marjorie Miller, had pointed out that under provisions of the newly enacted Interstate Domestic Violence Act, signed by President Bill Clinton in 1994, the federal government was authorized to prosecute anyone who'd crossed state borders in order to avoid prosecution for domestic violence. The law had been intended to protect women.

With the time for her to be charged with murder having elapsed, Rita Gluzman pleaded guilty to the trespassing and stolen-property charges, posted $250,000 bail pending sentencing, and was on her way out of the courthouse, and possibly out of the country, when she found herself stopped by agents of the FBI. They carried a warrant for her arrest under the Domestic Violence Act.

The United States Attorney for the Southern District of New York, Mary Jo White, said, "This is just the kind of case the new federal law was designed for." Ironically, the law was being invoked for the first time *against* a woman for killing a man. Should Rita Gluzman be convicted, she could get a sentence of life imprisonment with no possibility of parole or pardon.

Deprived of prosecuting Rita because of the lack of independent corroboration on Zelenin's story, Rockland County D.A. Michael Bongiorno put the best face on a bad situation. "When you have an investigation that cuts across state lines," he told reporters, "it is very difficult for a prosecutor's office, especially a small prosecutor's office, to effectively do everything the federal government can do."

In fact, the Rockland County D.A.'s office under former D.A. Kenneth Gribetz had prosecuted some of the largest and most sensational criminal cases in the recent history of New York. In addition to the "Death Mask" case, Gribetz had prosecuted a gang of political radicals for the murder of an armored-car guard and a policeman during an aborted holdup at a shopping mall. The star defendant in that case had been Kathy Boudin, a long-sought member of the Weatherman terrorist group, who was last seen fleeing stark naked from the explosion of a basement bomb factory in a Greenwich Village town house in the 1970s.

Hardly in that criminal category, Rita Gluzman was held without bail on the federal charge and would stand trial in federal court.

Said an FBI agent as Gluzman was led away, "She's a modern Lizzie Borden."

A colorful comparison, but not true, of course. The murder weapons were different. So were the victims' relationship to the accused. Rita had an accomplice; Lizzie was accused of acting alone. The bodies of Mr. and Mrs. Borden were left intact where they were killed; Yakov Gluzman's corpse had to be reassembled by a coroner. In Lizzie's case, there had been reasonable doubt that she'd done it, but no aura of wonder surrounded Rita.

Certainly, there was a parallel in terms of attention paid to the murders by the press. On April 19, 1996, the Associated Press wire reported, "A New Jersey woman was charged Thursday with taking part in the ax murder of her scientist husband and devising an attempted cover-up in which the body was cut into pieces and dumped in a New Jersey river."

Documents filed in federal court alleged that she killed Yakov Gluzman to gain control of the company they jointly owned. But eight months after the lodging of the murder charge, Rita Gluzman was also formally accused in a superseding indictment of having blackmailed Yakov with photos of him and another woman, tapping his phone, and threatening "the safety and reputations" of members of his family. According to the new bill of indictment filed by Assistant U.S. Attorney Cathy Seibel on December 13,

1996, Rita's attempt at extortion demanded "money and interests in businesses."

On the eve of the trial in the federal court in White Plains, New York, AP correspondent Jim Fitzgerald provided what is known in journalism as a "scene setter" and sometimes known as a "curtain raiser." The story began, "The prosecution says she's a calculating butcher, so fearful of divorce and a more frugal lifestyle that she killed her husband with an ax and had him cut into more than 60 pieces. The defense says she's an innocent out of 'The Crucible,' the victim of the real killer's deal with the government. The key witness is expected to be her cousin, Vladimir Zelenin, who has pleaded guilty to state and federal charges and has admitted taking part in the killing. Zelenin, who got out of Kazakhstan with the Gluzmans' help and worked for them, is hoping for a 2-year rather than a 25-year minimum term when he is sentenced."

The comparison to the 1950s drama about seventeenth-century witch hunts, trials, and executions by burning at the stake in Salem, Massachusetts, written by Arthur Miller as a metaphor for the investigation of communists by Senator Joseph R. McCarthy, had been made by Rita Gluzman's lawyer, Lawrence Hochheiser. "They get people to confess to being witches," he'd said after seeing the movie version of the play a week earlier. "If you confess, you don't get hanged. But you have to name names."

The trial opened on January 6, 1997, in Westchester County in the federal court of Judge Barrington Parker with no crowds gathered outside calling for leniency for Rita Gluzman as they had for Karla Faye Tucker. Yakov's family had come from Israel. So had Raisa Korenblit. Also attending were Yakov's former coworkers at Lederle. Lending support for Rita were her son, Ilan, her mother, Paula Shapiro, and sister Marianne Rabinowitz. They sat behind Rita and her lawyers, Larry Hochheiser and Michael Rosen.

Leading the prosecution was Cathy Seibel. Described in

one account of the trial as looking as tidy as the editor of a law journal, she was diminutive and liked her curly brown hair cut short. Her associates were Assistant U.S. Attorney Deirdre M. Daly and Lou Valvo from Rockland County's D.A.'s office, who was deputized for the purpose of the trial as Special Assistant U.S. Attorney. The team had spent nine months preparing for this climactic moment.

Opening for the government, Seibel declared, "This is a case about a brutal, cold-blooded murder, a murder that this defendant set in motion, this defendant planned, this defendant committed, and this defendant attempted to cover up. It is the murder of Yakov Gluzman, the defendant's husband." Rita Gluzman had done this "horrendous crime," she said, because Yakov had moved out and filed for divorce so he could start a new life with a girlfriend he'd met in Israel. "The defendant was angry, jealous, and desperately afraid that without her husband and his money, she would lose her business and her comfortable lifestyle. So she wiretapped the phone in her husband's apartment. She sent anonymous threatening letters to her husband and his father demanding large sums of money, and when neither of these crimes stopped her husband from going through with the divorce, she turned to the most monstrous crime of all: murder."

To do this, Seibel continued, she had recruited her cousin, "a recent Russian immigrant, a man who spoke little English, and was entirely dependent on her for his money, his job, his car, and his home."

On the night of April 6 of last year, Seibel went on, Vladimir Zelenin and Rita had armed themselves with axes and lay in wait in Yakov's apartment, and when he came through his door, "they attacked him with those axes and killed him. Later, the cousin dismembered the victim's body while the defendant cleaned up the blood that had been spilled."

Seibel then related a story that seemed to be the realization of "the American Dream" by a couple who had escaped from behind the Iron Curtain.

"When they were young," said Seibel, referring to Rita and Yakov, "the defendant [Rita] had struggled to get her husband permission to leave Russia. They and their son, Ilan, eventually settled in the United States. [Yakov] worked as a molecular biologist doing cancer research, and the defendant worked as a molecular biologist in the field of chemistry. In the late eighties, they started a company called ECI Technology, which specialized in electroplating equipment. Yakov Gluzman and the defendant co-owned the company. The defendant was president of ECI and worked there full time. While Yakov helped out with ECI, he worked full time elsewhere. At the time of his death, he worked in Lederle Labs, in Pearl River, New York, in Rockland County. ECI was located in East Rutherford, New Jersey, in Bergen County, right next to Rockland, and the Gluzman home was also in Bergen County, in Upper Saddle River."

Seibel's recitation of the biographies of the Gluzmans now took a dark turn.

"The evidence will show that the Gluzmans had marital problems. Finally, Yakov Gluzman moved out of the family home in early 1995 and took a small apartment in Pearl River, near his work. Through his lawyer, he tried to negotiate a property settlement with the defendant, but when she rejected the agreement, he filed for divorce. He also found a new woman in his life, Raisa Korenblit, who lived in Israel, as did Yakov Gluzman's brother and parents. When the defendant learned about Yakov's relationship with Raisa, she was furious and became obsessed with breaking up their relationship, even though she and Yakov were separated and living apart. The evidence will show that in fall 1995, the defendant hired a private investigator and asked him to try to keep Raisa Korenblit out of the United States, saying that Raisa was trying to break up an

American family, a family that in reality had already been broken up.

"The evidence will also show that in the fall of 1995, the defendant hired a security expert to go to Yakov Gluzman's apartment with her. The defendant had a key to the apartment. She lied and told the security man it was her own apartment and that she wanted him to search it for listening devices and bugs. What she wanted was information about her husband's phone lines and equipment she could use to secretly record her husband's calls. You'll learn that once the defendant got that information and equipment, she hid a small microcassette recorder behind the refrigerator in Yakov Gluzman's kitchen and illegally taped his telephone conversations and messages. You'll see the equipment she used and the tapes she made.

"The evidence will also show that Rita Gluzman committed another crime arising out of anger at her husband, her jealousy of his relationship with Raisa Korenblit, and the fear that the divorce would deprive her of the company and her lifestyle. In September of 1995, the defendant traveled to Israel. It was a business trip, but it had another purpose as well. Knowing that Yakov Gluzman was also in Israel at the time, the defendant hired an Israeli private investigator named David Rom and paid him to gather information about Raisa Korenblit, the woman Yakov Gluzman had been seeing. David Rom, in turn, hired another private investigator, Benny Lefkowitz, who took pictures of Raisa and Yakov together and gave the pictures, along with other information, to David Rom."

Seibel described Rita's futile attempts at extortion, then moved on to the murder plot.

"Rita Gluzman was becoming more and more desperate. The divorce case was proceeding and the defendant and her husband were battling over money and over control of ECI. The defendant was panicked at the thought of losing her husband to Raisa, losing the lifestyle her husband's substantial income had supported, and losing the company that she headed and that paid so much. That winter, the defendant contacted another private investigator, seeking his help in preventing Raisa Korenblit from coming to the United States. The defendant suggested that the private investigator plant cocaine on Raisa and have her arrested, and that he spread rumors that Raisa was HIV positive. When the private investigator didn't go along with the suggestions, and when her wiretapping and her extortionate threats didn't do anything to stop Yakov Gluzman's resolve to divorce, the defendant's thoughts turned to murder.

"And to whom did she turn to assist her in the murder? Her cousin, Vladimir Zelenin, the one individual in the world who was almost completely dependent on her. Zelenin, you will learn, was a widower, with two children, new to the United States, not authorized to work here, speaking little English. The defendant was good to Zelenin, giving him a job at ECI and an ECI company car, and letting him and his children stay in the apartment in Fair Lawn that ECI paid for.

"You are not going to like Vladimir Zelenin," she warned the jurors. "And rightfully so. He did an unspeakable thing and his reasons for doing so don't remotely begin to justify his actions. But the question of whether Vladimir Zelenin did something terrible is not an issue in this trial. Everyone is going to agree that he did it, including Zelenin himself.

"The issue is whether Vladimir Zelenin is telling the truth when he tells you about Rita Gluzman's participation in the murder," said Seibel. "It will be up to you to evaluate his testimony, to decide if he has more to gain by lying or telling the truth."

Now it was time for the defense attorney to address the jurors.

On the tallish side, rumpled-looking, and with the manner of a folksy country lawyer, but a veteran of innumerable courtroom frays, Larry Hochheiser began his opening statement by asserting that Rita Gluzman was "absolutely innocent" and that he found it "very difficult to stand here with the responsibility of a woman's fate in my hands" after hearing "a pretty awesome" opening statement by the prosecution. But on what did the government case rest? Who is Vladimir Zelenin? To say that he is an animal is to give a bad name to animals.

Recognizing a workable comparison when he saw one, Hochheiser returned to the analogy of the Salem witch trials dramatized in *The Crucible*. "The witch, the cold-blooded murderer, Vladimir Zelenin, comes in and says, 'I saw Rita Gluzman with the devil,' and the government takes this witness to their bosom. The government, these people who are the government, they accept what this guy says."

Hochheiser continued, "You may look at me and be saying, why should we listen to him? Sure, this guy, he gets paid by Rita Gluzman. You're absolutely right. You shouldn't be listening to me even if I am telling you the truth and His Honor told you that. She would swear it's this way, and I'd swear it's the other way, and she gets paid by the United States attorney and I get paid by the defendant, and that wouldn't work, would it? So I'm asking you to sit here and look at the evidence with us as it goes in and see what's really going on.

"When I say to you that I would look at me skeptically, I would also have to ask myself this question: Why am I so skeptical? Do I sit here and believe that innocent people do not go to trial? Do I sit here and believe that these three lawyers and these two FBI agents are so infallible that only guilty people come to trial? We wouldn't need jurors if that were true. We wouldn't have chosen you. So as you sit here and listen to me and listen to the evidence in the case, ask yourself: What does the trial of an innocent person look like? Now, the trial of an innocent person looks in this courtroom, and in all courtrooms across America, very much like the trial of a guilty person. The difference is in that question of 'he said, she said'—says who? If Vladimir

Zelenin were telling the truth, he would be corroborated, he would be verified."

Dismissing the star prosecution witness with contempt, he fired a broadside at prosecutors in general and Seibel in particular. "It's chilling to me when a prosecutor stands up—they all start with, 'This is a case about drugs and money and murder,' you know, it's like a book. This is a case about murder, and whatever. . . . Cathy Seibel is telling you in different words, 'I got a motive which is money and a body which is dead. Don't confuse me with the facts.' "

Faulting Seibel for following a tried-and-true script was ironic because Hochheiser's own opening statement was a variation of one he'd used in numerous criminal trials.

The defense attorney then turned to the key question in every criminal trial:

"The question is, did these people prove beyond a reasonable doubt Rita Gluzman's guilt, not whether I proved she is innocent. There are cases where sometimes a jury never knows what happened at the end. There are cases where lawyers never know what happened at the end, but you do not know that an innocent person is not going to be convicted if you follow those rules, that you will acquit unless the government proves the defendant guilty beyond a reasonable doubt. That's what innocence means to us under these rules."

Openings concluded, the prosecution began laying out its premise that Rita Gluzman had planned and carried out the murder with her cousin with a motive as old as murder itself. The same kind of jealousy that drove Rita to kill had prompted Cain to pick up the nearest blunt instrument and bang his brother Abel over the head with it. There was a second motive driving Rita, claimed the prosecutors— greed. To show this they brought to the witness stand the private eye Gluzman had asked to bug her husband's apartment in an attempt to learn more about his adulterous affair. Arguably the most colorful witness for the prosecution, private detective Joe Mullen specialized in matrimonial work. He told jurors of Rita Gluzman's "preoccupation" with Raisa Korenblit whom Rita saw as "a prostitute" and a threat to "an American family." During one visit to defense attorney Michael Rosen's office in New York, he testified, she inquired as to whether Rosen could find some way to keep Korenblit from being allowed to leave Israel. Next to the stand came a self-defined expert on bugging to enthrall jurors and spectators with an account of placing a bug behind a refrigerator in an apartment he'd been led to believe was Rita's but was actually Yakov's.

To bolster the greed aspect of the case, prosecutors called divorce lawyer Nicholas Nasarenko. He said Rita Gluzman had demanded Yakov give up his half-interest in ECI Technologies so that she would be in full control. Her obsession with money was the subject of testimony by Yakov's brother Michael. He told of Rita's clumsy attempts through anonymous letters demanding $100,000 and then $50,000 in order to prevent Yakov's affair with Korenblit from becoming a public scandal.

When Korenblit was put on the stand to describe her relationship with Yakov, jurors saw and heard not the prostitute of Rita's description, but an innocent-looking, shy young woman whose living was earned in Israel by working in agriculture.

Neighbors of Yakov Gluzman took the stand to tell of seeing a woman and a balding man entering Yakov's automobile on Easter morning.

With that, the government called its star witness, the balding Vladimir Zelenin, who had marked his fortieth birthday in the Rockland County jail. To lay the groundwork for what he was about to tell the jury the prosecution questioned him about the deal he had made—no less than twenty years, possibly more, depending on Judge Parker's evaluation of the worth of what he had to say about the murder. Asked what he'd done to warrant reduction of his penalty from one of life imprisonment, Zelenin answered and an interpreter translated his statement into English, "I acknowledged my guilt in the state court that I had committed the crime together with Rita Gluzman. I acknowledged the killing in the second degree, and I have acknowledged the guilt I had, in order to commit the crime together with Rita Gluzman, crossed the line."

By "crossing the line" he meant he and Rita had traversed state boundaries in violation of the federal domestic abuse law.

"We crossed the state line of New Jersey, New York," he said. "We used axes. We both attacked Yakov Gluzman when he returned home, and after he died, his body was cut up, by me. I was cutting the body, and Rita Gluzman was cleaning the blood that was on the floor."

Using the power she had over him, he said, Rita had forced him into doing her bidding. "I couldn't decline, because if I decline, then I would be thinking Rita will do everything to get rid of me and say return to Brooklyn or somewhere. I didn't have the means to do that."

After he told her he did not have access to a gun or an axe, he said, they went to a hardware store. "And we bought the ax, and the hacksaw," he continued. "The ax we were going to use in order to attack Yakov and kill him. The reason for the hacksaw was so that Yakov's body would be cut up. There was a conversation that Yakov was such a large man and that there was a problem how to get rid of the body out of the apartment, well, someone would notice it. That's why we decide that the body is going to be cut up."

The axe and hacksaw were produced for the jurors to see.

"For all these items," said Zelenin, "Rita paid."

He told of an attempt to kill Gluzman on March 29, 1996, and they had lain in wait in his apartment, but Gluzman didn't come home. They tried again on Saturday,

April 6, and succeeded. He described the murder, the accidental wound to his hand, and Rita cleaning up blood while he cut up the body. After he told how the knife blade had broken off in Yakov's body, Judge Parker declared the lunch recess and Rita Gluzman fell forward, her head slamming onto the defense table.

"Just note for the record," said the judge to the court stenographer as he left the bench, "that at the end of the morning session, around twelve-thirty, the defendant apparently fainted."

During the recess, Yakov's mother, Sophia, scornfully told reporters, "It's a game. She's an actress."

Before convening the afternoon session Judge Parker offered Rita Gluzman the option of not being in the courtroom. She could follow the proceedings on closed-circuit television. "I do not want to watch it on TV," Rita replied. "It was my husband. I'm not going to watch anything about my husband on TV."

Fainting was not the only dramatic moment during Zelenin's testimony. At another point when Rita burst into sobbing, Sophia Gluzman screamed, "When you kill, you cannot cry."

Now that Zelenin had kept his bargain with the federal prosecutors, he became fair game for cross-examination by Hochheiser. Despite attempts to undermine and discredit Zelenin, after four days of grueling questioning and gruesome answers, Vladimir and his terrible story remained intact.

On Tuesday, January 21, three weeks into the trial, the AP's Jim Fitzgerald summed up Zelenin's tale with this opening sentence: "The killers shopped at the Home Depot for an ax that could go through a man's head and a hacksaw that could chop him up, prosecutors say."

The dispatch continued, "At Grand Union, they allegedly bought the garbage bags that would hold the 60-some body parts. And after the deed was done, they allegedly made a quick stop at CVS for bandages, since one of the killers had accidentally swiped the other with a hatchet. As described by government witnesses, the plot to kill Yakov Gluzman combined the time-honored sins of jealousy and greed with the down-to-earth details of modern life."

Following testimony by a coroner and several tangential witnesses, Deirdre Daly took two hours to sum up for the government. In response, Larry Hochheiser directed his closing remarks, as he had focused in his opening statement, at the prosecution's star witness. "Without Vladimir Zelenin," he declared, "there is no case against Rita Gluzman."

The government made a deal with the devil, but they don't call it a deal with the devil, he said. "They call it a cooperative agreement. They elevate it. They tell you, 'Oh, we despise Vladimir Zelenin just as you do.' "

Prosecutor Daly rebutted with a defense of the plea bargain. "Zelenin will spend at least twenty years, perhaps the rest of his life, in jail for this horrendous crime," she reminded jurors, "and it was all the defendant's idea. She set it in motion. She recruited him. You can imagine the anger he must feel toward her."

Then she asked the jury to imagine Rita Gluzman's anger at the thought that Yakov Gluzman was leaving her. "This is the man who she fought for and got out of Russia. This is the man who she thought was no longer good in bed. This man was leaving her for another woman. She was furious. She was enraged."

Who was the one who would benefit from Yakov's death?

"She is responsible for this nightmare that has shattered so many lives."

After deliberating nine and a half hours, the jurors took their seats in the jury box on the last day of January and returned a verdict of guilty of murder and illegal wiretapping, but not guilty of extortion. Juror Joseph Novick later told reporters that they had been convinced by the testimony of Zelenin. "There was a lot of truth in it," he said.

"It seemed more clear than anything else that she was guilty. It was remarkable testimony."

Alternate juror Shari Laroff said, "The prosecution said it was like a puzzle, and every piece fit."

Prosecutor Cathy Seibel asked for life without parole, telling Judge Barrington Parker that the murder was "perhaps the most despicable crime any of us will encounter." She read from a letter from Yakov's parents: "For twenty-five years she gradually demolished him emotionally, and in the twenty-sixth year she dismembered him physically."

Judge Parker imposed the sentence requested by the government on May 1. "None of us can ever know what transpired between you and your husband," he said to Rita Gluzman. "The only thing we know is that nothing that occurred can possibly justify what you did to him. You are a woman of considerable courage, capacity, and accomplishment. For whatever reason, you allowed yourself to disintegrate around the relationship and the pain that grew out of it."

Rita replied, "I did not do it. Can I still say that in front of the world?"

When her son Ilan left the court with Paula Shapiro and Marianne Rabinowitz, Marianne told reporters, "She did and built many things in her life that should not be forgotten."

On May 15, 1997, Vladimir Zelenin's deal with the government was finalized with the imposition of a federal sentence of twenty-two and a half years in prison. Six days later he was given a twenty-year concurrent sentence by a Rockland County court, assuring that he would not be a free man until 2018.

Rita Gluzman was sent to a minimum-security federal prison in Danbury, Connecticut. Had New York prosecutors been able to convict her, she might have gone to death row.

Fourteen

Holy Homicide

Shortly before eleven o'clock on Sunday night, December 15, 1996, in the 7200 block of Dean Road in the residential section of Northminster, Indianapolis, Indiana, Kathy Anderson awoke and sniffed the acrid odor of something burning. Roughly shaking her sleeping husband, she said with alarm, "Robert, wake up. Wake up! I smell smoke."

Fearing that their Christmas tree had somehow caught fire, the couple raced downstairs in their pajamas. After assuring themselves that nothing was burning in their house, they went outside to see if they could locate the origin of the odor. Looking to the east, they saw tongues of flame and billowing thick black smoke in the home of their friends, the Reverend Frederick and Cleta Mathias.

While Kathy hurried to a phone to report the blaze, Robert dashed to the house. As he pounded upon the locked front door, he shouted, "Fire! Fire! Fred, Cleta, get out!"

He was still shouting and beating on the door when the Washington Township Fire Department arrived at 11:15 P.M. to find fire showing through second-floor windows. Kicking in the front door, fireman Wilbur Frey flashed his torch and saw a figure facedown on the floor in a doorway.

Bending over her, he found her hands tied behind her back. Peering through the dense smoke into the family room, he saw a man on the floor, hands tied behind his back, and the outline of an axe handle jutting from the head. Both bodies were wearing winter coats. Under the Christmas tree lay a cat, kicked to death. The fire apparently had been ignited with the contents of a can of lighter fluid found in the room.

Initial questioning of the Andersons and others determined that Reverend and Mrs. Mathias had left their home around 8:45 P.M. for an ecumenical Advent service held by his Northminster Presbyterian Church, a congregation of 1,700 in northeastern Indianapolis, and the Roman Catholic Christ the King Church. He had read from Chapter 5 of Thessalonians: "And the very God of peace sanctify you wholly; and I pray God your whole spirit and soul and body be preserved blameless unto the coming of our Lord Jesus Christ. Faithful is he that calleth you, who also will do it."

Preferring not to be addressed as "the Reverend Mr. Mathias" or "Doctor Mathias," but rather as Fred, he was an imposing six feet five inches and 250 pounds and had been chief pastor at Northminster for eleven years. Before assuming the Northminster pulpit in 1983 he ministered at the wealthier Westminster Presbyterian Church in Wilmington, Delaware. Under his direction, Northminster often lined up with churches of other denominations to provide social services.

A member of Mathias's church, *Indianapolis Star/News* columnist David Mannweiler, noted that Mathias was not a fire-and-brimstone preacher, except, perhaps, when he railed against efforts to exploit the environment. He'd also urged his congregation to reject a referendum that would have allowed pari-mutuel horse betting in Marion County. His wife, Cleta, assumed the traditional behind-the-scenes role of pastor's helpmate and the one in charge of the entertaining, which was expected of the minister of a large church. Devotees of classical music, they were regulars at the symphony and opera. They also enjoyed summer vacations in the Adirondack Mountains of New York.

Their murders, declared an editorial in the *Indianapolis Star/News* on December 17, 1996, "sent shock waves of disbelief and grief across the Indianapolis metropolitan area. Disbelief because it is so difficult to accept that such cruel and vicious killings could occur in one of the city's most placid neighborhoods. It is tragic irony that the good pastor and his wife appeared to have died in their Northeastside home at the foot of their Christmas tree, a symbol of a season Fred Mathias celebrated with great joy. But murder takes no holiday in Indianapolis these days. There have now been some 20 homicides investigated by the Marion County Sheriff's Department in 1996 and more than 100 murders within the Indianapolis Police Department district."

Marion County Prosecutor Scott Newman called the Mathias murders "truly the nightmare before Christmas."

To Captain Mike Russo of the sheriff's department, what had happened on Dean Road was the result of one of three scenarios: Mathias and his wife had returned home from church and surprised a burglar; the killer had accosted them as they arrived home and forced his way into the house with the intention of compelling them to hand over their valuables; someone had planned to kill the sixty-four-year-old minister, and his wife, the same age, had had the bad luck to be with him when it happened.

There was evidence that the Mathias house had been ransacked, but that could have been a ruse to conceal the true motive, just as the killer had set a fire in the hope that the flames would erase evidence. If robbery or burglary were not at the heart of the case, Russo and his team of detectives were left with the third motivation. Concluding that the murders were not a random act, they were left with the question: Who would want to kill a clergyman who, by all accounts, was a beloved figure, with plans to step down from the pulpit in July so he and his wife could move to the East Coast to spend their retirement years with their three children, who lived in Delaware and Maryland?

The morning after the discovery of the bodies, Russo said, "It was a very brutal and tragic homicide. These people had severe trauma to the head. Whoever perpetrated this crime did so in a brutal and malicious fashion. You don't see a burglary where the victims are treated in such a disgusting fashion. A burglar for the most part, if surprised, is going to want to flee, and we can't believe that these two victims would have presented any challenge to the burglar."

Hearing this, the Reverend William Enright of the Second Presbyterian Church in Indianapolis, and a longtime colleague of Mathias in the Whitewater Valley Presbytery, expressed shock. "It's just a devastating experience," he told a reporter for the *Christian Journal.* "It's the brutality of it that is so shocking, unsettling. Fred was a man who was very respected and deeply loved, a kind of gentle giant who had a strong sense of the church and abiding faithfulness to the church."

Worried by the assertion of investigators that the killings might not have been the random work of a thief, clergy members of the Whitewater Valley Presbytery ordered increased security around Mathias's church and advised members of the pastoral staff to be more cautious. Church attorney Mark Moore told the Presbyterian News Service, "If the police think this may not be a random act, we need to be more attentive to security. There are increasing police patrols in the church neighborhood. Extra people are on site at the church, and staff are being urged not to walk alone and to lock doors. The church has been a relatively open place, and that's not to say it won't be open for worship and that sort of thing. But physically we can't be as unconcerned about that kind of thing as we had."

On Thursday, December 19, a memorial service was held for the slain couple. "There is no tribute to a life such as Fred's that can ever be complete," said the Reverend Jill

Hudson. "For his gifts of personal integrity, his immense heart and willingness to serve, and his great love for Jesus Christ and his willingness to share that love with others are endless."

Several detectives attended the memorial. In keeping with a tradition as old as policing, they hoped that whoever had committed the crime would show up at the service and act in some fashion to either give himself away or arouse suspicions. Meanwhile, investigators had followed another well-established police procedure by issuing an appeal for public assistance.

One member of the public had come forward on the night of the murders to report having seen a young male walking near the Mathias home, and the day after the murders they'd gotten an anonymous tip suggesting they look into fifteen-year-old Sean Rich, who fit the description of the male. According to the tipster, Rich had been an usher at Northminster Presbyterian Church and been accused of several thefts. Fred Mathias had reached out to him and hadn't reported him to the police. Another tipster informed investigators that at school on the day after the murders Rich had flashed "a wad of cash."

Police also learned that on the day before the murders Rich had been in the Mathias house with a group of teenage boys who had volunteered to move a rug Mathias was donating to the church. The rug was taken from the basement through the garage. It was by way of the garage, detectives surmised, that the killer had gotten into the house. They also deduced that it was in the garage that the killer picked up Mathias's axe in a gloved hand that had left only a smudged print on the handle.

Questioned by detectives, Rich denied having killed the couple and said he had been at home on the phone at the time of the murders. This could not be confirmed in phone records.

Denial notwithstanding, Sheriff Jack Cottey of Marion County characterized Rich, without naming him, "the best suspect we have." Major Michael Turk of the sheriff's department said that the fifteen-year-old was the "lead suspect."

Unfortunately, the extinguishing of the fire in the Mathias house had left investigators with nothing in the form of physical clues and evidence. The water from hoses had washed away any strands of hair and fiber traces. Firefighters in boots had obliterated shoe prints. Smoke and water had made a search for fingerprints hopeless.

Feeling stymied by the lack of evidence, investigators took advantage of a relatively new resource in the world of criminal investigation. In the hope of obtaining advice on the killer's psychology, the Marion County Sheriff's Department provided a copy of the file on the Mathias murders to the FBI's Behavioral Sciences Division at Quantico, Virginia.

Begun in 1978 as an experiment, the FBI's criminal psychological profiling program had by 1983 interviewed thirty-five serial killers. The data collected was then analyzed in a computer program with the intention (and hope) that there would emerge commonalities as to how, when, where, and why the men had murdered, along with the nature of their victims.

The research resulted in defining offenders in two categories: organized and disorganized. These distinctions were noted in both the scene of the crime and the personality characteristics of the offender. In contrast to an organized perpetrator, a disorganized one left a crime scene that indicated a spontaneous act of sudden violence in which body and weapon were left at the scene. Such a person would be a male of below average intelligence, holding an unskilled job, feeling socially inadequate, and living or working near the crime scene. He would have a record of being in trouble at school and in the home. He would be someone who went out alone at night to prowl aimlessly. Whereas an organized killer targeted a stranger, the disorganized would know both the locale of the crime and the victim.

The method of murder and the condition of the Mathias crime scene pointed away from the killings having been organized. The use of Mathias's own axe indicated *disorganization*. An organized killer would not have come to the scene without a weapon. An organized killer would not have started a fire. An organized individual whose purpose was to kill and rob would not have done the former and departed without having done the latter. Clearly, Reverend and Mrs. Mathias, and their cat, had been killed on the spur of the moment and the fire set by someone who'd fled empty-handed in a state of panic.

If the killer had targeted Mathias solely he would not have arranged to kill him at a time when Mrs. Mathias would be present, unless his intent had been to kill both. But if that had been the goal, an organized individual would be unlikely to choose to do so when his victims were alert. He'd be more likely to intrude on them, catching them unaware, and unleash the attack, probably while they slept. And certainly not do so with an axe that just happened to be handy.

That Reverend and Mrs. Mathias had been bound with ropes before being killed was also instructive. Although it was possible to imagine one person being capable of trussing two people, especially elderly ones, the tying-up pointed to there having been more than one perpetrator.

While most of the individuals who had been arrested for murders, rapes, arson, and other crimes, and had been profiled by the FBI, had proved to fit the portraits provided by the Bureau's psychological sleuths to an astonishing degree, criminal psychological profiling could not point investigators to *the* man—definitely a man or men—they were seeking. Analysis of the psyche of a murderer was a guide, not a substitute for old-fashioned, laborious, time-consuming, brain-testing legwork of the homicide detective.

What stood out in the FBI's profile of the killer was a thread worth following. If these murders had been committed in a disorganized pattern, it was possible that the killer or killers had known Reverend and Mrs. Mathias and, perhaps, attended (or had attended) the Northminster Presbyterian Church. The thread led them back to where they'd started, but they still had nothing on which to obtain a warrant for the arrest of Sean Rich. Without some kind of break, whether through another tip, a confession, or some other equally dramatic development, the solution of the murders seemed increasingly unlikely.

That dismal outlook was expressed in a June 15, 1977, story in the *Star/News* by reporter Richard D. Walton. "Six months after the ax murders," he wrote, "police are locked in a stalemate with a suspect they can neither charge nor clear." Describing the suspect only as "a troubled teen who attended the couples' church," the item continued, "The investigation has been crippled by the absence of incriminating evidence from the crime scene."

A "forensics nightmare," Walton wrote, had left police with "little more than their instincts to go on. And those instincts keep drawing them back to the youth."

Walton quoted but did not name the boy's mother as saying police were obsessed over her "learning-disabled son." The woman asserted, "They need a scapegoat, and they need somebody to pin it on."

The portrait of Sean Rich provided by his mother, Pamela, when questioned by police was chillingly close to the FBI profile. In attempting to deal with her troubled son she had filed a court document in which she said he was "physically violent." He threw things or slammed a fist into a wall. He once fired a BB gun down the hallway of the house, then stalked out carrying an eleven-inch knife. He went out at night alone. If she left $10 in her bedroom, her son would take it. And there'd been the trouble at the church over missing money.

On the night of the murders, Rich's mother told police,

she, Sean, and her other children had gone Christmas caroling. At eight o'clock she'd dropped Sean at home, which was not far from the Mathias house. When her husband returned home at 8:40 P.M., she said, he found Sean in shorts and a tank top talking on the phone. Sean was still in his room, she said, when she came in at nine o'clock. "The kid," she vowed, "never left the house."

From Sean Rich, who was now represented by an attorney, the detectives got nothing more than his story about being on the phone at the time of the murders.

Might the most sensational murder case in the history of Indianapolis go unsolved?

"We've by no means given up," Detective John Gray told reporter Walton. Also vowing not to allow the investigation to languish, Sheriff Cottey expressed a belief that "somebody out there" knew who'd killed the Mathiases and one day might want to come forward and clear his conscience.

But in the meantime, detectives had other cases to work. Along with cops in virtually every community in the country, those in Indianapolis and environs were engaged in a continuing war against those who dealt in illicit drugs. A veteran of that seemingly futile battle, Detective John Gray reported to work on Thursday, January 22, 1998, prepared for another day in which a call to the front lines often took the form of a telephone call from someone who, for a host of reasons, decided to become a police informant. One such anonymous tipster whispered into Gray's attentive ear that a youth, Paul Brightman, an eighteen-year-old dropout from North Central High School and a service-station cashier, was dealing drugs, namely marijuana, from his house on East Meadow Lane, in the suburb of Carmel. The informant also said that Brightman might know something about the Mathias murders.

On Monday night, January 26, Gray and others executed a search warrant at Brightman's address, found a small quantity of marijuana, and turned their attention to Brightman's association with Sean Rich. During the questioning, they suggested that Brightman's marijuana problem and any other legal difficulty he could find himself facing in the matter of the Mathias murders might be greatly alleviated if he leveled with them about December 15, 1996.

Just as police in East Rutherford, New Jersey, and Rockland County, New York, persuaded Vladimir Zelenin that his interest lay in becoming a cooperative witness against Rita Gluzman, the Indianapolis detectives laid before Paul Brightman the prospect of avoiding a possible death sentence if he testified against Rich.

At some point during the long night Brightman admitted he'd gone to the Mathias house with Rich for the purpose of burglarizing it. Mathias and his wife walked in on them as they were ransacking the downstairs. He said he'd hit them on the head with a .22-caliber pistol that Rich had brought along, then held the gun on the couple as Rich tied them up.

"I went out to the garage," Brightman said. "Sean told me to get something—something long, kind of solid." When he realized he'd grabbed an axe, he continued, he'd thrown it on the floor. "We got in a tiff. He wanted me to do it. I'm not a murderer. I'm a very sensitive person. He picked up the ax and hit Mrs. Mathias."

Watching in horror, Fred Mathias exclaimed, "You're going to hell, Sean, you're going to hell." Rich responded by hitting him with the axe.

"I don't know how many times," said Brightman. "I wasn't watching."

Brightman was arrested on two preliminary murder charges and one count of robbery. A few hours later, Sean Rich was taken into custody on the same charges.

"For members of Northminster Presbyterian Church, it was their worst fears come true," reported Fort Wayne's *News Sentinel* on Wednesday, January 28, 1998. "One of their own was under arrest for the brutal ax slaying of their minister and his wife."

Said the Reverend Ronald Smith, who had succeeded Mathias in the pulpit of the church in June 1997, "All of us breathed a sigh of relief. That's not to say there's a sense of jubilation. There's nothing here to be jubilant about."

A church spokesman told reporters, "If Sean is guilty, we'd like him to acknowledge that. He broke the law. He was part of a heinous set of circumstances and is going to pay a penalty for that."

It would be more than a year before Sean Rich faced a trial on an indictment alleging two counts of murder, burglary, confinement, arson, battery, theft, and cruelty to an animal (the Mathias cat). An attempt by Rich's lawyer to have him tried as a juvenile because the crimes had been committed when he was fifteen was denied. Marion County Juvenile Court judge James Payne ruled that the state had shown enough evidence to convince him that Rich, now sixteen, should be tried as an adult.

Rich's lawyer claimed that the police coerced Brightman into confessing by talking about the death penalty. Attorney Glenn Huelskamp asserted, "They convinced Paul that they could take his life."

The police were not alone in having questioned Brightman. While in custody on the evening of January 27, 1998, he agreed to be interviewed in jail by newspaper reporters and a reporter taping the interview for WTHR-TV. He said that after Rich had tied up the Mathiases, the minister had pleaded for their lives and told them they could take anything they wanted from the house, but Rich killed them with the axe. Admitting only to hitting the Mathiases with a gun and kicking the cat to death, he said, "I just wanted to get out of that house."

A reporter asked why he hadn't tried to stop the killings. With a burst of nervous laughter, Brightman replied, "I'm not going to turn around and jump in front of an ax blade. I feared for my own life. I didn't know what was going to happen. I went home, locked myself in my room, and cried for the rest of the night."

Fearing the effect showing the tape in court might have on Brightman's pending trial, his attorney, Mark Inman, fought to have it excluded as evidence. In a hearing before Judge Gary Miller out of the presence of the jury, Inman asked Brightman why he signed a release agreeing to grant the station the interview.

Brightman answered that he didn't recall signing the form because he had been awake for more than a day and a half. "I don't remember much of the twenty-sixth or twenty-seventh," he said. "I was tired."

Dennis Pickens, a corrections officer for the Marion County Sheriff's Department, testified that he'd read the waiver to Brightman twice and afforded him time to read it before signing.

"He said he wanted to tell his side of the story," said Pickens, "because he felt he had been railroaded."

Judge Miller declared, "He was aware he did not have to talk to the media. He didn't have to talk to anyone."

As a result of the ruling to admit the complete tape of the interview, jurors in the Sean Rich trial would be allowed to judge Brightman's veracity. But before that proceeding began, Paul Brightman's fate would be in the hands of another jury. While he had admitted being present when the killings had been committed, he had pleaded not guilty to murder.

When his trial opened on Wednesday, January 20, 1999, his lawyer, Mark Inman, told jurors his client had been targeted by the police because of his friendship with Sean Rich. "They wanted to take him down," said Inman. "They continually pounded on him and threatened him."

Deputy Prosecutor Carole Johnson opened by talking about the manner in which Mathias and his wife had been killed. With autopsy photos shown to the jury, Dr. Dean Hawlay, the pathologist from Indiana University's School of Medicine, described the wounds. He testified that the axe head was completely embedded in Reverend Mathias's head and tore a nine-inch gash along the base of the skull, killing him instantly. Cleta died from a similar "incised, chopping wound."

As he testified, the children of the murdered couple turned their heads away from the witness. Jurors who had to look at the photos wept.

However, the jury was not called upon to render a verdict against Brightman. Three days into the trial he pleaded guilty in the hope of getting a greatly reduced sentence if he admitted guilt and agreed to testify against Sean Rich. He received a sixty-five-year sentence.

The triumphant Marion County prosecutor Scott Newman declared, "At least here we have a person who assisted in that crime willing to accept responsibility and tell a jury exactly what happened."

Glenn Huelskamp, Sean Rich's lawyer, said Brightman's plea deal "is just another example of his manipulation of the system."

The Mathiases' son, Mark, saw "a sense of justice" and said, "It's fair to the extent that we'll keep Paul Brightman out of society for many, many years."

Following two days of jury selection, Rich's trial began on Tuesday, February 23, 1999. Deputy Prosecutor Carole Johnson opened by describing the savagery of the killings of "busy, well-loved leaders of the church," and asked, "Who could have hated them enough to do that?"

The Reverend Donna Wells, assistant pastor at the time of the murders, assumed the witness chair to relate that Sean Rich had been an usher at the church but had been removed from the job when Mathias and other parish staff suspected him of stealing money from an offering plate.

Paul Brightman kept his bargain with the state and told his version of what had happened on the night of December 15, 1996, then was cross-examined by Rich's defense counsel who strove to portray him as an unreliable witness who'd been bullied by police into placing Rich at the crime scene in order to gain the best possible deal for himself.

This was not the first time, of course, nor the last, that

a defense lawyer in a case that came down to "he said/he said" sought to attack the prosecution's case by attacking police tactics in obtaining a confession and questioning the believability of the resulting witness.

After an adjournment for the weekend, the trial proceeded for two more days of testimony, summations, and the judge's charge to the jury of six men and six women, including a computer analyst, two nurses, a college student, two teachers, and a retiree.

After eleven hours of deliberation they convicted Rich of one count each of burglary and theft and two counts of confinement but found him not guilty of cruelty to an animal. Then the foreman, Gene Mosley, an elementary-school teacher, announced a deadlock on arson, battery, and murder.

Said attorney Huelskamp, "I think that the verdict really shows the jury didn't believe Paul Brightman."

The astonished Marion County prosecutor Scott Newman speculated that the jurors had been confused on the difference between murder and felony murder. He was right. Interviewed by *Indianapolis Star/News* reporters William J. Booher and Stephen Beaven, members of the jury related an eleven-hour debate amid tears and temper in which four jurors struggled with what constituted felony murder. State law defined murder as intentional killing of a human and felony murder the killing of a human during the course of committing a felony, in this case the crime of burglary. Three requests to the judge for a clarification had been denied because Judge Miller "didn't find it appropriate." He had provided jurors at the start of the trial with standard written instructions and legal definitions. He sent them notes stating, "I cannot answer your question. Please re-read the instructions and continue your deliberations."

Prosecutor Newman immediately announced that he would retry the charges on which the jury had failed to agree.

As members of the Mathias family and the church congregation shook their heads in disbelief that the jury had not found Rich guilty of murder, Mark Moore, the spokesman for the Northminster Presbyterian Church, declared, "It is beyond comprehension that the jury could find Sean Rich guilty of burglary, of criminal confinement, and of theft, yet not find Sean guilty of the vicious murders that resulted from his acts."

On April 8, 1999, Sean Rich stood before Judge Miller for sentencing. Quoting the son of the murdered minister and his wife, he termed Rich a fiendish sociopath. "These were elderly people surprised in their own home," he said, "their hands bound, heads bashed in with an ax and their house burned to cover up this dastardly deed.

"You are not a typical teenager. You are not a good brother, you are not a good son," he continued, citing evidence that Rich had acted violently toward his sister, had problems with his mother, and disobeyed rules while incarcerated in the Marion County Jail. "You have a temper. You seem to be the type of person who has the ability to commit the crimes in this case."

He sentenced Rich to the maximum, ninety-three years. He would serve that time no matter of what additional crimes a future trial jury might find him guilty.

In an editorial on April 14, 1999, titled "When the Steel Door Closes," the *Star/News* said, "Imagine that you're 17 years old. Your life is ahead of you—dating, college, marriage, employment and children. Then you hear a judge sentence you to 93 years in prison. Your life is crushed beneath the pounding of his wooden gavel. In an instant, your dreams become your nightmares. The place you never wanted to call home becomes the only residence you'll ever know. There, behind prison's cold, steel bars, you'll become an adult and a senior citizen and, eventually, die. The realization that you threw your life away in a stupid, selfish, murderous rage that lasted minutes will haunt you."

The editorial concluded, "Although it's hard to see anything good in this case—at least four lives have been destroyed, not to mention the devastation to families of all parties—there is one resounding message to teens and others who think crime pays: It doesn't. Rich faces 93 years—more than an average life span—in jail. We applaud [Judge] Miller's decision because it serves justice and gives would-be criminals reason to pause before committing a crime."

Fifteen

Welcome to the Morgue

When Rebecca Holberton didn't show up for her new job at the Denver, Colorado, airport facility of USWest on Wednesday, July 8, 1998, her supervisor, Barb Anders, was worried. A USWest employee for twenty-five years who'd transferred to Denver from Portland, Oregon, early in 1995, Rebecca said she was excited about taking up the new assignment after taking a short vacation. She was expected on the job on Monday, July 5, but had not shown up. When she didn't arrive the next day, a USWest employee had gone to her house and found no one home. If Rebecca had elected to extend the vacation, Anders assumed, based on her stellar record with USWest, she would have notified someone at the airline. Increasingly concerned, Anders phoned the Jefferson County sheriff's office and asked if someone could go to Rebecca's town house in Trappers Glen on West Chananago.

A deputy was dispatched. Noting that there was no car parked at the house, he went to the front door and rang the bell. Unanswered, he walked to the rear of the house, scaled a wooden fence, and peered through a sliding glass door.

A shout of "Is anybody home?" brought no reply. Trying the door and finding it unlocked, he slid it open, took a step inside, and immediately saw a large, bulky plastic bag sealed with duct tape. Nearby, a blanket appeared to have been thrown over a bulky object in a chair. Approaching it, he saw what appeared to be the ankles of a woman bound with tape.

A call for backup was quickly answered by several deputies. After confirming the woman in the chair was dead and that the plastic bag contained another woman's corpse, they searched the house and found a third body beneath bloodstained blankets. Preliminary examination of the bodies indicated that at least one had been killed by a blow with an axe. With the discovery of a triple-homicide, in which an axe may have been used, it seemed to the people of Colorado that the state renowned for the pristine beauty of the Rocky Mountains, clear waters, and tranquil vistas had become a killing ground.

Pending in Colorado courts at the moment were a dozen murder cases that qualified under a law that had taken effect in 1996 for imposition of the death penalty if a review of a panel of judges so ordered. The effect of the new statute, claimed defense lawyers, would be to encourage prosecutors to swell the number of candidates eligible for cells on death row.

Among them was thirty-nine-year-old Robert Riggan, convicted of raping and killing a twenty-one-year-old Denver prostitute, Anita Paley. Also facing the possibility of death were Danny and Francisco Martinez, the unrelated twenty-five-year-old members of a gang of six who on May 30, 1997, raped, tortured, and stabbed fourteen-year-old Brandy Duvall twenty-eight times, then left her to bleed to death in a ditch along Clear Creek. Eighteen days later twenty-eight-year-old Jaques Richardson, while burglarizing the apartment of thirty-four-year-old tour guide Janey Benedict, hog-tied his victim so tightly she died of strangulation. In the same year, twenty-three-year-old Lucas

Salmon had abducted college student Jacine Gielinski from a parking lot and raped, beat, and murdered her with repeated stabbings.

Noting that between 1967 and 1977 Colorado had executed only one person, David Kaplan, the attorney for Francisco Martinez, said, "The floodgates have opened up. There are a dozen death-penalty cases pending right now in the state. This time next year, who knows how death row will look?" Pointing out that Texas had executed 173 inmates since the U.S. Supreme Court ruled executions constitutional in 1976 and had 441 on death row, he continued, "I call it the Texasification of Colorado's death penalty."

Another defense attorney, David Lane, said, "Murders here haven't all of a sudden gotten worse. Prosecutors know they're going to start filling up death row here and are champing at the bit trying to do it."

While murders were nothing new in Colorado, killing with an axe had been a rarity. But barely two years before the discovery of the three bodies in the house on West Chanango, Coloradans had been horrified by an axe murder in Edgewater. On July 26, 1996, a German national, thirty-three-year-old Manuela Garcia, finally had taken enough abuse from her husband, Henry Anthony Garcia. She had told her daughter Lorianne that she was going to kill him. She even showed Lorianne an axe. Later, as Lorianne and two other children slept, she carried it into another bedroom and struck Henry twenty-three times. Despite the fact that Henry was asleep when attacked, Manuela's attorneys claimed she had acted in self-defense, explaining that after being repeatedly beaten and raped and fearing more assaults, Manuela had "snapped." But the prosecution argued that the murder had been premeditated. Therefore, Manuela had committed a first-degree murder, punishable by life imprisonment or the death penalty. On August 27, 1997, a jury of eleven women and one man convicted Manuela of second-degree murder with a term of twenty-four to forty-eight years. Quickly overshadowing Manuela's settling of her domestic situation with an axe was the Jon Benet Ramsey murder in Colorado that horrified and fascinated the entire country and much of the world.

Jefferson County launched an investigation into the horrors of West Chanango, hoping for a quick result.

As in most homicides where there was a mystery, they started by identifying victims. The easiest of the three was the one whose nonappearance at USWest had triggered the discovery of her death and the others. A native of Oregon, Rebecca Holberton was forty-four years old and a graduate of Oregon State University. In 1980 she had married Rodney Holberton, an airline pilot. They had no children and had divorced in 1992. She liked her job, was good at it, and was liked and respected by coworkers.

In contrast to Rebecca's rather staid biography, twenty-eight-year-old, five-foot-five, blond Angela "Angie" Fite's story was tempestuous and marked with alcohol abuse, domestic discord, and violence. Trained as a dental assistant, the second victim had been a resident of Aurora, Colorado. She'd been arrested five times between 1994 and 1997 for assault related to her common law marriage to thirty-four-year-old Michael Vernon Kelly. They had two small children, Kayla, age two, and Kyle, five. According to neighbors, Angie and Kelly enjoyed riding his motorcycle. A check of Kelly's past disclosed arrests for assault, carrying a concealed weapon, brandishing a knife, driving under the influence, and disturbing the peace. Angela had sought a restraining order against him in 1996 and the next year Kelly sought one against her. Angela had moved out of their Salem Street home that autumn.

Forty-eight-year-old Candace "Candy" Walters, the third victim, worked for Premiere Home Lending, a real estate firm owned by her daughter, Holly. Her tasks included checking applications for loans and processing other paperwork. She had previously been employed by the Gates Energy Company. An animal lover, she often took care of Holly's dogs and was a member of the Natural History Museum and the Denver Zoo. An enthusiast of the outdoors, she liked to watch birds and deer.

When detectives contacted Rebecca Holberton's ex-husband in his Portland, Oregon, home, he said he'd last spoken to her by phone in April when he was passing through Denver. "It couldn't have happened to a person more undeserving," he said. "She always had a smile on her face. I mean she was a kind, gentle person. What more can you want? I don't know how somebody could do it. The only thing I could think of is that to do something like this he would have to be high on drugs."

Of great interest to the investigators was what circumstance had brought these three very different women together in Rebecca's house. Might Holberton be aware of any of Rebecca's other friends? He had been told, he replied, that she had a boyfriend named "Cody."

In questioning Holly Walters about Candy's friends, the detectives learned that Cody was the nickname of William Neal. She told them that her mother and Neal were to have gone to Las Vegas for the July Fourth weekend. When her mother did not return, Holly began paging Neal. He called her around three in the morning Wednesday and said Candy had hit a deer, run her car off the road, and was going to the hospital. After hearing nothing from her mother, Holly called the police and reported her missing. Was Holly certain the man's name was William Neal? Yes.

The name rang a disturbing bell for the investigators. In the sordid culture of people who used speed and methamphetamine, got arrested, and jumped bail, Neal was known to a group of bounty hunters employed by bail bondsmen. According to Duane "Dog" Chapman, a bounty hunter, of the three hundred "speed freaks" in Denver, Neal knew "about a quarter of them." Neal had illusions of grandeur. He often dressed in cowboy clothes and called himself "Cody" while trying to pass himself off as a bounty hunter or occasionally an undercover cop.

As detectives organized a search for Neal as a possible suspect in the murders, Neal was reaching out to a man he had known for several years, Steve Grund, news director at Denver television station KWGN. Taking Neal's phone call, Grund listened with amazement to a murder confession. Sounding exhausted, Neal wondered if Grund would be willing to act as a go-between with the police in arranging his surrender.

At approximately the same time, Denver police were listening to a woman who claimed to have been taken to a house on West Chanango on Sunday, July 5, by a man who showed her two bodies. He then blindfolded her, tied her to a bed, and raped her. During this assault, she said, another woman had been tied to a nearby chair. Finished with the rape, the caller continued, he untied the other woman, waved a handgun, and retied the woman. Rubbing the other woman's leg, he asked her, "What kind of day are you having?" With that, he picked up an axe and clubbed her.

Not until now, Wednesday, July 8, said the woman, had she been able to report these horrifying events because the man had forced her to drive to her own apartment, where he'd held her hostage for three days, along with another woman and a man who shared the apartment. He'd left around 6 P.M., handing her his pager number and telling her that if she paged him he would confess to the police.

Using the number provided by the woman, a Jefferson County deputy reached Neal and for three hours listened to him provide gruesome details of the murders that only the killer could have known. The conversation ended with Neal promising to meet the deputy in the parking lot of a Target store on West Cross Drive in nearby Littleton. At 12:41 A.M., Thursday, July 9, he pulled into the lot in a pickup truck and was promptly arrested.

Announcing the stunning break in a triple-homicide case, which was barely twelve hours old, Jefferson County Sheriff's spokesman Steve Davis could provide no motive for the murders. "That's what we're trying to piece together," he told reporters. "How did he know these people? Did they know each other? How long did they know one another? How did they meet?"

Lieutenant John Kiekbush said, "We don't know what kind of ruse was used. We don't know how he got them to the house on Chanango."

Rebecca Holberton's neighbor, Preston Rell, reported having seen Neal going in and out of the house "a lot" but said he knew "very little about him."

Interviewed by a reporter from Steve Gund's television station, Jennifer Neal (Cody's third ex-wife and mother of Neal's five-year-old daughter) said she'd been scared of Neal for years.

When a nephew of Neal's, D. J. Hardy, was interviewed, he portrayed his uncle as "pretty distant from the family." A biographical sketch of William Lee Neal, which he provided, appeared to bear him out. Born in 1952 in Virginia, he'd moved frequently with his parents, an older brother, and three sisters, before the family settled in San Antonio, Texas. A high-school graduate, he enlisted in the U.S. Army and said he'd served with the Airborne Rangers. A search of army records showed, however, that he'd done nothing so glamorous. Between 1972 and 1975 he had been a light-weapons infantryman, machine-gunner, and grenadier.

In Portage, Alaska, on September 10, 1989, he'd married for the first time. It lasted about thirteen months. After visiting his nephew he decided to settle in Denver and became associated with a firm in Englewood that installed fire and security alarm systems, but had parted with the company for unknown reasons.

He married Jennifer on February 26, 1993, in Las Vegas, and their daughter was born in July. The marriage broke up in August 1995 with Neal hauling away all their furniture except a TV set. In divorce papers he claimed debts of $51,000 and gave his occupation as "unemployed alarm technician." He listed assets consisting of a 1993 Toyota and $4.

His widowed mother died in 1995.

The nephew's account of Neal's life provided *Denver Post* reporters Kevin Simpson, Marilyn Robinson, and Kieran Nicholson the following lead to a July 11 story: "The death of his mother, a divorce and the loss of a business combined to widen an already gaping chasm between suspected triple-murderer William 'Cody' Neal and relatives, a family member said Friday."

The same day the *Rocky Mountain News* published a story by Lisa Levitt Ryckman, Cathy Cummins, John C. Ensslin, and Manny Gonzales that withheld the name of the woman who had witnessed one of the murders. "She was raped, forced to watch as another woman was hacked to death, then held hostage for almost three days," it said. "And she had just turned 21."

The story went on to quote the former leasing manager of an apartment complex where Neal had lived that the suspect frequently wore full cowboy regalia with a brace of holstered guns. "He's scary looking," said Beck Coca. "I can't understand what kind of hold he had over women."

Searching for an explanation and for a motive to kill three women were ten investigators. They knew from Candace Walters's daughter Holly that Candace claimed to have met Neal in a hotel bar several years earlier.

As the detectives sought a motive and an explanation of the relationships between Neal and the three women, and theirs to one another—if any—Jefferson County sheriff's spokesman Steve Davis reported the autopsy findings. He said the women had died from blunt trauma by "undisclosed weapons." That an axe had been wielded was attested to by the woman he'd held hostage. As to other weapons, said Davis, "Only the suspect knows what was used on whom."

From the scene of the murders, investigators had removed about four hundred pieces of evidence, but whether an axe had been found was not disclosed. Neither was the nature of weapons found in the pickup truck that Neal drove into the parking lot, expecting to be arrested.

Arraigned six days after his surrender, Neal was charged with thirteen felonies, including three counts of first-degree homicide, two counts of first-degree sexual assault upon the woman he'd forced to watch as he killed Angela Fite, two counts each of second-degree kidnapping and criminal extortion related to the hostage-taking, two counts of "violent crime" for threatening the hostages with "a knife and/or gun," and various counts of theft involving cash and credit cards that were taken from Holberton and Walters.

Remanded to jail without bail to await further court proceedings that could result in the death penalty, Neal demonstrated a remarkable desire to talk. In a telephone interview from jail with KCNC News4 reporter Rick Salinger, he said, "There are two bodies they haven't found yet." Where they might be located, he did not choose to state.

Investigators were openly dubious. Unless he was to "start providing names, dates and locations," said Sergeant Jim Parr of the sheriff's office, "we haven't come up with any other missing people or unsolved homicides that fit this MO [modus operandi, or method of operation]."

Neal also told Salinger, "I will state as fact that I was not under the influence of any drugs, speed, etc., during the time of the murders."

The murders were committed, he said, over six days. He killed Holberton on June 30 because he knew she was going on vacation and he could use her town house; Walters on July 3, and Fite on July 5. Between these homicides, he said, he'd gone "partying" and had rented a limousine for one of his outings. As to why he killed, he said, "I will do my best to answer that at a later time and place."

That moment came when investigators interviewed him on September 14, 1998. He said during seven hours of questioning that he had liked all three of his victims but feared they would expose his criminal activities, which included "theft, extortion, fraud, embezzlement, forgery." They were "potential snitches" and "none of them were trustable."

"They pushed me to my limit," he asserted. "I don't want to say I 'snapped.' All three had fair warning. I could imagine those three women were going to nail me."

He said he'd taken more than $70,000 from Holberton and about $6,000 from Walters.

The killings were committed with an axe instead of a gun, he said, because he didn't want to attract attention. "Then I would have had to kill the neighbors," he said. "I would have gone on a real killing spree."

He'd let the fourth woman go because "her testimony alone could put me in the death penalty phase" following his conviction. "I always believed in the death penalty, myself," he said. "And I still believe in the death penalty. I do have a heart and I do have a conscience."

During a preliminary hearing on November 3, 1998, the woman Neal had kidnapped and shown the bodies to told the court that when he lifted up a blanket to reveal a woman's foot, he had said, "Welcome to the mortuary."

Testimony from investigators, based on Neal's confessions, revealed how he'd killed the women. After telling Holberton he had a surprise for her and making her stand holding a briefcase over her head, he threw a blanket over her and bludgeoned her repeatedly with an axe. The same ruse was used on Walters as she sat in a chair. He'd brought Angela Fite to the house and tricked her into a chair, told her it was time for him to feed his cat, went into the kitchen, and came back to club her to death with an axe.

"I felt remorse the whole way," he told the police. "I wanted them to go as quickly as possible. I killed them instantly."

Brought to trial in February 1999, he pleaded guilty and announced that for the penalty phase he would be his own lawyer. Accordingly, he said, he needed time to prepare.

Whether he would be allowed to represent himself would depend on the findings of psychiatric examinations to evaluate his mental competency. Craig Truman, a veteran defense counsel, harbored no doubt regarding the outcome. "He has to be so sick as to not understand the nature of the charges or the penalties he would face," he declared. "There are small minerals that meet that test."

The public defender whom Neal had fired, Jim Aber, exclaimed, "This is a total farce. Seeking the death penalty against a person not represented by counsel is like trying to kill an unarmed man. There is no morality or justice in this."

In keeping with the action of the Colorado legislature in 1996 that stripped juries of the right to decide on executions, for the first time in Colorado history a panel of three judges would convene to decide whether a murderer was to live or die. In doing so, the panel would have before it a man who had been convicted as the most heinous multiple-murderer in the annals of Colorado, and a case in which the confessed killer had declared that he wished to die.

Was he, as many in Colorado believed, demonstrating a capacity to manipulate the law, as he had cruelly and cunningly manipulated women into a murderous trap? Legalistic terms aside, were not the deeds committed in the house on West Chanango obviously those of a madman? Or was he the embodiment of evil?

A week before the panel of judges was scheduled to hold a hearing on the death penalty, columnist Bill Johnson wrote in the *Denver Rocky Mountain News,* "I wouldn't want to be one of those three judges, but I've got a buck that says they'll decide to kill that obviously crazy man."

The column continued, "Of all the senseless killings we've witnessed the past two years, William Cody Neal's rampage has to be amongst the most—well, perplexing. It is as eerily senseless as it was bloody, as bizarre as it is tragic."

Noting that Neal would represent himself before the panel of judges, Johnson saw Neal as manipulative and found it "sickening."

"No, he doesn't want a lawyer," he wrote. "He says he doesn't want them grilling his victims' families. They deserve their retribution and justice, he says. He doesn't want a circus, no legal sideshows, some 'lawyer guy' finding loopholes, making unreal the reality of what he's done. He's cooked. He's given the three judges deciding his fate no discernible choice. He's co-opted us into yet another killing. His own. Some will call it justice when they pull the needle from his arm, wheel him out and bury him. But I believe it will be just another murder. And that it won't deter the next rampage. Still, why'd he do it at all? Why are those three women dead? With all he's said, not even William Cody Neal has an explanation. As if one really matters."

The three-judge panel convened to determine Neal's penalty on September 12, 1999. The judges were Thomas Woodford of Jefferson County and William Meyer and Frank Martinez of Denver. What they heard from Neal was not a demand that he be put to death, but a plea for life in prison. Accompanied by a spiritual counselor, Randy Canney, Neal claimed to have found God and said he wanted to live in order to serve God in prison.

"How could anyone have mercy on someone like me?" he asked rhetorically. "To those three beautiful women that I ruthlessly murdered, I gave no mercy or they would be here today. So I find it difficult to ask that of this court. The person who did those crimes deserves none."

However, Neal said, he was no longer that person. He'd changed.

"My heart was stone, and only God can change a heart," he said.

Speaking of viewing a tape of his confession in the seven-hour interview by investigators, he said, "I shake my head. It's me, but it's not me now. I ask all the people who have known me to forgive me."

Spiritual counselor Randy Canney testified that Neal's claim was true. He said he'd found Neal truly remorseful for what he'd done and that Neal's religious conversion was genuine.

This contention was greeted with scorn by the prosecutor.

"Those words have no meaning coming from him," said Charles Tingle. "He is a manipulator of the highest degree, a schemer, a con artist of unequaled ability."

Tingle told the judges, "He does not deserve your mercy. Your compassion should be reserved for his murder victims. The death penalty is justice in this case. To be merciful and not impose the death penalty is wrong. The horror is truly unimaginable."

On Friday, September 24, 1999, relatives of the murdered women had their say before the judicial panel.

Angela Fite's father, Phillip Wayne Fite, glared at Neal and described his daughter as "a gift to this world." He said Angela's two children were devastated and could not understand why their mother was gone.

Telling them she was dead, said Angela's ex-husband, Mike Kelly, "was the hardest thing I've ever had to do in my life." He said his children, six-year-old Kyle and three-year-old Kayla, had been robbed of their mother's love. "They pick out the brightest star in the sky," he said, "and they say, 'There's Mama.' "

Candace Walters's sister, Barbara Watkins, told the judges their eighty-year-old mother still had not accepted Candace's death and had begun having imaginary conversations with her and other dead relatives.

On Wednesday, September 29, 1999, the judges sentenced Neal to death.

A thirty-six-page decision stated that the murders were committed entirely without conscience.

"William Neal was unaffected by the enormity of his

bloody, ruthless, unprovoked attacks," said Judge Woodford. "After each murder, William Neal went out socializ-
ing, shopping, dining, preparing for the next murder and
generally performing his usual daily activities without any
feelings about the person he had just slaughtered."

He continued, "The judges have determined from the
overwhelming evidence that these brutal, needless killings
visited emotional devastation upon the children and families of these three kind and lovely ladies that the defendant
purported to love."

The panel found Neal "so self-absorbed" that his capacity for remorse was questionable and the timing of his religious conversion was suspect.

"William Neal's plea rings hollow in light of his past
deceits and evil deeds," they said. "William Neal was a
self-admitted con artist and manipulator, tools which he
used to take advantage of the victims."

When the judges announced their decision in court, family and friends of the dead women reacted with a collective
"Yes!" One person clapped.

Neal showed no reaction and left the courtroom without
a word or a glance at the families of his victims.

"This is not going to be over for us for a very, very long
time," said Wayne Fite. "The anger is less, but we'll never
recover from this." Vowing to be present at Neal's execution, he said, "This doesn't really have anything to do with
vengeance. This person is a menace to society and needed
to be taken out of action."

Said Holly Walters, Candace's daughter, "This brings
some closure, but it does not bring back my mom, Angela
or Rebecca."

No matter what had motivated William Neal and all the
others whose horrible acts have been recounted in this
book, the moment they took an axe and committed the sin
of Cain they were destined to be called to account one way

or another by a humanity haunted by the lament of the pained God of the Bible's Book of Genesis:

> "The voice of thy brother's blood
> crieth unto me from the ground."

APPENDIX

An inquest was convened by Judge Josiah Blaisdell five days after Andrew and Abby Borden had been found murdered. Despite the fact that Lizzie Borden was under suspicion and had a constitutional right not to testify, she was quizzed by District Attorney Hosea Knowlton over a period of three days, August 9–11, 1892.

The following transcript of her testimony was published by the New Bedford newspaper *The Evening Standard*. It is historically significant not only because it records the only testimony given by Lizzie Borden, but because the circumstances leading up to it would ultimately undermine the prosecution's case at trial.

Tuesday, August 9, 1892

Q. (Mr. Knowlton) Give me your full name.
A. Lizzie Andrew Borden.
Q. Is it Lizzie or Elizabeth?
A. Lizzie.
Q. You were so christened?
A. I was so christened.
Q. What is your age, please?
A. Thirty-two.
Q. Your mother is not living?
A. No sir.
Q. When did she die?
A. She died when I was two and a half years old.
Q. You do not remember her, then?
A. No sir.

Q. What was your father's age?

A. He was seventy next month.

Q. What was his whole name?

A. Andrew Jackson Borden.

Q. And your stepmother, what is her whole name?

A. Abby Durfee Borden.

Q. How long had your father been married to your stepmother?

A. I think about twenty-seven years.

Q. How much of that time have they lived in that house on Second street?

A. I think, I am not sure, but I think about twenty years last May.

Q. Always occupied the whole house?

A. Yes sir.

Q. Somebody told me it was once fitted up for two tenements.

A. When we bought it it was for two tenements, and the man we bought it off stayed there a few months until he finished his own house. After he finished his own house and moved into it there was no one else ever moved in; we always had the whole.

Q. Have you any idea how much your father was worth?

A. No sir.

Q. Have you ever heard him say?

A. No sir.

Q. Have you ever formed any opinion?

A. No sir.

Q. Do you know something about his real estate?

A. About what?

Q. His real estate?

A. I know what real estate he owned, part of it; I don't know whether I know it all or not.

Q. Tell me what you know of.

A. He owns two farms in Swanzey, the place on Sec-

ond street and the A. J. Borden building and corner, and the land on South Main street where
McMannus is, and then a short time ago he bought
some real estate up further south that, formerly,
he said belonged to a Mr. Birch.

Q. Did you ever deed him any property?

A. He gave us some years ago, Grandfather Borden's
house on Ferry street, and he bought that back
from us some weeks ago, I don't know just how
many.

Q. As near as you can tell.

A. Well, I should say in June, but I am not sure.

Q. What do you mean by bought it back?

A. He bought it of us, and gave us the money for it.

Q. How much was it?

A. How much money? He gave us $5,000 for it.

Q. Did you pay him anything when you took a deed
from him?

A. Pay him anything? No sir.

Q. How long ago was it you took a deed from him?

A. When he gave it to us?

Q. Yes.

A. I can't tell you; I should think five years.

Q. Did you have any other business transactions with
him besides that?

A. No sir.

Q. In real estate?

A. No sir.

Q. Or in personal property?

A. No sir.

Q. Never?

A. Never.

Q. No transfer of property one way or the other?

A. No sir.

Q. At no time?

A. No sir.

Q. And I understand he paid you the cash for this property?

A. Yes sir.

Q. You and Emma equally?

A. Yes sir.

Q. How many children has your father?

A. Only two.

Q. Only you two?

A. Yes sir.

Q. Any others ever?

A. One that died.

Q. Did you ever know of your father making a will?

A. No sir, except I heard somebody say once that there was one several years ago; that is all I ever heard.

Q. Who did you hear say so?

A. I think it was Mr. Morse.

Q. What Morse?

A. Uncle John V. Morse.

Q. How long ago?

A. How long ago I heard him say it? I have not any idea.

Q. What did he say about it?

A. Nothing, except just that.

Q. What?

A. That Mr. Borden had a will.

Q. Did you ask your father?

A. I did not.

Q. Did he ever mention the subject of will to you?

A. He did not.

Q. He never told you that he had made a will, or had not?

A. No sir.

Q. Did he have a marriage settlement with your stepmother that you knew of?

A. I never knew of any.

Q. Had you heard anything of his proposing to make a will?

A. No sir.

Q. Do you know of anybody that your father was on bad terms with?

A. There was a man that came there that he had trouble with, I don't know who the man was.

Q. When?

A. I cannot locate the time exactly. It was within two weeks. That is I don't know the date or day of the month.

Q. Tell all you saw and heard.

A. I did not see anything. I heard the bell ring, and father went to the door and let him in. I did not hear anything for some time, except just the voices; then I heard the man say, "I would like to have that place, I would like to have that store." Father says, "I am not willing to let your business go in there." And the man said, "I thought with your reputation for liking money, you would let your store for anything." Father said, "You are mistaken." Then they talked a while, and then their voices were louder, and I heard father order him out, and went to the front door with him.

Q. What did he say?

A. He said that he had stayed long enough, and he would thank him to go.

Q. Did he say anything about coming again?

A. No sir.

Q. Did your father say anything about coming again, or did he?

A. No sir.

Q. Have you any idea who that was?

A. No sir. I think it was a man from out of town, because he said he was going home to see his partner.

Q. Have you had any efforts made to find him?

A. We have had a detective, that is all I know.

Q. You have not found him?

A. Not that I know of.

Q. You can't give us any other idea about it?

A. Nothing but what I have told you.

Q. Beside that do you know of anybody that your father had bad feelings toward, or who had bad feelings toward your father?

A. I know of one man that has not been friendly with him; they have not been friendly for years.

Q. Who?

A. Mr. Hiram C. Harrington.

Q. What relation is he to him?

A. He is my father's brother-in-law.

Q. Your mother's brother?

A. My father's only sister married Mr. Harrington.

Q. Anybody else that was on bad terms with your father, or that your father was on bad terms with?

A. Not that I know of.

Q. You have no reason to suppose that man you speak of a week or two ago, had ever seen your father before, or has since?

A. No sir.

Q. Do you know of anybody that was on bad terms with your stepmother?

A. No sir.

Q. Or that your stepmother was on bad terms with?

A. No sir.

Q. Had your stepmother any property?

A. I don't know, only that she had half the house that belonged to her father.

Q. Where was that?

A. On Fourth Street.

Q. Who lives in it?

A. Her half sister.

Q. Any other property beside that that you know of?

A. I don't know.

Q. Did you ever know of any?

A. No sir.

Q. Did you understand that she was worth anything more than that?

A. I never knew.

Q. Did you ever have any trouble with your stepmother?

A. No sir.

Q. Have you, within six months, had any words with her?

A. No sir.

Q. Within a year?

A. No sir.

Q. Within two years?

A. I think not.

Q. When last that you know of?

A. About five years ago.

Q. What about?

A. Her stepsister, half sister.

Q. What name?

A. Her name now is Mrs. George W. Whitehead.

Q. Nothing more than hard words?

A. No sir, they were not hard words; it was simply a difference of opinion.

Q. You have been on pleasant terms with your stepmother since then?

A. Yes sir.

Q. Cordial?

A. It depends upon one's idea of cordiality, perhaps.

Q. According to your idea of cordiality?

A. Quite so.

Q. What do you mean by "quite so"?

A. Quite cordial. I do not mean the dearest of friends in the world, but very kindly feelings, and pleasant. I do not know how to answer you any better than that.

Q. You did not regard her as your mother?

A. Not exactly, no; although she came here when I was very young.

Q. Were your relations towards her that of daughter and mother?

A. In some ways it was, and in some it was not.

Q. In what ways was it?

A. I decline to answer.

Q. Why?

A. Because I don't know how to answer it.

Q. In what ways was it not?

A. I did not call her mother.

Q. What name did she go by?

A. Mrs. Borden.

Q. When did you begin to call her Mrs. Borden?

A. I should think five or six years ago.

Q. Before that time you had called her mother?

A. Yes sir.

Q. What led to the change?

A. The affair with her stepsister.

Q. So that the affair was serious enough to have you change from calling her mother, do you mean?

A. I did not choose to call her mother.

Q. Have you ever called her mother since?

A. Yes, occasionally.

Q. To her face, I mean?

A. Yes.

Q. Often?

A. No sir.

Q. Seldom?

A. Seldom.

Q. Your usual address was Mrs. Borden?

A. Yes sir.

Q. Did your sister Emma call her mother?

A. She always called her Abby from the time she came into the family.

Q. Is your sister Emma older than you?

A. Yes sir.

Q. What is her age?

A. She is ten years older than I am. She was some-where about fourteen when she came there.

Q. What was your stepmother's age?

A. I don't know. I asked her sister Saturday, and she said sixty-four. I told them sixty-seven; I did not know. I told as nearly as I knew. I did not know there was so much difference between she and fa-ther.

Q. Why did you leave off calling her mother?

A. Because I wanted to.

Q. Is that all the reason you have to give me?

A. I have not any other answer.

Q. Can't you give me any better reason than that?

A. I have not any reason to give, except that I did not want to.

Q. In what other respect were the relations between you and her not that of mother and daughter, be-sides not calling her mother?

A. I don't know that any of the relations were changed. I had never been to her as a mother in many things. I always went to my sister, because she was older and had the care of me after my mother died.

Q. In what respects were the relations between you and her that of mother and daughter?

A. That is the same question you asked before; I can't answer you any better now than I did before.

Q. You did not say before you could not answer, but that you declined to answer.

A. I decline to answer because I do not know what to say.

Q. That is the only reason?

A. Yes sir.

Q. You called your father father?

A. Always.

Q. Were your father and mother happily united?
(PAUSE)

A. Why, I don't know but that they were.

Q. Why do you hesitate?

A. Because I don't know but that they were, and I am telling the truth as nearly as I know it.

Q. Do you mean me to understand that they were happy entirely, or not?

A. So far as I know they were.

Q. Why did you hesitate then?

A. Because I did not know how to answer you any **better than what came into my mind.** I was trying to think if I was telling it as I should; that is all.

Q. Do you have any difficulty in telling it as you should, any difficulty in answering my questions?

A. Some of your questions I have difficulty in answering because I don't know just how you mean them.

Q. Did you ever know of any difficulty between her and your father?

A. No sir.

Q. Did he seem to be affectionate?

A. I think so.

Q. As man and woman who are married ought to be?

A. So far as I have ever had any chance of judging.

Q. They were?

A. Yes.

Q. What dress did you wear the day they were killed?

A. I had on a navy blue, sort of a bengaline; or India silk skirt, with a navy blue blouse. In the afternoon they thought I had better change it. I put on a pink wrapper.

Q. Did you change your clothing before the afternoon?

A. No sir.

Q. You dressed in the morning, as you have described, and kept that clothing on until afternoon?

A. Yes sir.

Q. When did Morse come there first, I don't mean this visit, I mean as a visitor, John V. Morse?

A. Do you mean this day that he came and stayed all night?

Q. No. Was this visit his first to your house?

A. He has been in the east a year or more.

Q. Since he has been in the east has he been in the habit of coming to your house?

A. Yes; came in any time he wanted to.

Q. Before that had he been at your house, before he came east?

A. Yes, he has been here, if you remember the winter that the river was frozen over and they went across, he was here that winter, some 14 years ago, was it not?

Q. I am not answering questions, but asking them.

A. I don't remember the date. He was here that winter.

Q. Has he been here since?

A. He has been here once since, I don't know whether he has or not since.

Q. How many times this last year has he been at your house?

A. None at all to speak of, nothing more than a night or two at a time.

Q. How often did he come to spend a night or two?

A. Really I don't know; I am away so much myself.

Q. Your last answer is that you don't know how much he had been here, because you had been away yourself so much?

A. Yes.

Q. That is true the last year, or since he has been east?

A. I have not been away the last year so much, but other times I have been away when he has been here.

Q. Do I understand you to say that his last visit before this one was 14 years ago?

A. No, he has been here once between the two.

Q. How long did he stay then?

A. I don't know.

Q. How long ago was that?

A. I don't know.

Q. Give me your best remembrance.

A. Five or six years, perhaps six.

Q. How long has he been east this time?

A. I think over a year; I am not sure.

Q. During the last year how much of the time has he been at your house?

A. Very little that I know of.

Q. Your answer to that question before was, I don't know because I have been away so much myself.

A. I did not mean I had been away very much myself the last year.

Q. How much have you been away the last year?

A. I have been away a great deal in the daytime, occasionally at night.

Q. Where in the daytime, any particular place?

A. No, around town.

Q. When you go off nights, where?

A. Never unless I have been off on a visit.

Q. When was the last time when you have been away for more than a night or two before this affair?

A. I don't think I have been away to stay more than a night or two since I came from abroad, except about three or four weeks ago I was in New Bedford for three or four days.

Q. Where at New Bedford?

A. At 20 Madison street.

Q. How long ago were you abroad?

A. I was abroad in 1890.

Q. When did he come to the house the last time before your father and mother were killed?

A. He stayed there all night Wednesday night.

Q. My question is when he came there.

A. I don't know; I was not at home when he came; I was out.

Q. When did you first see him there?

A. I did not see him at all.

Q. How did you know he was there?

A. I heard his voice.

Q. You did not see him Wednesday evening?

A. I did not; I was out Wednesday evening.

Q. You did not see him Thursday morning?

A. I did not; he was out when I came down stairs.

Q. When was the first time you saw him?

A. Thursday noon.

Q. You had never seen him before that?

A. No sir.

Q. Where were you Wednesday evening?

A. I spent the evening with Miss Russell.

Q. As near as you can remember, when did you return?

A. About nine o'clock at night.

Q. The family had then retired?

A. I don't know whether they had or not. I went right to my room; I don't remember.

Q. You did not look to see?

A. No sir.

Q. Which door did you come in at?

A. The front door.

Q. Did you lock it?

A. Yes sir.

Q. For the night?

A. Yes sir.

Q. And went right up stairs to your room?

A. Yes sir.

Q. When was it that you heard the voice of Mr. Morse?

A. I heard him down there about supper time—no, it was earlier than that. I heard him down there

somewhere about three o'clock, I think, I was in
my room Wednesday, not feeling well, all day.

Q. Did you eat supper at home Wednesday night?

A. I was at home; I did not eat any supper, because I
did not feel able to eat supper; I had been sick.

Q. You did not come down to supper?

A. No sir.

Q. Did you hear him eating supper?

A. No sir. I did not know whether he was there or not.

Q. You heard him in the afternoon?

A. Yes sir.

Q. Did you hear him go away?

A. I did not.

Q. You did not go down to see him?

A. No sir.

Q. Was you in bed?

A. No sir. I was on the lounge.

Q. Why did you not go down?

A. I did not care to go down, and I was not feeling
well, and kept my room all day.

Q. You felt better in the evening?

A. Not very much better. I thought I would go out
and see if the air would make me feel any better.

Q. When you came back at nine o'clock, you did not
look in to see if the family were up?

A. No sir.

Q. Why not?

A. I very rarely do when I come in.

Q. You go right to your room?

A. Yes sir.

Q. Did you have a night key?

A. Yes sir.

Q. How did you know it was right to lock the front
door?

A. That was always my business.

Q. How many locks did you fasten?

A. The spring locks itself, and there is a key to turn, and you manipulate the bolt.

Q. You manipulated all those?

A. I used them all.

Q. Then you went to bed?

A. Yes, directly.

Q. When you got up the next morning, did you see Mr. Morse?

A. I did not.

Q. Had the family breakfasted when you came down?

A. Yes sir.

Q. What time did you come down stairs?

A. As near as I can remember, it was a few minutes before nine.

Q. Who did you find down stairs when you came down?

A. Maggie and Mrs. Borden.

Q. Did you inquire for Mr. Morse?

A. No sir.

Q. Did you suppose he had gone?

A. I did not know whether he had or not; he was not there.

Q. Your father was there?

A. Yes sir.

Q. Then you found him?

A. Yes sir.

Q. Did you speak to either your father or Mrs. Borden?

A. I spoke to them all.

Q. About Mr. Morse?

A. I did not mention him.

Q. Did not inquire anything about him?

A. No sir.

Q. How long before that time had he been at the house?

A. I don't know.

Q. As near as you can tell?

A. I don't know. He was there in June sometime, I don't know whether he was there after that or not.

Q. Why did you not go to Marion with the party that went?

A. Because they went sooner than I could, and I was going Monday.

Q. Why did they go sooner than you could· what was there to keep you?

A. I had taken the secretaryship and treasurer of our C. E. society, had the charge, and the roll call was the first Sunday in August, and I felt I must be there and attend to that part of the business.

Q. Where was your sister Emma that day?

A. What day?

Q. The day your father and Mrs. Borden were killed?

A. She had been in Fairhaven.

Q. Had you written to her?

A. Yes sir.

Q. When was the last time you wrote to her?

A. Thursday morning, and my father mailed the letter for me.

Q. Did she get it at Fairhaven?

A. No sir, it was sent back. She did not get it at Fairhaven, for we telegraphed for her, and she got home here Thursday afternoon, and the letter was sent back to this post office.

Q. How long had she been in Fairhaven?

A. Just two weeks to a day.

Q. You did not visit in Fairhaven?

A. No sir.

Q. Had there been anybody else around the house that week, or premises?

A. No one that I knew of, except the man that called to see him on this business about the store.

Q. Was that that week?

A. Yes sir.

Q. I misunderstood you probably, I thought you said a week or two before.

A. No, I said that week. There was a man came the week before and gave up some keys, and I took them.

Q. Do you remember of anybody else being then around the premises that week?

A. Nobody that I know of or saw.

Q. Nobody at work there?

A. No sir.

Q. Nobody doing any chores there?

A. No sir, not that I know of.

Q. Nobody had access to the house, so far as you know, during that time?

A. No sir.

Q. I ask you once more how it happened that, knowing Mr. Morse was at your house, you did not step in and greet him before you retired?

A. I have no reason, except that I was not feeling well Wednesday, and so did not come down.

Q. No, you were down. When you came in from out.

A. Do you mean Wednesday night?

Q. Yes.

A. Because I hardly ever do go in. I generally went right up to my room, and I did that night.

Q. Could you then get to your room from the back hall?

A. No sir.

Q. From the back stairs?

A. No sir.

Q. Why not? What would hinder?

A. Father's bedroom door was kept locked, and his door into my room was locked and hooked, I think, and I had no keys.

Q. That was the custom of the establishment?

A. It had always been so.

Q. It was so Wednesday, and so Thursday?

A. It was so Wednesday, but Thursday they broke the door open.

Q. That was after the crowd came; before the crowd came?

A. It was so.

Q. There was no access, except one had a key, and one would have to have two keys?

A. They would have to have two keys if they went up the back way to get into my room. If they were in my room; they would have to have a key to get into his room, and another to get into the back stairs.

Q. Where did Mr. Morse sleep?

A. In the next room over the parlor in front of the stairs.

Q. Right up the same stairs that your room was?

A. Yes sir.

Q. How far from your room?

A. A door opened into it.

Q. The two rooms connected directly?

A. By one door, that is all.

Q. Not through the hall?

A. No sir.

Q. Was the door locked?

A. It has been locked and bolted, and a large writing desk in my room kept up against it.

Q. Then it was not a practical opening?

A. No sir.

Q. How otherwise do you get from your room to the next room?

A. I have to go into the front hall.

Q. How far apart are the two doors?

A. Very near, I don't think more than so far (measuring).

Q. Was it your habit when you were in your room to keep your door shut?

A. Yes sir.

Q. That time, that Wednesday afternoon?

A. My door was open part of the time, and part of the time I tried to get a nap and their voices annoyed me, and I closed it. I kept it open in summer more or less, and closed in winter.

Q. Then, unless for some special reason, you kept your door open in the summer?

A. Yes sir, if it was a warm day. If it was a cool day, I should have closed it.

Q. Where was your father when you came down Thursday morning?

A. Sitting in the sitting room in his large chair, reading the *Providence Journal.*

Q. Where was your mother? Do you prefer me to call her Mrs. Borden?

A. I had as soon you called her mother. She was in the dining room with a feather duster dusting.

Q. When she dusted did she wear something over her head?

A. Sometimes when she swept, but not when dusting.

Q. Where was Maggie?

A. Just come in the back door with the long pole, brush, and put the brush on the handle, and getting her pail of water; she was going to wash the windows around the house. She said Mrs. Borden wanted her to.

Q. Did you get your breakfast that morning?

A. I did not eat any breakfast; I did not feel as though I wanted any.

Q. Did you get any breakfast that morning?

A. I don't know whether I ate half a banana; I don't think I did.

Q. You drank no tea or coffee that morning?

A. No sir.

Q. And ate no cookies?

A. I don't know whether I did or not. We had some

molasses cookies; I don't know whether I ate any that morning or not.

Q. Were the breakfast things put away when you got down?

A. Everything except the coffee pot; I am not sure whether that was on the stove or not.

Q. You said nothing about Mr. Morse to your father or mother?

A. No sir.

Q. What was the next thing that happened after you got down?

A. Maggie went out of doors to wash the windows and father came out into the kitchen and said he did not know whether he would go down to the post office or not. And then I sprinkled some handkerchiefs to iron.

Q. Tell me again what time you came down stairs.

A. It was a little before nine, I should say about quarter; I don't know sure.

Q. Did your father go down town?

A. He went down later.

Q. What time did he start away?

A. I don't know.

Q. What were you doing when he started away?

A. I was in the dining room I think; yes, I had just commenced; I think, to iron.

Q. It may seem a foolish question. How much of an ironing did you have?

A. I only had about eight or ten of my best handkerchiefs.

Q. Did you let your father out?

A. No sir, he went out himself.

Q. Did you fasten the door after him?

A. No sir.

Q. Did Maggie?

A. I don't know. When she went up stairs she always locked the door, she had charge of the back door.

Q. Did she go out after a brush before your father went away?

A. I think so.

Q. Did you say anything to Maggie?

A. I did not.

Q. Did you say anything about washing the windows?

A. No sir.

Q. Did you speak to her?

A. I think I told her I did not want any breakfast.

Q. You do not remember of talking about washing the windows?

A. I don't remember whether I did or not; I don't remember it. Yes, I remember; yes, I asked her to shut the parlor blinds when she got through, because the sun was so hot.

Q. About what time do you think your father went down town?

A. I don't know, it must have been after nine o'clock. I don't know what time it was.

Q. You think at that time you had begun to iron your handkerchiefs?

A. Yes sir.

Q. How long a job was that?

A. I did not finish them; my flats were not hot enough.

Q. How long a job would it have been if the flats had been right?

A. If they had been hot, not more than 20 minutes, perhaps.

Q. How long did you work on the job?

A. I don't know, sir.

Q. How long was your father gone?

A. I don't know that.

Q. Where were you when he returned?

A. I was down in the kitchen.

Q. What doing?

A. Reading an old magazine that had been left in the cupboard, an old *Harper's Magazine*.

Q. Had you got through ironing?

A. No sir.

Q. Had you stopped ironing?

A. Stopped for the flats.

Q. Were you waiting for them to be hot?

A. Yes sir.

Q. Was there a fire in the stove?

A. Yes sir.

Q. When your father went away, you were ironing them?

A. I had not commenced, but I was getting the little ironing board and the flats.

Q. Are you sure you were in the kitchen when your father returned?

A. I am not sure whether I was there or in the dining room.

Q. Did you go back to your room before your father returned?

A. I think I did carry up some clean clothes.

Q. Did you stay there?

A. No sir.

Q. Did you spend any time up the front stairs before your father returned?

A. No sir.

Q. Or after he returned?

A. No sir. I did stay in my room long enough when I went up to sew a little piece of tape on a garment.

Q. What was the time when your father came home?

A. He came home after I came down stairs.

Q. You were not up stairs when he came home?

A. I was not up stairs when he came home; no sir.

Q. What was Maggie doing when your father came home?

A. I don't know whether she was there or whether she had gone up stairs; I can't remember.

Q. Who let your father in?

A. I think he came to the front door and rang the bell,

and I think Maggie let him in, and he said he had
forgotten his key; so I think she must have been
down stairs.

Q. His key would have done him no good if the locks
were left as you left them?

A. But they were always unbolted in the morning.

Q. Who unbolted them that morning?

A. I don't think they had been unbolted; Maggie can
tell you.

Q. If he had not forgotten his key it would have been
no good?

A. No, he had his key and could not get in. I understood Maggie to say he said he had forgotten his
key.

Q. You did not hear him say anything about it?

A. I heard his voice, but I don't know what he said.

Q. I understood you to say he said he had forgotten
his key?

A. No, it was Maggie said he said he had forgotten
the key.

Q. Where was Maggie when the bell rang?

A. I don't know, sir.

Q. Where were you when the bell rang?

A. I think in my room up stairs.

Q. Then you were up stairs when your father came
home?

A. I don't know sure, but I think I was.

Q. What were you doing?

A. As I say, I took up these clean clothes, and stopped
and basted a little piece of tape on a garment.

Q. Did you come down before your father was let in?

A. I was on the stairs coming down when she let him
in.

Q. Then you were up stairs when your father came to
the house on his return?

A. I think I was.

Q. How long had you been there?

A. I had only been upstairs just long enough to take the clothes up and baste the little loop on the sleeve. I don't think I had been up there over five minutes.

Q. Was Maggie still engaged in washing windows when your father got back?

A. I don't know.

Q. You remember, Miss Borden, I will call your attention to it so as to see if I have any misunderstanding, not for the purpose of confusing you; you remember, that you told me several times that you were down stairs, and not up stairs when your father came home? You have forgotten, perhaps?

A. I don't know what I have said. I have answered so many questions and I am so confused I don't know one thing from another. I am telling you just as nearly as I know.

Q. Calling your attention to what you said about that a few minutes ago, and now again to the circumstance you have said you were up stairs when the bell rang, and were on the stairs when Maggie let your father in; which now is your recollection of the true statement, of the matter, that you were down stairs when the bell rang and your father came?

A. I think I was down stairs in the kitchen.

Q. And then you were not up stairs?

A. I think I was not; because I went up almost immediately, as soon as I went down, and then came down again and stayed down.

Q. What had you in your mind when you said you were on the stairs as Maggie let your father in?

A. The other day somebody came there and she let them in and I was on the stairs; I don't know whether the morning before or when it was.

Q. You understood I was asking you exactly and explicitly about this fatal day?

A. Yes sir.

Q. I now call your attention to the fact that you had specifically told me you had gone up stairs, and had been there about five minutes when the bell rang, and were on your way down, and were on the stairs when Maggie let your father in that day—.

A. Yes, I said that, and then I said I did not know whether I was on the stairs or in the kitchen.

Q. Now how will you have it?

A. I think, as nearly as I know, I think I was in the kitchen.

Q. How long was your father gone?

A. I don't know, sir, not very long.

Q. An hour?

A. I should not think so.

Q. Will you give me the best story you can, so far as your recollection serves you, of your time while he was gone?

A. I sprinkled my handkerchiefs, and got my ironing board and took them in the dining room. I took the ironing board in the dining room and left the handkerchiefs in the kitchen on the table and whether I ate any cookies or not I don't remember. Then I sat down looking at the magazine waiting for the flats to heat. Then I went in the sitting room and got the *Providence Journal,* and took that into the kitchen. I don't recollect of doing anything else.

Q. Which did you read first, the *Journal* or the magazine?

A. The magazine.

Q. You told me you were reading the magazine when your father came back?

A. I said in the kitchen, yes.

Q. Was that so?

A. Yes, I took the *Journal* out to read, and had not read it. I had it near me.

Q. You said a minute or two ago you read the magazine awhile, and then went and got the *Journal* and took it out to read?

A. I did, but I did not read it; I tried my flats then.

Q. And went back to reading the magazine?

A. I took the magazine up again, yes.

Q. When did you last see your mother?

A. I did not see her after when I went down in the morning and she was dusting the dining room.

Q. Where did you or she go then?

A. I don't know where she went. I know where I was.

Q. Did you or she leave the dining room first?

A. I think I did. I left her in the dining room.

Q. You never saw her or heard her afterwards?

A. No sir.

Q. Did she say anything about making the bed?

A. She said she had been up and made the bed up fresh, and had dusted the room and left it all in order. She was going to put some fresh pillow slips on the small pillows at the foot of the bed, and was going to close the room, because she was going to have company Monday and she wanted everything in order.

Q. How long would it take to put on the pillow slips?

A. About two minutes.

Q. How long to do the rest of the things?

A. She had done that when I came down.

Q. All that was left was what?

A. To put on the pillow slips.

Q. Can you give me any suggestions as to what occupied her when she was up there, when she was struck dead?

A. I don't know of anything except she had some cotton cloth pillow cases up there, and she said she was going to commence to work on them. That is all I know. And the sewing machine was up there.

Q. Whereabouts was the sewing machine?

A. In the corner between the north and west side.

Q. Did you hear the sewing machine going?

A. I did not.

Q. Did you see anything to indicate that the sewing machine had been used that morning?

A. I had not. I did not go in there until after everybody had been in there, and the room had been overhauled.

Q. If she had remained down stairs, you would undoubtedly have seen her?

A. If she had remained down stairs, I should have, if she had remained in her room, I should not have.

Q. Where was that?

A. Over the kitchen.

Q. To get to that room she would have to go through the kitchen?

A. To get up the back stairs.

Q. That is the way she was in the habit of going?

A. Yes sir, because the other doors were locked.

Q. If she had remained down stairs, or had gone to her own room, you undoubtedly would have seen her?

A. I should have seen her if she had stayed downstairs; if she had gone to her room, I would not have seen her.

Q. She was found a little after 11 in the spare room, if she had gone to her own room she must have gone through the kitchen and up the back stairs, and subsequently have gone down and gone back again?

A. Yes sir.

Q. Have you any reason to suppose you would not have seen her if she had spent any portion of the time in her own room, or down stairs?

A. There is no reason why I should not have seen her if she had been down there, except when I first came down stairs, for two or three minutes I went down cellar to the water closet.

Q. After that you were where you practically commanded the view of the first story the rest of the time?

A. I think so.

Q. When you went up stairs for a short time, as you say you did, you then went in sight of the sewing machine?

A. No, I did not see the sewing machine, because she had shut that room up.

Q. What do you mean?

A. I mean the door was closed. She said she wanted it kept closed to keep the dust and everything out.

Q. Was it a room with a window?

A. It has three windows.

Q. A large room?

A. The size of the parlor; a pretty fair sized room.

Q. It is the guest room?

A. Yes, the spare room.

Q. Where the sewing machine was was the guest room?

A. Yes sir.

Q. I ask again, perhaps you have answered all you care to, what explanation can you give, can you suggest, as to what she was doing from the time she said she had got the work all done in the spare room until 11 o'clock?

A. I suppose she went up and made her own bed.

Q. That would be in the back part?

A. Yes sir.

Q. She would have to go by you twice to do that?

A. Unless she went when I was in my room that few minutes.

Q. That would not be time enough for her to go and make her own bed and come back again?

A. Sometimes she stayed up longer and sometimes shorter; I don't know.

Q. Otherwise than that, she would have to go in your sight?

A. I should have to have seen her once; I don't know that I need to have seen her more than once.

Q. You did not see her at all?

A. No sir, not after the dining room.

Q. What explanation can you suggest as to the whereabouts of your mother from the time you saw her in the dining room, and she said her work in the spare room was all done, until 11 o'clock?

A. I don't know. I think she went back into the spare room, and whether she came back again or not, I don't know; that has always been a mystery.

Q. Can you think of anything she could be doing in the spare room?

A. Yes sir. I know what she used to do sometimes. She kept her best cape she wore on the street in there, and she used occasionally to go up there to get it and to take it into her room. She kept a great deal in the guest room drawers; she used to go up there and get things and put things; she used those drawers for her own use.

Q. That connects her with her own room again, to reach which she had to go down stairs and come up again?

A. Yes.

Q. Assuming that she did not go into her own room, I understand you to say she could not have gone to her own room without your seeing her?

A. She could while I was down cellar.

Q. You went down immediately you came down, within a few minutes, and you did not see her when you came back?

A. No sir.

Q. After that time she must have remained in the guest chamber?

A. I don't know.

Q. So far as you can judge?

A. So far as I can judge she might have been out of the house, or in the house.

Q. Had you any knowledge of her going out of the house?

A. No sir.

Q. Had you any knowledge of her going out of the house?

A. She told me she had had a note, somebody was sick, and said "I am going to get the dinner on the way," and asked me what I wanted for dinner.

Q. Did you tell her?

A. Yes, I told her I did not want anything.

Q. Then why did you not suppose she had gone?

A. I supposed she had gone.

Q. Did you hear her come back?

A. I did not hear her go or come back, but I supposed she went.

Q. When you found your father dead you supposed your mother had gone?

A. I did not know. I said to the people who came in "I don't know whether Mrs. Borden is out or in; I wish you would see if she is in her room."

Q. You supposed she was out at the time?

A. I understood so; I did not suppose anything about it.

Q. Did she tell you where she was going?

A. No sir.

Q. Did she tell you who the note was from?

A. No sir.

Q. Did you ever see the note?

A. No sir.

Q. Do you know where it is now?

A. No sir.

Q. She said she was going out that morning?

A. Yes sir.

Wednesday, August 10, 1892

Mr. Knowlton asks:

Q. I shall have to ask you once more about that morning. Do you know what the family ate for breakfast?

A. No sir.

Q. Had the breakfast all been cleared away when you got down?

A. Yes sir.

Q. I want you to tell me just where you found the people when you got down that you did find there?

A. I found Mrs. Borden in the dining room. I found my father in the sitting room.

Q. And Maggie?

A. Maggie was coming in the back door with her pail and brush.

Q. Tell me what talk you had with your mother at that time?

A. She asked me how I felt. I said I felt better than I did Tuesday, but I did not want any breakfast. She asked me what I wanted for dinner, I told her nothing. I told her I did not want anything. She said she was going out, and would get the dinner. That is the last I saw her, or said anything to her.

Q. Where did you go then?

A. Into the kitchen.

Q. Where then?

A. Down cellar.

Q. Gone perhaps five minutes?

A. Perhaps. Not more than that; possibly a little bit more.

Q. When you came back did you see your mother?

A. I did not; I supposed she had gone out.

Q. She did not tell you where she was going?

A. No sir.

Q. When you came back was your father there?

A. Yes sir.

Q. What was he doing?

A. Reading the paper.

Q. Did you eat any breakfast?

A. No sir, I don't remember whether I ate a molasses cookie or not. I did not eat any regularly prepared breakfast.

Q. Was it usual for your mother to go out?

A. Yes sir, she went out every morning nearly, and did the marketing.

Q. Was it usual for her to be gone away from dinner?

A. Yes sir, sometimes, not very often.

Q. How often, say?

A. O, I should not think more than—well I don't know, more than once in three months, perhaps.

Q. Now I call your attention to the fact that twice yesterday you told me, with some explicitness, that when your father came in you were just coming down stairs?

A. No, I did not, I beg your pardon.

Q. That you were on the stairs at the time your father was let in, you said with some explicitness. Do you now say you did not say so?

A. I said I thought first I was on the stairs; then I remembered I was in the kitchen when he came in.

Q. First you thought you were in the kitchen; afterwards you remembered you were on the stairs?

A. I said I thought I was on the stairs; then I said I knew I was in the kitchen. I still say that now. I was in the kitchen.

Q. Did you go into the front part of the house after your father came in?

A. After he came in from down street I was in the sitting room with him.

Q. Did you go into the front hall afterwards?

A. No sir.

Q. At no time?

A. No sir.

Q. Excepting the two or three minutes you were down cellar, were you away from the house until your father came in?

A. No sir.

Q. You were always in the kitchen or dining room excepting when you went up stairs?

A. I went up stairs before he went out.

Q. You mean you went up there to sew a button on?

A. I basted a piece of tape on.

Q. Do you remember you did not say that yesterday?

A. I don't think you asked me. I told you yesterday I went up stairs directly after I came up from down cellar, with the clean clothes.

Q. You now say after your father went out, you did not go up stairs at all?

A. No sir, I did not.

Q. When Maggie came in there washing the windows, you did not appear from the front part of the house?

A. No sir.

Q. When your father was let in, you did not appear from up stairs?

A. No sir. I was in the kitchen.

Q. That is so?

A. Yes sir, to the best of my knowledge.

Q. After your father went out, you remained there either in the kitchen or dining room all the time?

A. I went in the sitting room long enough to direct some paper wrappers.

Q. One of the three rooms?

A. Yes sir.

Q. So it would have been extremely difficult for anybody to have gone through the kitchen and dining
room and front hall, without your seeing them?

A. They could have gone from the kitchen into the
sitting room while I was in the dining room, if
there was anybody to go.

Q. Then into the front hall?

A. Yes sir.

Q. You were in the dining room ironing?

A. Yes sir, part of the time.

Q. You were in all of the three rooms?

A. Yes sir.

Q. A large portion of that time, the girl was out of
doors?

A. I don't know where she was, I did not see her. I
supposed she was out of doors, as she had the pail
and brush.

Q. You know she was washing windows?

A. She told me she was going to, did not see her do
it.

Q. For a large portion of the time, you did not see the
girl?

A. No sir.

Q. So far as you know you were alone in the lower
part of the house a large portion of the time, after
your father went away, and before he came back?

A. My father did not go away, I think until somewhere
about 10, as near as I can remember, he was with
me down stairs.

Q. A large portion of the time after your father went
away, and before he came back, so far as you know,
you were alone in the house?

A. Maggie had come in and gone up stairs.

Q. After he went out, and before he came back; a
large portion of the time after your father went
out, and before he came back, so far as you know,
you were the only person in the house?

A. So far as I know, I was.

Q. And during that time, so far as you know, the front door was locked?

A. So far as I know.

Q. And never was unlocked at all?

A. I don't think it was.

Q. Even after your father came home, it was locked up again?

A. I don't know whether she locked it up again after that or not.

Q. It locks itself?

A. The spring lock opens.

Q. It fastens it so it cannot be opened from the outside?

A. Sometimes you can press it open.

Q. Have you any reason to suppose the spring lock was left so it could be pressed open from the out side?

A. I have no reason to suppose so.

Q. Nothing about the lock was changed before the people came?

A. Nothing that I know of.

Q. What were you doing in the kitchen when your father came home?

A. I think I was eating a pear when he came in.

Q. What had you been doing before that?

A. Been reading a magazine.

Q. Were you making preparations to iron again?

A. I had sprinkled my clothes, and was waiting for the flat. I sprinkled the clothes before he went out.

Q. Had you built up the fire again?

A. I put in a stick of wood. There was a few sparks. I put in a stick of wood to try to heat the flat.

Q. You had then started the fire?

A. Yes sir.

Q. The fire was burning when he came in?

A. No sir, but it was smoldering and smoking as though it would come up.

Q. Did it come up after he came in?

A. No sir.

Q. Did you do any more ironing?

A. I did not. I went in with him, and did not finish.

Q. You did not iron any more after your father came in?

A. No sir.

Q. Was the ironing board put away?

A. No sir, it was on the dining room table.

Q. When was it put away?

A. I don't know. Somebody put it away after the affair happened.

Q. You did not put it away?

A. No sir.

Q. Was it on the dining room table when you found your father killed?

A. I suppose so.

Q. You had not put it away then?

A. I had not touched it.

Q. How soon after your father came in, before Maggie went up stairs?

A. I don't know. I did not see her.

Q. Did you see her after your father came in?

A. Not after she let him in.

Q. How long was your father in the house before you found him killed?

A. I don't know exactly, because I went out to the barn. I don't know what time he came home. I don't think he had been home more than fifteen or twenty minutes; I am not sure.

Q. When you went out to the barn, where did you leave your father?

A. He had laid down on the sitting room lounge, taken off his shoes, and put on his slippers, and taken off his coat and put on the reefer. I asked him if he wanted the window left that way.

Q. Where did you leave him?

A. On the sofa.

Q. Was he asleep?

A. No sir.

Q. Was he reading?

A. No sir.

Q. What was the last thing you said to him?

A. I asked him if he wanted the window left that way. Then I went into the kitchen, and from there to the barn.

Q. Whereabouts in the barn did you go?

A. Up stairs.

Q. To the second story of the barn?

A. Yes sir.

Q. How long did you remain there?

A. I don't know, fifteen or twenty minutes.

Q. What doing?

A. Trying to find lead for a sinker.

Q. What made you think there would be lead for a sinker up there?

A. Because there was some there.

Q. Was there not some by the door?

A. Some pieces of lead by the open door, but there was a box full of old things up stairs.

Q. Did you bring any sinker back from the barn?

A. I found no sinker.

Q. Did you bring any sinker back from the barn?

A. Nothing but a piece of a chip I picked up on the floor.

Q. Where was that box you say was up stairs, containing lead?

A. There was a kind of a workbench.

Q. Is it there now?

A. I don't know, sir.

Q. How long since have you seen it there?

A. I have not been out there since that day.

Q. Had you been in the barn before?

A. That day, no sir.

Q. How long since you had been in the barn before?

A. I don't think I had been into it. I don't know as I had in three months.

Q. When you went out did you unfasten the screen door?

A. I unhooked it to get out.

Q. It was hooked until you went out?

A. Yes sir.

Q. It had been left hooked by Bridget if she was the last one in?

A. I suppose so; I don't know.

Q. Do you know when she did get through washing the outside?

A. I don't know.

Q. Did you know she washed the windows inside?

A. I don't know.

Q. Did you see her washing the windows inside?

A. I don't know.

Q. You don't know whether she washed the dining room and sitting room windows inside?

A. I did not see her.

Q. If she did, would you not have seen her?

A. I don't know. She might be in one room and I in another.

Q. Do you think she might have gone to work and washed all the windows in the dining room and sitting room and you not know it?

A. I don't know. I am sure, whether I should or not, I might have seen her, and not know it.

Q. Miss Borden, I am trying in good faith to get all the doings that morning of yourself and Miss Sullivan, and I have not succeeded in doing it. Do you desire to give me any information or not?

A. I don't know it—I don't know what your name is.

Q. It is certain beyond reasonable doubt she was engaged in washing the windows in the dining room or sitting room when your father came home. Do you mean to say you know nothing of either of those operations?

A. I knew she washed the windows outside; that is, she told me so. She did not wash the windows in the kitchen, because I was in the kitchen most of the time.

Q. The dining room and sitting room; I said.

A. I don't know.

Q. It is reasonably certain she washed the windows in the dining room and sitting room, inside while your father was out, and was engaged in this operation when your father came home; do you mean to say you know nothing of it?

A. I don't know whether she washed the windows in the sitting room and dining room or not.

Q. Can you give me any information how it happened at that particular time you should go into the chamber of the barn to find a sinker to go to Marion with to fish the next Monday?

A. I was going to finish my ironing; my flats were not hot. I said to myself "I will go and try and find that sinker, perhaps by the time I get back the flats will be hot." That is the only reason.

Q. How long had you been reading an old magazine before you went to the barn at all?

A. Perhaps half an hour.

Q. Had you got a fish line?

A. Not here; we had some at the farm.

Q. Had you got a fish hook?

A. No sir.

Q. Had you any apparatus for fishing at all?

A. Yes, over there.

Q. Had you any sinkers over there?

A. I think there were some. It is so long since I have been there; I think there were some.

Q. You had no reason to suppose you were lacking sinkers?

A. I don't think there were any on my lines.

Q. Where were your lines?

A. My fishlines were at the farm here.

Q. What made you think there were no sinkers at the farm on your lines?

A. Because some time ago when I was there I had none.

Q. How long since you used the fishlines?

A. Five years, perhaps.

Q. You left them at the farm then?

A. Yes sir.

Q. And you have not seen them since?

A. Yes sir.

Q. It occurred to you after your father came in it would be a good time to go to the barn after sinkers, and you had no reason to suppose there was not abundance of sinkers at the farm and abundance of lines?

A. The last time I was there there were some lines.

Q. Did you not say before you presumed there were sinkers at the farm?

A. I don't think I said so.

Q. You did say so exactly. Do you now say you presume there were not sinkers at the farm?

A. I don't think there were any fishlines suitable to use at the farm; I don't think there were any sinkers on any line that had been mine.

Q. Do you remember telling me you presumed there were lines, and sinkers and hooks at the farm?

A. I said there were lines I thought, and perhaps hooks. I did not say I thought there were sinkers on my lines. There was another box of lines over there beside mine.

Q. You thought there were not sinkers?

A. Not on my lines.

Q. Not sinkers at the farm?

A. I don't think there were any sinkers at the farm. I don't know whether there were or not.

Q. Did you then think there were no sinkers at the farm?

A. I thought there were no sinkers anywhere, or I should not have been trying to find some.

Q. You thought there were no sinkers at the farm to be had?

A. I thought there were no sinkers at the farm to be had.

Q. That is the reason you went into the second story of the barn to look for a sinker?

A. Yes sir.

Q. What made you think you would find sinkers there?

A. I heard Father say, and I knew there was lead there.

Q. You thought there might be lead there made into sinkers?

A. I thought there might be lead there with a hole in it.

Q. Did you examine the lead that was down stairs near the door?

A. No sir.

Q. Why not?

A. I don't know.

Q. You went straight to the upper story of the barn?

A. No, I went under the pear tree and got some pears first.

Q. Then went to the second story of the barn to look for sinkers for lines you had at the farm, as you supposed as you had seen them there five years before that time?

A. I went up to get some sinkers, if I could find them. I did not intend to go to the farm for lines; I was going to buy some lines here.

Q. You then had no intention of using your own line and hooks at Marion?

A. I could not get them.

Q. What was the use of telling me a little while ago you had no sinkers on your line at the farm?

A. I thought I made you understand that those lines at the farm were no good to use.

Q. Did you not mean for me to understand one of the reasons you were searching for sinkers was that the lines you had at the farm, as you remembered them had no sinkers on them?

A. I said the lines at the farm had no sinkers on them.

Q. I did not ask you what you said. Did you not mean for me to understand that?

A. I meant for you to understand I wanted the sinkers and was going to have new lines.

Q. You had not then bought your lines?

A. No sir, I was going out Thursday noon.

Q. You had not bought any apparatus for fishing?

A. No hooks.

Q. Had bought nothing connected with your fishing trip?

A. No sir.

Q. Going to go fishing the next Monday, were you?

A. I don't know that we should go fishing Monday.

Q. Going to the place to go fishing Monday?

A. Yes sir.

Q. This was Thursday and you had no idea of using any fishing apparatus before the next Monday?

A. No sir.

Q. You had no fishing apparatus you were proposing to use the next Monday until then?

A. No sir, not until I bought it.

Q. You had not bought anything?

A. No sir.

Q. Had not started to buy anything?

A. No sir.

Q. The first thing in preparation for your fishing trip the next Monday was to go to the loft of that barn to find some old sinkers to put on some hooks and lines that you had not then bought?

A. I thought if I found no sinkers I would have to buy the sinkers when I bought the lines.

Q. You thought you would be saving some thing by hunting in the loft of the barn before you went to see whether you should need lines or not?

A. I thought I would find out whether there were any sinkers before I bought the lines; and if there was, I should not have to buy any sinkers. If there were some, I should only have to buy the lines and the hooks.

Q. You began the collection of your fishing apparatus by searching for the sinkers in the barn?

A. Yes sir.

Q. You were searching in a box of old stuff in the loft of the barn?

A. Yes sir, up stairs.

Q. That you had never looked at before?

A. I had seen them.

Q. Never examined them before?

A. No sir.

Q. All the reason you supposed there was sinkers there was your father had told you there was lead in the barn?

A. Yes, lead; and one day I wanted some old nails; he said there was some in the barn.

Q. All the reason that gave you to think there was sinkers was your father said there was old lead in the barn?

A. Yes sir.

Q. Did he mention the place in the barn?

A. I think he said up stairs; I am not sure.

Q. Where did you look up stairs?

A. On that workbench, like.

Q. In anything?

A. Yes, it was a box, sort of a box, and then some

things lying right on the side that was not in the box.

Q. How large a box was it?

A. I could not tell you. It was probably covered up with lumber, I think.

Q. Give me the best idea of the size of the box you can.

A. Well, I should say, I don't know, I have not any idea.

Q. Give me the best idea you have.

A. I have given you the best idea I have.

Q. What is the best idea you have?

A. About that large (measuring with hands).

Q. That long?

A. Yes.

Q. How wide?

A. I don't know.

Q. Give me the best idea you have.

A. Perhaps about as wide as it was long.

Q. How high?

A. It was not very high.

Q. About how high?

(Witness measures with her hands.)

Q. About twice the length of your forefinger?

A. I should think so. Not quite.

Q. What was in the box?

A. Nails, and some old locks, and I don't know but there was a door knob.

Q. Anything else?

A. I don't remember anything else.

Q. Any lead?

A. Yes, some pieces of tea lead, like.

Q. Foil, what we call tin foil, the same as you use on tea chests?

A. I don't remember seeing any tin foil; not as thin as that.

Q. Tea chest lead?

A. No sir.

Q. What did you see in shape of lead?

A. Flat pieces of lead, a little bigger than that; some of them were doubled together.

Q. How many?

A. I could not tell you.

Q. Where else did you look beside in the box?

A. I did not look anywhere for lead except on the workbench.

Q. How full was the box?

A. It was nearly as full as it could have been.

Q. You looked on the bench, beside that, where else?

A. Nowhere except on the bench.

Q. Did you look for anything else beside lead?

A. No sir.

Q. When you got through looking for lead did you come down?

A. No sir. I went to the west window over the hay, to the west window, and the curtain was slanted a little. I pulled it down.

Q. What else?

A. Nothing.

Q. That is all you did?

A. Yes sir.

Q. That is the second story of the barn?

A. Yes sir.

Q. Was the window open?

A. I think not.

Q. Hot?

A. Very hot.

Q. How long do you think you were up there?

A. Not more than fifteen or twenty minutes, I should not think.

Q. Should you think what you have told me would occupy four minutes?

A. Yes, because I ate some pears up there.

Q. Do you think all you have told me would take you four minutes?

A. I ate some pears up there.

Q. I asked you to tell me all you did.

A. I told you all I did.

Q. Do you mean to say you stopped your work, and then, additional to that, sat still and ate some pears?

A. While I was looking out of the window, yes sir.

Q. Will you tell me all you did in the second story of the barn?

A. I think I told you all I did that I can remember.

Q. Is there anything else?

A. I told you. I took some pears up from the ground when I went up; I stopped under the pear tree and took some pears up when I went up.

Q. Have you now told me everything you did up in the second story of the barn?

A. Yes sir.

Q. I now call your attention, and ask you to say whether all you have told me—I don't suppose you stayed there any longer than necessary?

A. No sir, because it was very close.

Q. I suppose that was the hottest place there was on the premises?

A. I should think so.

Q. Can you give me any explanation why all you have told me would occupy more than three minutes?

A. Yes, it would take me more than three minutes.

Q. To look in that box that you have described the size of on the bench and put down the curtain and then get out as soon as you conveniently could; would you say you were occupied in that business twenty minutes?

A. I think so, because I did not look at the box when I first went up.

Q. What did you do?

A. I ate my pears.

Q. Stood there eating the pears, doing nothing?

A. I was looking out of the window.

Q. Stood there, looking out of the window eating the pears?

A. I should think so.

Q. How many did you eat?

A. Three, I think.

Q. You were feeling better than you did in the morning?

A. Better than I did the night before.

Q. You were feeling better than you were in the morning?

A. I felt better in the morning than I did the night before.

Q. That is not what I asked you. You were then, when you were in that hot loft, looking out of the window and eating three pears, feeling better, were you not, than you were in the morning when you could not eat any breakfast?

A. I never eat any breakfast.

Q. You did not answer my question, and you will, if I have to put it all day. Were you, then when you were eating those three pears in that hot loft, looking out of that closed window, feeling better than you were in the morning when you ate no breakfast?

A. I was feeling well enough to eat the pears.

Q. Were you feeling better than you were in the morning?

A. I don't think I felt very sick in the morning, only—Yes, I don't know but I did feel better. As I say, I don't know whether I ate any breakfast or not, or whether I ate a cookie.

Q. Were you then feeling better than you did in the morning?

A. I don't know how to answer you, because I told you I felt better in the morning anyway.

Q. Do you understand my question? My question is whether, when you were in the loft of that barn, you were feeling better than you were in the morning when you got up?

A. No, I felt about the same.

Q. Were you feeling better than you were when you told your mother you did not care for any dinner?

A. No sir, I felt about the same.

Q. Well enough to eat pears, but not well enough to eat anything for dinner?

A. She asked me if I wanted any meat.

Q. I ask you why you should select that place, which was the only place which would put you out of sight of the house, to eat those three pears in?

A. I cannot tell you any reason.

Q. You observe that fact, do you not? You have put yourself in the only place perhaps, where it would be impossible, for you to see a person going into the house?

A. Yes sir, I should have seen them from the front window.

Q. From anywhere in the yard?

A. No sir, not unless from the end of the barn.

Q. Ordinarily in the yard you could see them, and in the kitchen where you had been, you could have seen them?

A. I don't think I understand.

Q. When you were in the kitchen, you could see persons who came in at the back door?

A. Yes sir.

Q. When you were in the yard, unless you were around the corner of the house, you could see them come in at the back door?

A. No sir, not unless I was at the corner of the barn; the minute I turned I could not.

Q. What was there?

A. A little jog like, the walk turns.

Q. I ask you again to explain to me why you took those pears from the pear tree?

A. I did not take them from the pear tree.

Q. From the ground, wherever you took them from. I thank you for correcting me, going into the barn, going up stairs into the hottest place in the barn, in the rear of the barn, the hottest place, and there standing and eating those pears that morning?

A. I beg your pardon, I was not in the rear of the barn. I was in the other end of the barn that faced the street.

Q. Where you could see anybody coming into the house?

A. Yes sir.

Q. Did you not tell me you could not?

A. Before I went into the barn, at the jog on the outside.

Q. You now say when you were eating the pears, you could see the back door?

A. Yes sir.

Q. So nobody could come in at that time without you seeing them?

A. I don't see how they could.

Q. After you got through eating your pears you began your search?

A. Yes sir.

Q. Then you did not see into the house?

A. No sir, because the bench is at the other end.

Q. Now I have asked you over and over again, and will continue the inquiry, whether anything you did at the bench would occupy more than three minutes?

A. Yes, I think it would, because I pulled over quite a lot of boards in looking.

Q. To get at the box?

A. Yes sir.

Q. Taking all that, what is the amount of time you think you occupied in looking for that piece of lead which you did not find?

A. Well, I should think perhaps I was ten minutes.

Q. Looking over those old things?

A. Yes sir, on the bench.

Q. Now can you explain why you were ten minutes doing it?

A. No, only that I can't do anything in a minute.

Q. When you came down from the barn, what did you do then?

A. Came into the kitchen.

Q. What did you do then?

A. I went into the dining room and laid down my hat.

Q. What did you do then?

A. Opened the sitting room door, and went into the sitting room, or pushed it open; it was not latched.

Q. What did you do then?

A. I found my father, and rushed to the foot of the stairs.

Q. What were you going into the sitting room for?

A. To go up stairs.

Q. What for?

A. To sit down.

Q. What had become of the ironing?

A. The fire had gone out.

Q. I thought you went out because the fire was not hot enough to heat the flats.

A. I thought it would burn, but the fire had not caught from the few sparks.

Q. So you gave up the ironing and was going up stairs?

A. Yes sir, I thought I would wait till Maggie got dinner and heat the flats again.

Q. When you saw your father where was he?

A. On the sofa.

Q. What was his position?

A. Lying down.

Q. Describe anything else you noticed at that time.

A. I did not notice anything else, I was so frightened and horrified. I ran to the foot of the stairs and called Maggie.

Q. Did you notice that he had been cut?

A. Yes; that is what made me afraid.

Q. Did you notice that he was dead?

A. I did not know whether he was or not.

Q. Did you make any search for your mother?

A. No sir.

Q. Why not?

A. I thought she was out of the house; I thought she had gone out. I called Maggie to go to Dr. Bowen's. When they came I said, "I don't know where Mrs. Borden is." I thought she had gone out.

Q. Did you tell Maggie you thought your mother had come in?

A. No sir.

Q. That you thought you heard her come in?

A. No sir.

Q. Did you say to anybody that you thought she was killed up stairs?

A. No sir.

Q. To anybody?

A. No sir.

Q. You made no effort to find your mother at all?

A. No sir.

Q. Who did you send Maggie for?

A. Dr. Bowen. She came back and said Dr. Bowen was not there.

Q. What did you tell Maggie?

A. I told her he was hurt.

Q. When you first told her?

A. I says "Go for Dr. Bowen as soon as you can. I think father is hurt."

Q. Did you then know that he was dead?

A. No sir.

Q. You saw him?

A. Yes sir.

Q. You went into the room?

A. No sir.

Q. Looked in at the door?

A. I opened the door and rushed back.

Q. Saw his face?

A. No, I did not see his face, because he was all covered with blood.

Q. You saw where the face was bleeding?

A. Yes sir.

Q. Did you see the blood on the floor?

A. No sir.

Q. You saw his face covered with blood?

A. Yes sir.

Q. Did you see his eyeball hanging out?

A. No sir.

Q. See the gashes where his face was laid open?

A. No sir.

Q. Nothing of that kind?

A. No sir. (Witness covers her face with her hand for a minute or two; then examination is resumed.)

Q. Do you know of any employment that would occupy your mother for the two hours between nine and eleven in the front room?

A. Not unless she was sewing.

Q. If she had been sewing you would have heard the machine?

A. She did not always use the machine.

Q. Did you see, or were there found, anything to indicate that she was sewing up there?

A. I don't know. She had given me a few weeks before some pillow cases to make.

Q. My question is not that. Did you see, or were there

found, anything to indicate that she had done any
sewing in that room that morning?

A. I don't know. I was not allowed in that room; I did
not see it.

Q. Was that the room where she usually sewed?

A. No sir.

Q. Did you ever know her to use that room for sewing?

A. Yes sir.

Q. When?

A. Whenever she wanted to use the machine.

Q. When she did not want to use the machine, did
you know she used that room for sewing?

A. Not unless she went up to sew a button on; or
something.

Q. She did not use it as a sitting room?

A. No sir.

Q. Leaving out the sewing, do you know of anything
else that would occupy her for two hours in that
room?

A. No, not if she had made the bed up, and she said
she had when I went down.

Q. Assuming the bed was made?

A. I don't know anything.

Q. Did she say she had done the work?

A. She said she had made the bed, and was going to
put on the pillow cases, about 9 o'clock.

Q. I ask you now again, remembering that—

A. I told you that yesterday.

Q. Never mind about yesterday. Tell me all the talk
you had with your mother when you came down
in the morning?

A. She asked me how I felt. I said I felt better, but
did not want any breakfast. She said what kind of
meat did I want for dinner. I said I did not want
any. She said she was going out, somebody was
sick, and she would get the dinner, get the meat,
order the meat. And, I think she said something

about the weather being hotter, or something; and I don't remember that she said anything else. I said to her, "Won't you change your dress before you go out." She had on an old one. She said "No, this is good enough." That is all I can remember.

Q. In this narrative you have not again said anything about her having said that she had made the bed?

A. I told you that she said she made the bed.

Q. In this time saying, you did not put that in. I want the conversation that you had with her that morning. I beg your pardon again, in this time of telling me, you did not say anything about her having received a note.

A. I told you that before.

Q. Miss Borden, I want you now to tell me all the talk you had with your mother, when you came down, and all the talk she had with you. Please begin again.

A. She asked me how I felt. I told her. She asked me what I wanted for dinner. I told her not anything, what kind of meat I wanted for dinner. I told her not any. She said she had been up and made the spare bed, and was going to take up some linen pillow cases for the small pillows at the foot, and then the room was done. She says: "I have had a note from somebody that is sick and I am going out, and I will get the dinner at the same time." I think she said something about the weather. I don't know. She also asked me if I would direct some paper wrappers for her, which I did.

Q. She said she had had a note?

A. Yes sir.

Q. You told me yesterday you never saw the note?

A. No sir, I never did.

Q. You looked for it?

A. No sir, but the rest have.

Q. She did not say where she was going?

A. No sir.

Q. Does she usually tell you where she is going?

A. She does not generally tell me.

Q. Did she say when she was coming back?

A. No sir.

Q. Did you know that Mr. Morse was coming to dinner?

A. No sir, I knew nothing about him.

Q. Was he at dinner the day before?

A. Wednesday noon? I don't know. I had not seen him; I don't think he was.

Q. Were you at dinner?

A. I was in the house. I don't know whether I went down to dinner or not. I was not feeling well.

Q. Whether you ate dinner or not?

A. I don't remember.

Q. Do you remember who was at dinner the day before?

A. No sir. I don't remember, because I don't know whether I was down myself or not.

Q. Were you at tea Wednesday night?

A. I went down, but I think, I don't know, whether I had any tea or not.

Q. Did you sit down with the family?

A. I think I did, but I am not sure.

Q. Was Mr. Morse there?

A. No sir, I did not see him.

Q. Who were there to tea?

A. Nobody.

Q. The family were there, I suppose?

A. Yes sir; I mean nobody but the family.

Q. Did you have an apron on Thursday?

A. Did I what?

Q. Have an apron on Thursday?

A. No sir, I don't think I did.

Q. Do you remember whether you did or not?

A. I don't remember sure, but I don't think I did.

Q. You had aprons, of course?

A. I had aprons, yes sir.

Q. Will you try and think whether you did or not?

A. I don't think I did.

Q. Will you try and remember?

A. I had no occasion for an apron on that morning.

Q. If you can remember, I wish you would.

A. I don't remember.

Q. That is all the answer you can give me about that?

A. Yes sir.

Q. Did you have any occasion to use the axe or hatchet?

A. No sir.

Q. Did you know where they were?

A. I knew there was an old axe down cellar; that is all I knew.

Q. Did you know anything about a hatchet down cellar?

A. No sir.

Q. Where was the old axe down cellar?

A. The last time I saw it it was stuck in the old chopping block.

Q. Was that the only axe or hatchet down cellar?

A. It was all I knew about.

Q. When was the last you knew of it?

A. When our farmer came to chop wood.

Q. When was that?

A. I think a year ago last winter; I think there was so much wood on hand he did not come last winter.

Q. Do you know of anything that would occasion the use of an axe or hatchet?

A. No sir.

Q. Do you know of anything that would occasion the getting of blood on an axe or hatchet down cellar?

A. No sir.

Q. I do not say there was, but assuming an axe or hatchet was found down cellar with blood on it?

A. No sir.

Q. Do you know whether there was a hatchet down there before the murder?

A. I don't know.

Q. You are not able to say your father did not own a hatchet?

A. I don't know whether he did or not.

Q. Did you know there was found at the foot of the stairs a hatchet and axe?

A. No sir, I did not.

Q. Assume that is so, can you give me any explanation of how they came there?

A. No sir.

Q. Assume they had blood on them, can you give any occasion for there being blood on them?

A. No sir.

Q. Can you tell of any killing of an animal? or any other operation that would lead to their being cast there, with blood on them?

A. No sir, he killed some pigeons in the barn last May or June.

Q. What with?

A. I don't know, but I thought he wrung their necks.

Q. What made you think so?

A. I think he said so.

Q. Did anything else make you think so?

A. All but three or four had their heads on, that is what made me think so.

Q. Did all of them come into the house?

A. I think so.

Q. Those that came into the house were all headless?

A. Two or three had them on.

Q. Were any with their heads off?

A. Yes sir.

Q. Cut off or twisted off?

A. I don't know which.

Q. How did they look?

A. I don't know, their heads were gone, that is all.

Q. Did you tell anybody they looked as though they were twisted off?

A. I don't remember whether I did or not. The skin I think was very tender, I said why are these heads off? I think I remember of telling somebody that he said they twisted off.

Q. Did they look as if they were cut off?

A. I don't know, I did not look at that particularly.

Q. Is there anything else besides that that would lead, in your opinion so far as you can remember, to the finding of instruments in the cellar with blood on them?

A. I know of nothing else that was done.

(Judge Blaisdell)—Was there any effort made by the witness to notify Mrs. Borden of the fact that Mr. Borden was found?

Q. Did you make any effort to notify Mrs. Borden of your father being killed?

A. No sir, when I found him I rushed right to the foot of the stairs for Maggie. I supposed Mrs. Borden was out. I did not think anything about her at the time, I was so—

Q. At any time did you say anything about her to anybody?

A. No sir.

Q. To the effect that she was out?

A. I told father when he came in.

Q. After your father was killed?

A. No sir.

Q. Did you say you thought she was up stairs?

A. No sir.

Q. Did you ask them to look up stairs?

A. No sir.

Q. Did you suggest to anybody to search up stairs?

A. I said, "I don't know where Mrs. Borden is;" that is all I said.

Q. You did not suggest that any search be made for her?

A. No sir.

Q. You did not make any yourself?

A. No sir.

Q. I want you to give me all that you did, by way of word or deed, to see whether your mother was dead or not, when you found your father was dead.

A. I did not do anything, except what I said to Mrs. Churchill. I said to her: "I don't know where Mrs. Borden is. I think she is out, but I wish you would look."

Q. You did ask her to look?

A. I said that to Mrs. Churchill.

Q. Where did you intend for her to look?

A. In Mrs. Borden's room.

Q. When you went out to the barn did you leave the door shut, the screen door?

A. I left it shut.

Q. When you came back did you find it shut or open?

A. No sir; I found it open.

Q. Can you tell me anything else that you did, that you have not told me, during your absence from the house?

A. No sir.

Q. Can you tell me when it was that you came back from the barn, what time it was?

A. I don't know what time it was.

Q. Have you any idea when it was that your father came home?

A. I am not sure, but I think it must have been after 10, because I think he told me he did not think he should go out until about 10. When he went out I did not look at the clock to see what time it was. I think he did not go out until 10, or a little after. He was not gone so very long.

Q. Will you give me the best judgment you can as to

the time your father got back? If you have not any, it is sufficient to say so.

A. No sir, I have not any.

Q. Can you give me any judgment as to the length of time that elapsed after he came back, and before you went to the barn?

A. I went right out to the barn.

Q. How soon after he came back?

A. I should think not less than five minutes; I saw him taking off his shoes and lying down; it only took him two or three minutes to do it. I went right out.

Q. When he came into the house did he not go into the dining room first?

A. I don't know.

Q. And there sit down?

A. I don't know.

Q. Why don't you know?

A. Because I was in the kitchen.

Q. It might have happened, and you not have known.

A. Yes sir.

Q. You heard the bell ring?

A. Yes sir.

Q. And you knew when he came in?

A. Yes sir.

Q. You did not see him?

A. No sir.

Q. When did you first see him?

A. I went into the sitting room, and he was there; I don't know whether he had been in the dining room before or not.

Q. What made you go into the sitting room?

A. Because I wanted to ask him a question.

Q. What question?

A. Whether there was any mail for me.

Q. Did you not ask him that question in the dining room?

A. No sir, I think not.

Q. Was he not in the dining room sitting down?

A. I don't remember his being in the dining room sitting down.

Q. At that time was not Maggie washing the windows in the sitting room?

A. I thought I asked him for the mail in the sitting room; I am not sure.

Q. Was not the reason he went in the dining room because she was in the sitting room washing windows?

A. I don't know.

Q. Did he not go upstairs to his own room before he sat down in the sitting room?

A. I did not see him go.

Q. He had the key to his room down there?

A. I don't know whether he had it; it was kept on the shelf.

Q. When you did go into the sitting room to ask him a question, if it was the sitting room, what took place then?

A. I asked him [if] he had any mail. He said, "None for you." He had a letter in his hand. I supposed it was for himself. I asked him how he felt. He said he should lie down. I asked him if he thought he should have a nap. He said he would try to. I asked him if he wanted the window left the way it was or if he felt a draught. He said, "No." That is all.

Q. Did you help him about lying down?

A. No sir.

Q. Fix his pillows or head?

A. No sir; I did not touch the sofa.

Q. Did he lie down before you left the room?

A. Yes sir.

Q. Did anything else take place?

A. Not that I remember of.

Q. Was he then under medical treatment?

A. No sir.

Q. The doctor had not given him any medicine that you know of?

A. No sir; he took some medicine; it was not doctor's medicine; it was what we gave him.

Q. What was it?

A. We gave him castor oil first and then Garfield tea.

Q. When was that?

A. He took the castor oil some time Wednesday. I think some time Wednesday noon, and I think the tea Wednesday night; Mrs. Borden gave it to him. She went over to see the doctor.

Q. When did you first consult Mr. Jennings?

A. I can't tell you that; I think my sister sent for him; I don't know.

Q. Was it you or your sister?

A. My sister.

Q. You did not send for him?

A. I did not send for him. She said did we think we ought to have him. I said do as she thought best. I don't know when he came first.

Q. Now, tell me once more, if you please, the particulars of that trouble that you had with your mother four or five years ago.

A. Her father's house on Fourth street was for sale—

Q. Whose father's house?

A. Mrs. Borden's father's house. She had a stepmother and a half sister, Mrs. Borden did, and this house was left to the stepmother and a half sister, if I understood it right, and the house was for sale. The stepmother, Mrs. Oliver Gray, wanted to sell it, and my father bought out the Widow Gray's share. She did not tell me and he did not tell me, but some outsiders said that he gave it to her. Put it in her name. I said if he gave that to her, he ought to give us something. Told Mrs. Borden so.

She did not care anything about the house herself. She wanted it so this half sister could have a home, because she had married a man that was not doing the best he could, and she thought her sister was having a very hard time and wanted her to have a home. And we always thought she persuaded father to buy it. At any rate, he did buy it, and I am quite sure she did persuade him. I said what he did for her people, he ought to do for his own children. So he gave us Grandfather's house. That was all the trouble we ever had.

Q. You have not stated any trouble yet between you and her?

A. I said there was feeling four or five years ago when I stopped calling her mother. I told you that yesterday.

Q. That is all there is to it then?

A. Yes sir.

Q. You had no words with your stepmother then?

A. I talked with her about it and said what he did for her he ought to do for us; that is all the words we had.

Q. That is the occasion of his giving you the house that you sold back to him?

A. Yes sir.

Q. Did your mother leave any property?

A. I don't know.

Q. Your own mother?

A. No sir; not that I ever knew of.

Q. Did you ever see that thing? (Wooden club.)

A. Yes sir, I think I have.

Q. What is it?

A. My father used to keep something similar to this, that looked very much like it under his bed. He whittled it out himself at the farm one time.

Q. How long since you have seen it?

A. I have not seen it in years.

Q. How many years?

A. I could not tell you. I should think ten to fifteen years; not since I was quite a little girl, if that is the one. I can't swear that it is the one; it was about that size.

Q. How many years, ten or fifteen?

A. I was a little girl, it must be as much as that.

Q. When was the last time the windows were washed before that day?

A. I don't know.

Q. Why don't you know?

A. Because I had nothing to do with the work down stairs.

Q. When was the last time that you ate with the family, that you can swear to, before your mother was killed?

A. Well, I ate with them all day Tuesday, that is, what little we ate, we sat down to the table; and I think I sat down to the table with them Wednesday night, but I am not sure.

Q. All day Tuesday?

A. I was down at the table.

Q. I understand you to say you did not come down to breakfast?

A. That was Wednesday morning.

Q. I understood you to say that you did not come down to breakfast?

A. I came down, but I did not eat breakfast with them. I did not eat any breakfast. Frequently I would go into the dining room and sit down to the table with them and not eat any breakfast.

Q. Did you give to the officer the same skirt you had on the day of the tragedy?

A. Yes sir.

Q. Do you know whether there was any blood on the skirt?

A. No sir.

Q. Assume that there was, do you know how it came there?

A. No sir.

Q. Have you any explanation of how it might come there?

A. No sir.

Q. Did you know there was any blood on the skirt you gave them?

A. No sir.

Q. Assume that there was, can you give any explanation of how it came there, on the dress skirt?

A. No sir.

Q. Assume that there was, can you suggest any reason how it came there?

A. No sir.

Q. Have you offered any?

A. No sir.

Q. Have you ever offered any?

A. No sir.

Q. Have you said it came from flea bites?

A. On the petticoats I said there was a flea bite. I said it might have been. You said you meant the dress skirt.

Q. I did. Have you offered any explanation how that came there?

A. I told those men that were at the house that I had had fleas; that is all.

Q. Did you offer that as an explanation?

A. I said that was the only explanation that I knew of.

Q. Assuming that the blood came from the outside, can you give any explanation of how it came there?

A. No sir.

Q. You cannot now?

A. No sir.

Q. What shoes did you have on that day?

A. A pair of ties.

Q. What color?

A. Black.

Q. Will you give them to the officer?

A. Yes.

Q. Where are they?

A. At home.

Q. What stockings did you have on that day?

A. Black.

Q. Where are they?

A. At home.

Q. Have they been washed?

A. I don't know.

Q. Will you give them to the officer?

A. Yes sir.

Q. The window you was at is the window that is nearest the street in the barn?

A. Yes sir; the west window.

Q. The pears you ate, you got from under the tree in the yard?

A. Yes sir.

Q. How long were you under the pear tree?

A. I think I was under there very nearly four or five minutes. I stood looking around. I looked up at the pigeon house that they have closed up. It was no more than five minutes, perhaps not as long. I can't say sure.

Q. (Judge Blaisdell) Was this witness on Thursday morning in the front hall or front stairs or front chamber, any part of the front part of the house at all?

Q. What do you say to that?

A. I had to come down the front stairs to get into the kitchen.

Q. When you came down first?

A. Yes sir.

Q. Were you afterwards?

A. No sir.

Q. Not at all?

A. Except the few minutes I went up with the clean clothes, and I had to come back again.

Q. That you now say was before Mr. Borden went away?

A. Yes sir.

Thursday, August 11, 1892

Q. Is there anything you would like to correct in your previous testimony?

A. No sir.

Q. Did you buy a dress pattern in New Bedford?

A. A dress pattern?

Q. Yes, a dress pattern.

A. I think I did.

Q. Where is it?

A. It is at home.

Q. Where?

A. Where at home?

Q. Please.

A. It is in a trunk.

Q. In your room?

A. No sir; in the attic.

Q. Not made up?

A. O, no sir.

Q. Where did you buy it?

A. I don't know the name of the store.

Q. On the principal street there?

A. I think it was on the street that Hutchinson's book store is on. I am not positive.

Q. What kind of a one was it, please?

A. It was a pink stripe and a white stripe, and a blue stripe corded gingham.

Q. Your attention has already been called to the circumstance of going into the drug store of Smith's, on the corner of Columbia and Main streets, by some officer, has it not, on the day before the tragedy?

A. I don't know whether some officer has asked me, somebody has spoke of it to me; I don't know who it was.

Q. Did that take place?

A. It did not.

Q. Do you know where the drug store is?

A. I don't.

Q. Did you go into any drug store and inquire for prussic acid?

A. I did not.

Q. Where were you on Wednesday morning that you remember?

A. At home.

Q. All the time?

A. All day, until Wednesday night.

Q. Nobody there but your parents and yourself and the servant?

A. Why, Mr. Morse came sometime in the afternoon, or at noon time, I suppose, I did not see him.

Q. He did not come so to see you?

A. No sir, I did not see him.

Q. He did not come until afternoon anyway, did he?

A. I don't think he did; I am not sure.

Q. Did you dine with the family that day?

A. I was down stairs, yes sir. I did not eat any breakfast with them.

Q. Did you go into the drug store for any purpose whatever?

A. I did not.

Q. I think you said yesterday that you did not go into the room where your father lay, after he was killed, on the sofa, but only looked in at the door?

A. I looked in; I did not go in.

Q. You did not step into the room at all?

A. I did not.

Q. Did you ever, after your mother was found killed, go into that room?

A. No sir.

Q. Did you afterwards go into the room where your father was found killed, any more than to go through it to go up stairs?

A. When they took me up stairs they took me through that room.

Q. Otherwise than that did you go into it?

A. No sir.

Q. Let me refresh your memory. You came down in the night to get some water with Miss Russell, along towards night, or in the evening, to get some water with Miss Russell?

A. Thursday night? I don't remember it.

Q. Don't you remember coming down sometime to get some toilet water?

A. No sir, there was no toilet water down stairs.

Q. Or to empty the slops?

A. I don't know whether I did Thursday evening or not. I am not sure.

Q. You think it may have been some other evening?

A. I don't remember coming down with her to do such a thing. I may have, I can't tell whether it was Thursday evening or any other evening.

Q. Other than that, if that did take place, you don't recollect going into that room for any purpose at any time?

A. No sir.

Q. Was the dress that was given to the officers the same dress that you wore that morning?

A. Yes sir.

Q. The India silk?

A. No, it is not an India silk. It is silk and linen; some call it bengaline silk.

Q. Something like that dress there? (Pongee.)

A. No, it was not like that.

Q. Did you give to the officer the same shoes and stockings that you wore?

A. I did, sir.

Q. Do you remember where you took them off?

A. I wore the shoes even after that, all around the house Friday, and Saturday until I put on my shoes for the street.

Q. That is to say you wore them all that day, Thursday, until you took them off for the night?

A. Yes sir.

Q. Did you tell us yesterday all the errand that you had at the barn?

A. Yes sir.

Q. You have nothing to add to what you said?

A. No sir.

Q. You had no other errand than when you have spoken of?

A. No sir.

Q. Miss Borden, of course you appreciate the anxiety that everybody has to find the author of this tragedy, and the questions that I put to you have been in that direction; I now ask you if you can furnish any other fact, or give any other, even suspicion, that will assist the officers in any way in this matter?

A. About two weeks ago—

Q. Was you going to tell the occurrence about the man that called at the house?

A. No sir. It was after my sister went away. I came home from Miss Russell's one night, and as I came up, I always glanced towards the side door as I came along by the carriage way, I saw a shadow on the side steps. I did not stop walking, but I walked slower. Somebody ran down the steps, around the east end of the house. I thought it was a man, because I saw no skirts, and I was frightened, and of course I did not go around to see. I hurried to the front door as fast as I could and locked it.

Q. What time of night was that?

A. I think about quarter of 9; it was not after 9 o'clock, anyway.

Q. Do you remember what night that was?

A. No sir; I don't. I saw somebody run around the house once before last winter.

Q. One thing at a time. Do you recollect about how long ago that last occurrence was?

A. It was after my sister went away. She has been away two weeks today, so it must have been within two weeks.

Q. Two weeks today? Or two weeks at the time of the murder?

A. Is not today Thursday?

Q. Yes, but I thought you said she was gone two weeks the day of the murder?

A. Is not today Thursday?

Q. Yes, but that would be three weeks; I thought you said the day your father was murdered she had been away just two weeks?

A. Yes, she had.

Q. Then it would be three weeks today—your sister went away, a week has elapsed?

A. Yes, I had forgotten that a whole week had passed since the affair.

Q. Different from that you cannot state?

A. No sir; I don't know what the date was.

Q. This form when you first saw it was on the steps of the back door?

A. Yes sir.

Q. Went down the rear steps?

A. Went down towards the barn.

Q. Around the back side of the house?

A. Disappeared in the dark; I don't know where they went.

Q. Have you ever mentioned that before?

A. Yes sir; I told Mr. Jennings.

Q. To any officer?

A. I don't think I have, unless I told Mr. Hanscom.

Q. What was you going to say about last winter?

A. Last winter when I was coming home from church one Thursday evening, I saw somebody run around the house again. I told my father of that.

Q. Did you tell your father of this last one?

A. No sir.

Q. Of course you could not identify who it was either time?

A. No, I could not identify who it was, but it was not a very tall person.

Q. Have you sealskin sacks?

A. Yes sir.

Q. Where are they?

A. Hanging in a large white bag in the attic, each one separate.

Q. Put away for the summer?

A. Yes sir.

Q. Do you ever use prussic acid on your sacks?

A. Acid? No sir; I don't use anything on them.

Q. Is there anything else that you can suggest that even amounts to anything whatever?

A. I know of nothing else, except the man who came, and father ordered him out, that is all I know.

Q. That you told about the other day?

A. I think I did; yes sir.

Q. You have not been able to find that man?

A. I have not; I don't know whether anybody else has or not.

Q. Have you caused search to be made for him?

A. Yes sir.

Q. When was the offer of reward made for the detection of the criminals?

A. I think it was made Friday.

Q. Who suggested that?

A. We suggested it ourselves, and asked Mr. Buck if he did not think it was a good plan.

Q. Whose suggestion was it, yours or Emma's?

A. I don't remember. I think it was mine.

ABOUT THE AUTHOR

H. Paul Jeffers is a former broadcast newsman with more than forty published books of fiction and nonfiction. Among his true crime titles are *Wanted by the FBI*, a history of the Bureau's Ten Most Wanted list; *Who Killed Precious?*, the story and cases of the FBI's criminal psychological profiling unit; *Murder Along the Way*, with former Rockland County, New York, District Attorney Kenneth Gribetz; and *Bloody Business*, an anecdotal history of Scotland Yard.

He lives in New York City.